KINGSHIP ACCORDING TO THE
DEUTERONOMISTIC HISTORY

SOCIETY
OF BIBLICAL
LITERATURE

DISSERTATION SERIES

J. J. M. Roberts, Old Testament Editor
Charles Talbert, New Testament Editor

Number 87

KINGSHIP ACCORDING TO THE
DEUTERONOMISTIC HISTORY

by
Gerald Eddie Gerbrandt

Gerald Eddie Gerbrandt

KINGSHIP ACCORDING TO THE DEUTERONOMISTIC HISTORY

Scholars Press
Atlanta, Georgia

1986

KINGSHIP ACCORDING TO THE DEUTERONOMISTIC HISTORY

Gerald Eddie Gerbrandt

BS
1199
.K5
G47
1986

Th.D., 1979
Union Theological Seminary
Richmond, Virginia

Advisor:
W. Sibley Towner

Library of Congress Cataloging-in-Publication Data

Gerbrandt, Gerald Eddie.
  Kingship according to the Deuteronomistic history.

  (Dissertation series / Society of Biblical
Literature ; no. 87)
  Thesis (Doctor of Theology)—Union Theological
Seminary, Richmond, 1979
  Bibliography: p.
  1. Kings and rulers—Biblical teachings. 2. Bible.
O.T. Criticism, interpretation, etc.
3. Bible. O.T. Former Prophets—Criticism, interpre-
tation, etc. 4. D Document (Biblical criticism)
I. Title. II. Series: Dissertation series (Society of
Biblical Literature) ; no. 87.
BS1199.K5G47   1986   222'.06   86-6660

ISBN 0-89130-968-3 (alk. paper)
ISBN 0-89130-969-1 (pbk. : alk. paper)

Printed in the United States of America
on acid-free paper

To my Parents,
Henry and Susan Gerbrandt

Contents

PREFACE xi

ABBREVIATIONS xiii

Chapter

1. INTRODUCTION AND REVIEW OF RESEARCH 1

   A Review of Research on the Composition
   of the Deuteronomistic History 1

      Martin Noth 1
      Rejection of Martin Noth's Thesis 2
      Confirmation of Martin Noth's Thesis 5
      Modification of Martin Noth's Thesis 6

         Gerhard von Rad 7
         The Two-Redaction Theory 8
         DtrG - DtrP - DtrN 11

   A Response to the Research on the Composition of the Deuteronomistic History 13

   A Review of Research on Kingship According
   to the Deuteronomistic History 18

      The Traditional Position 18
      Recent Alternative Proposals 23

   A Response to the Research on Kingship According
   to the Deuteronomistic History 36

   The Purpose of This Dissertation 38

2. KINGSHIP IN 2 KINGS 18-23 45

   King Josiah, 2 Kings 22-23 45

      The Deuteronomist's Evaluation of
        King Josiah 46

      The Basis of the Deuteronomist's
        Evaluation 57

         The Discovery of the Lawbook,
          2 Kings 22:3-20 59

         The Covenant Renewal Ceremony,
          2 Kings 23:1-3 61

         The Reform of the Cult,
          2 Kings 23:4-20, 24 64

         The Passover Celebration,
          2 Kings 23:21-23. 66

      Conclusion 67

   King Hezekiah, 2 Kings 18-20 68

      The Deuteronomist's Evaluation of
        King Hezekiah 72

      The Basis of the Deuteronomist's
        Evaluation 75

         Introduction, 2 Kings 18:9-16. 79

         Yahweh's Deliverance of Jerusalem,
          2 Kings 18:17-19:37 81

         Hezekiah's Illness, 2 Kings
          20:1-11 85

         The Envoys from Babylon,
          2 Kings 20:12-19. 86

      Conclusion 88

   A Proposal: The Role of the King According
   to the Deuteronomistic Historian. 89

      The Deuteronomist's Theology 90

      The Role of the King According to
        the Deuteronomistic Historian. 96

3. KINGSHIP IN THE REMAINDER OF THE
   DEUTERONOMISTIC HISTORY 103

   Deuteronomy 17:14-20—The Law
      of Kingship 103

Preliminary Critical Considerations 103

Kingship in the Deuteronomic Law
of Kingship 108

Kingship in the Deuteronomistic
Addition to the Law of Kingship 113

Joshua 116

Judges 123

Gideon and Kingship, Judges 8:22-23 123

Jotham's Fable and the Story of
Abimelech, Judges 9 129

Judges 17-21 134

The Deuteronomist and the Time of
the Judges 138

The Rise of Kingship 140

Preliminary Critical Concerns 140

1 Samuel 8-12 and Anti-Kingship
Rhetoric 143

The Function of 1 Samuel 8-12 in the
Deuteronomistic History 145

1 Samuel 8-12 Warns of the
Dangers of Kingship 146

1 Samuel 8-12 Integrates Kingship
with Israelite Theology 149

The Rejection of Saul,
1 Samuel 13-15 154

King David in the Deuteronomistic
History 158

Preliminary Critical Concerns 158

The Davidic Covenant 160

The Prophecy of Nathan,
2 Samuel 7 160

The Davidic Promise in the
Remainder of the Deuteron-
omistic History 164

King David and the Deuteronomist's View
of Kingship 170

1 and 2 Kings 173

The Deuteronomist and King
   Solomon........................... 174
The Sin of Jeroboam and the End
   of the North....................... 177
Prophets, Kings, and the Battles
   of Israel........................... 180
The Coronation of Joash,
   1 Kings 11 182

4. SUMMARY AND CONCLUSION 189

APPENDIX:
   A REVIEW OF RESEARCH ON 2 KINGS 22-23 195

BIBLIOGRAPHY   201

INDEX   227

Preface

This study was presented to Union Theological Seminary in Virginia in August, 1979 as a doctoral dissertation. The seven years since have resulted in numerous monographs and articles bearing on the topic. Ideally the dissertation should have been revised and refined in light of more recent research. Such a revision could also have ameliorated the awkward dissertation style of the work. In keeping with the nature of the SBL Dissertation Series, however, I am submitting the original study virtually unchanged.

Many people have made a significant contribution to the ultimate production of this book. I wish to express my deepest gratitude to them. The dissertation was directed by Professor W. Sibley Towner who devoted many hours of consultation to me. His continuous support and encouragement aided the task immeasurably. My committee members, Professor James L. Mays and Professor Patrick D. Miller, Jr., influenced the work at many points with their helpful questions and insightful comments. These were always appreciated.

I owe a special debt to Dr. Waldemar Janzen, formerly my teacher, and now colleague and friend. He first whetted my appetite for the academic study of Old Testament in an undergraduate course on the history of Old Testament criticism. His support and guidance in the past 20 years can not be repaid.

The contribution of my family in this project was immense. The patience and love of Esther, my wife, made doctoral studies a relative pleasure. It was she who pushed that we remain at school, away from home and family, until the dissertation was completely finished. For this I am thankful. My three children, Nathan, Bradley and Virginia regularly drew me from my study for times of play. Finally, I want to express thanks to my parents, Henry and Susan Gerbrandt. They instilled in me a love for the scriptures, and they gave me the opportunity and desire to pursue formal study beyond what was possible for their generation. It is this combination which made this book possible, and thus I dedicate it to them.

Gerald E. Gerbrandt

Winnipeg, Manitoba
May, 1986

Abbreviations

AB	The Anchor Bible
AnBib	Analecta Biblica
AOAT	Alter Orient und Altes Testament
ATANT	Abhandlungen zur Theologie des Alten und Neuen Testaments
ATD	Das Alte Testament Deutsch
BASOR	*Bulletin of the American Schools of Oriental Research*
BAT	Die Botschaft des Altes Testaments
BBB	Bonner Biblische Beiträge
BFCT	Beiträge zur christlicher Theologie
BHT	Beiträge zur historischen Theologie
Bib	*Biblica*
BJRL	*Bulletin of the John Rylands University Library of Manchester*
BKAT	Biblischer Kommentar: Altes Testament
BR	*Biblical Research*
BWANT	Beiträge zur Wissenschaft vom Alten und Neuen Testament
BWAT	Beiträge zur Wissenschaft vom Alten Testament

BZ	*Biblische Zeitschrift*
BZAW	Beiheft zur *Zeitschrift für die alttestamentliche Wissenschaft*
CB	The Century Bible
CBC	The Cambridge Bible Commentary
CBQ	*Catholic Biblical Quarterly*
FRLANT	Forschungen zur Religion und Literatur des Alten und Neuen Testaments
HAT	Handkommentar zum Alten Testament
HTR	*Harvard Theological Review*
HUCA	*Hebrew Union College Annual*
IB	*Interpreter's Bible*
ICC	The International Critical Commentary
Int	*Interpretation*
JBL	*Journal of Biblical Literature*
JNES	*Journal of Near Eastern Studies*
JSOTSup	Journal for the Study of the Old Testament, Supplements
JSS	*Journal of Semitic Studies*
JTS	*Journal of Theological Studies*
KAT	Kommentar zum Alten Testament
KHCAT	Kurzer Hand-Commentar zum Alten Testament
NICOT	The New International Commentary on the Old Testament
OTL	Old Testament Library
SBLDS	SBL Dissertation Series
SBLMS	SBL Monograph Series
SBT	Studies in Biblical Theology

SJT	*Scottish Journal of Theology*
TLZ	*Theologische Literaturzeitung*
TRu	*Theologische Rundschau*
TS	*Theological Studies*
TZ	*Theologische Zeitschrift*
VT	*Vetus Testamentum*
VTSup	Vetus Testamentum, Supplements
WMANT	Wissenschaftliche Monographien zum Alten und Neuen Testament
ZAW	*Zeitschrift für die alttestamentliche Wissenschaft*
ZTK	*Zeitschrift für Theologie und Kirche*

Biblical quotations have been taken from the Revised Standard Version.

1

Introduction and Review of Research

A REVIEW OF RESEARCH ON THE COMPOSITION OF THE DEUTERONOMISTIC HISTORY[1]

Martin Noth

1943 marks a turning point in the study of the composition of Deuteronomy and the Former Prophets. In that year Martin Noth published his ground-breaking *Überlieferungsgeschichtliche Studien,*[2] a volume which has become the starting point for research in this area ever since.

Prior to Noth, research within the Former Prophets had been dominated by literary-critical methods and the attempt to trace the

---

[1] For a more detailed history of critical studies on the composition of the Deuteronomistic History see especially Arnold Nicolaas Radjawane, "Das deuteronomistische Geschichtswerk: Ein Forschungsbericht," *TRu* 38 (1974) 177-216; and Ernst Jenni, "Zwei Jahrzehnte Forschung an den Büchern Josua bis Könige," *TRu* 27 (1961) 1-32, 97-146. Other helpful sources on this history are Norman Snaith, "The Historical Books," in *The Old Testament and Modern Study* (ed. H. H. Rowley; London: Oxford, 1961) 84-114; Hans-Joachim Kraus, *Geschichte der historisch-kritischen Erforschung des Alten Testaments von der Reformation bis zur Gegenwart* (Neukirchen Kries Moers: Buchhandlung des Erziehungsvereins, 1956) 411-16; Ronald E. Clements, *One Hundred Years of Old Testament Interpretation* (Philadelphia: Westminster, 1976) 31-50, as well as various OT introductions.

[2] Martin Noth, *Überlieferungsgeschichtliche Studien I. Die sammelnden und bearbeitenden Geschichtswerke im Alten Testament* (Halle: Max Niemeyer, 1943).

Pentateuchal sources into these OT books. Julius Wellhausen[3] and others[4] saw the Former Prophets bound together by a Deuteronomic redaction, but the role attributed to this redactor in the final composition was really quite minimal. Noth's most significant contribution at this point was his thesis that the books Deuteronomy to 2 Kings were part of a unified work of history produced by a single author living in Palestine during the exile. He argued that these individual books then need to be treated as part of this Deuteronomistic History and not as separate books. Naturally the author of this history used many smaller and larger old sources, but these were not to be equated with the Pentateuchal sources. The author gave this history his own distinctive stamp by the way in which he adopted or rejected his sources, by the order he gave to them through the composition of linking passages, and most importantly, by the composition and insertion of speeches and summary-like passages at key points within the history. Noth briefly summarized his thesis as follows:

> The goal of the foregoing investigation was to show that we should not speak of a "deuteronomistic redaction" of an already more or less completed, older, historical account, but that *Dtr was the author of a comprehensive history (Traditionswerkes)*. To be sure, Dtr conscientiously took up the extant tradition and had it speak for itself, but still, he himself organized and arranged the whole, and through retrospective and forward-looking synopses he systematized and interpreted it.[5] (Translation mine).

Rejection of Martin Noth's Thesis

A number of OT scholars who were used to literary criticism and source analysis when studying Deuteronomy and the Former Prophets

---

[3]Julius Wellhausen, *Die Composition des Hexateuchs und der historischen Bücher des Alten Testaments* (Berlin: Walter de Gruyter, 1963); and Wellhausen, *Prolegomena to the History of Ancient Israel* (Cleveland: Meridian, 1957) 228-93.

[4]For two examples of this, notice the Old Testament introduction, Carl Cornill, *Introduction to the Canonical Books of the Old Testament* (New York: G. P. Putnam, 1907); and the commentaries by Karl Budde, *Das Buch der Richter*, KHCAT, Abt. 7 (Freiburg: J. C. B. Mohr [Paul Siebeck], 1897); and Budde, *Die Bücher Samuel*, KHCAT, Abt. 8 (Tübingen: J. C. B. Mohr [Paul Siebeck], 1902).

[5]Noth, *ÜgS*, p. 89.

were simply not convinced by Noth's new proposal based on his traditio-historical approach. Like Wellhausen, Cornill, Budde and others of the pre-Noth period they admitted the existence of a Deuteronomic redactor working during the time of the exile or later, but this redactor was certainly not the purposeful historian envisioned by Noth. For these scholars true history writing in Israel arose during the period of enlightenment which blossomed at the time of David and Solomon, and not during the oppressive years of the exile. The redactor of the exile then merely combined the major histories of Israel available to him (J and E, or some variation thereof), and brought them up to date.

Three scholars who could be characterized in this way are Gustav Hölscher, Otto Eissfeldt and Cuthbert Simpson. All three began their OT research before 1943, and after studying Noth remained convinced that the older methods and results were more valid and accurate. Hölscher had already written on the sources and redaction of Kings,[6] and on the origins of history writing in Israel[7] before Noth published his important study. Yet he felt little need to change his basic views when in 1952 he wrote another work on history writing in Israel, tracing the work of J and E from Genesis to Kings.[8] In this study of J and E Hölscher accepted neither a Pentateuch nor a Deuteronomistic History, but argued that Genesis to 2 Kings "form, as their contents reveal, in reality a single coherent work which only later was divided into nine individual books."[9] (Translation mine). The true historians of the OT were J and E and not some Deuteronomist.

Eissfeldt first published his OT introduction in 1934.[10] Here he presented the classic picture of the Pentateuch and the Former Prophets. Like Hölscher, Eissfeldt was not persuaded to change his basic approach

---

[6]Gustav Hölscher, "Das Buch der Könige, seine Quellen und seine Redaktion," in *Eucharisterion*, Fs. Hermann Gunkel, FRLANT, hft. 36, T. 1 (ed. Hans Schmidt; Göttingen: Vandenhoeck & Ruprecht, 1923) 158-213.

[7]Gustav Hölscher, *Die Anfänge der hebräischen Geschichtsschreibung*, Sitzungsberichte der Heidelberger Akademie der Wissenschaften, Philosophisch-historische Klasse, Jahrgang 1941/42, 3 Abh. (Heidelberg: Carl Winter's Universitätsbuchhandlung, 1942).

[8]Gustav Hölscher, *Geschichtsschreibung in Israel. Untersuchungen zum Jahwisten und Elohisten*. Skrifter Utgivna av Kungl. Humanistiska Vetenskapssamfundet I Lund, Nr. 50 (Lund: C. W. K. Gleerup, 1952).

[9]Ibid., p. 8.

[10]Otto Eissfeldt, *Einleitung in das Alte Testament*, Neue theologische Grundrisse (Tübingen: J. C. B. Mohr [Paul Siebeck], 1934).

by Noth's work, and the third edition of his introduction still left little room for a creative historian like the Deuteronomist.[11] His clearest rejection of Noth is expressed in his review of Noth's book.[12] Here he focussed upon Joshua 1 and 1 Samuel 7-12 and argued that both passages are better explained by positing two parallel strands rather than as the product of an author who carefully picked his sources and then added his own comments to them. Again it is evident that for Eissfeldt J and E, together with L, are the important Old Testament historians, and the role of the Deuteronomist is that of a compiler and redactor.

Although Simpson wrote two books on the early traditions and history of Israel, both after 1943, neither makes any significant use of Noth's study.[13] In his introduction to the *Composition of the Book of Judges* Simpson suggested that the literary structure of the Hexateuch (for Simpson there existed three strands, J^1, J^2 which was a later revision of J^1, and E) continued not only through Judges, but also through 1 and 2 Samuel up to 1 Kings 13. He is then also part of this approach to the Former Prophets.

The views of Hölscher, Eissfeldt and Simpson on the Former Prophets have found very few followers in recent years. One exception to this is Hannelis Schulte, a student of Hölscher's. In a recent work she argues that the Yahwist, writing shortly after the division of the kingdom, was the first real historian in Israel. It was he who compiled the old traditions, recorded oral history, and added his own contributions thus producing a history extending from the beginning of time till the death of Solomon.[14] Such a picture does not allow for the kind of Deuteronomistic historian proposed by Noth.

Noth's thesis is not only rejected by those who continue to work in the source analysis tradition, but also by some who are not satisfied by it for

---

[11]Otto Eissfeldt, *The Old Testament. An Introduction* (New York: Harper & Row, 1965).

[12]Otto Eissfeldt, "Die Geschichtswerke im Alten Testament," *TLZ* 72 (1947) 71-76.

[13]Cuthbert Simpson, *The Early Traditions of Israel. A Critical Analysis of the Pre-deuteronomic Narrative of the Hexateuch* (Oxford: Basil Blackwell, 1948); and Simpson, *Composition of the Book of Judges* (Oxford: Basil Blackwell, 1957).

[14]Hannelis Schulte, *Die Entstehung der Geschichtsschreibung im alten Israel,* BZAW, Nr. 128 (Berlin: Walter de Gruyter, 1972).

other reasons. Artur Weiser[15] and Georg Fohrer[16] are two who represent this approach. Both see the Pentateuchal strands as continuing into Joshua at least, and argue for an original Hexateuch. Both deny a literary unity for all the books placed into the Deuteronomistic History by Noth. Each emphasizes that the books of Judges to Kings need to be studied and analyzed individually since each had its own history. In this way both decidedly downplay the significance of the Deuteronomist in the final form of the history and so see no common Deuteronomistic theology uniting the books of Deuteronomy to 2 Kings. As Fohrer stated, "There never was a Deuteronomistic History as a unified literary entity; instead, we have a series of books Deuteronomy-Kings, each composed or edited in a different way."[17]

Confirmation of Martin Noth's Thesis

Two scholars who did their research at approximately the same time as Noth, and who arrived at conclusions which tended to support or confirm Noth's thesis of a Deuteronomistic History were Alfred Jepsen and Ivan Engnell. During the 1930's Jepsen analyzed the sources and composition of 1 and 2 Kings. By 1939 his work was finished and accepted for publication, but because of the Second World War it was not published until 1953.[18] Jepsen made virtually no changes in the manuscript in these intervening years, so that a significant value of his conclusions is that they were arrived at completely independently from Noth. In contrast to many scholars of his time Jepsen denied that J and E could be found in Kings. He saw Kings as based primarily upon two sources, a synchronistic chronicle of the kings of Israel and Judah, and the annals of the kings. These two major sources were combined by a priestly redactor working in Jerusalem early during the exile, and then incorporated into a story beginning at least with the rise of David. This story then received a second, more major redaction or revision based on the book of Deuteronomy and biased toward the prophetic movement. The whole history was reinterpreted on the basis of a prophetic theology, various prophetic traditions were added

---

[15]Artur Weiser, *Introduction to the Old Testament* (New York: Association, 1961).

[16]Georg Fohrer, *Introduction to the Old Testament* (Nashville: Abingdon, 1968).

[17]Ibid., p. 195.

[18]Alfred Jepsen, *Die Quellen des Königsbuches* (Halle: Max Niemeyer, 1953).

(the stories of Elijah, Elisha and Isaiah are a few examples), and the history was extended backward to the time of Moses (traditions of the conquest, of the judges and of Samuel, as well as the book of Deuteronomy were incorporated). A deuteronomistic History had been produced extending from Deuteronomy to 2 Kings by a prophetically inclined individual working in Palestine during the exile. This Deuteronomistic History then received a final minor redaction by a levitical editor. Jepsen thus independently supported Noth's thesis of a Deuteronomistic History even though he differed considerably from Noth on his analysis of the prehistory of 1 and 2 Kings. It is questionable whether Jepsen's work has received the attention and consideration it deserves.[19]

In 1945 the Swedish scholar Engnell published an introduction to the OT based on his own traditio-historical methods of research.[20] In this work he argued that the OT contains three major literary complexes: the P-work (Genesis to Numbers), the D-work (Deuteronomy to 2 Kings), and the K-work (Ezra to 2 Chronicles). The author of each of these independent complexes had adopted and reworked the various traditions available to him (these traditions were seen as being primarily oral) to produce a unified literary composition. The individual behind the Deuteronomistic History was clearly an author and historian in his own right, and not just a redactor. The important aspect to note here is that Engnell came to conclusions similar to those of Noth regarding the unity and literary independence of the Deuteronomistic History despite the fact that Engnell's methods of research were radically different from Noth's.

Modification of Martin Noth's Thesis

During the 35 years since the publication of Noth's *Überlieferungsgeschichtliche Studien* the phrase "Deuteronomistic History"[21] has

---

[19]It sometimes appears as if Jepsen is simply categorized as confirming Noth's thesis, and then ignored. One exception to this is the recent commentary by Klaus Dietrich Fricke, *Das zweite Buch von den Königen*, Die Botschaft des Alten Testaments, Bd. 12, T. 2 (Stuttgart: Calwer, 1972), which makes considerable use of Jepsen's conclusions.

[20]Ivan Engnell, *Gamla Testementet. En Traditionshistorisk Inledning* (Stockholm: Svensk Krykans Diakonistyrelses Bokföflag, 1945). Note also Engnell, A Rigid Scrutiny: Critical Essays on the Old Testament (Nashville: Vanderbilt, 1969).

[21]Some scholars speak of a "Deuteronomic History" instead of a "Deuteronomistic History." Since this is a question of style rather than of

become a commonplace in OT studies. An examination of popular introductions to the OT reveals that virtually all speak of such a history, and
consider at least Judges to 2 Kings to be a literary unity of some sort.[22]
The arguments of scholars such as Hölscher and Eissfeldt against Noth
have not received general support, and it is possible today to speak of a
near-consensus on at least the existence of a Deuteronomistic History.[23]
Despite this high degree of agreement, few scholars have accepted Noth's
views exactly as he presented them. Most would probably consider Noth's
thesis to be too simple and in need of considerable modification and/or
further expansion. The following are some of the major ways in which
Noth's thesis has been adapted or modified.

Gerhard von Rad. Gerhard von Rad's response to Noth's study was
decidedly mixed. On the one hand von Rad recognized the outstanding
contribution that Noth had made to an area of OT studies which had been
in dire need of some new work. On the other hand von Rad disagreed with
Noth's thesis at a number of rather important places. Von Rad had earlier
already argued for the literary (the Pentateuchal strands begin in Genesis
and continue through Joshua) and theological (the promise of land in
Genesis is fulfilled in the account of the settlement in Joshua) unity of
the Hexateuch,[24] and he was not persuaded by Noth to change his mind on

---

meaning this difference has no real significance and does not affect the
statement made. In time a more uniform vocabulary will hopefully be
adopted.

[22]A few representative introductions which speak of a Deuteronomistic
History are: Henry Jackson Flanders, Jr., Robert Wilson Crapps, and
David Anthony Smith, *People of the Covenant: An Introduction to the Old
Testament* (New York: Ronald, 1963) 165-66; Bernhard W. Anderson,
Understanding the Old Testament, 2nd ed. (Englewood Cliffs: Prentice-
Hall, 1966) 77; J. Alberto Soggin, *Introduction to the Old Testament*, OTL
(Philadelphia: Westminster, 1976) 161-64; Otto Kaiser, *Introduction to the
Old Testament* (Minneapolis: Augsburg, 1975) 169-75.

[23]It should be noted that some of conservative scholarship does not
accept the existence of a continuous Deuteronomistic History, but deals
with each book independently. Two examples of this are: Edward J.
Young, *An Introduction to the Old Testament*, 2nd ed. (Grand Rapids:
Eerdmans, 1970); Norman L. Geisler, *A Popular Survey of the Old Testament* (Grand Rapids: Baker, 1977).

[24]Gerhard von Rad, "The Form-critical Problem of the Hexateuch,"
first published as "Das formgeschichtliche Problem des Hexateuch" in
1938, in *The Problem of the Hexateuch and Other Essays* (Edinburgh:
Oliver & Boyd, 1966) 1-78.

this.[25] According to von Rad the histories behind the Hexateuch were expansions of early Credos which summarized Israel's salvation history from its early beginnings till the settlement in Palestine and thus the books Genesis to Joshua were inextricably tied together. A Deuteronomistic History could only extend from Judges to 2 Kings. Further, even after taking away Deuteronomy and Joshua, von Rad was impressed by the different ways in which the Deuteronomist had worked in the remainder of Noth's Deuteronomistic History. In Judges the Deuteronomist had given the material a cyclical schema, in 1 and 2 Samuel he had interfered very little with the sources, and in 1 and 2 Kings he had produced a history of the prophetic word with no sign of a cyclical view.[26] In light of these major differences between von Rad and Noth it is not surprising that the former has often been categorized among those rejecting Noth's thesis.[27]

Despite von Rad's pointed criticisms of Noth, however, he accepts the existence of a historical work produced by someone or a group with a particular theology and purpose. Because of the rather different styles in Judges and Kings he treats them and their theology separately, but at both places he freely speaks of the Deuteronomist. Von Rad is especially helpful when he describes how the Deuteronomist wrote his history as a history moved forward by the prophetic word.[28] Such an approach to either Judges or Kings would have been unheard of before Noth's claim that the Deuteronomist was a purposeful historian and not just a redactor combining two or more histories. In this von Rad accepts far more of Noth than is usually recognized.

The Two-Redaction Theory.[29] The most common way of adapting Noth's thesis is to accept the existence of a Deuteronomistic History, but

---

[25]Gerhard von Rad, "Hexateuch oder Pentateuch," *Verkündigung und Forschung* (1949/50) 52-56; von Rad, *Old Testament Theology* (2 vols.; New York: Harper & Row, 1962) 1:105-305.

[26]Von Rad, *OTT*, 1:327-47.

[27]One example of this is Radjawane, "Das deuteronomistische Geschichtswerk."

[28]Von Rad, *OTT*, 1:327-47; von Rad, "Theologische Geschichtsschreibung im Alten Testament," *TZ* 4 (1948) 161-74; von Rad, *Studies in Deuteronomy*, SBT, no. 9 (London: SCM, 1953) 74-91.

[29]For a good history of the two-redaction theory see Richard Donald Nelson, "The Redactional Duality of the Deuteronomistic History" (Th.D dissertation, Union Theological Seminary in Virginia, 1973) 1-38.

to argue that to speak of one single author[30] or redaction is too simplistic. In other words, it is suggested that there were at least two editions of the Deuteronomistic History, the first probably having been written before the beginning of the exile, and the second some time during the exile. Such an adaptation has its roots in OT studies going back well behind Noth. Abraham Kuenen had already observed that some of the editorial material in Kings assumed the destruction of Jerusalem and the beginning of the exile while other editorial comments suggested a composition before 587 B.C. He concluded that the basic structure of Kings had been supplied by a pre-exilic editor, and that this work then received some expansion bringing it up to date, and a slight revision during the exile.[31] Wellhausen[32] as well as a number of other scholars of the pre-Noth era[33] accepted Kuenen's proposals.

It is then not surprising that a number of scholars who followed the basic outline of Noth's thesis adapted it according to some of these earlier insights. Jepsen's research, although supporting Noth's basic thesis, also

---

[30]A number of Old Testament scholars prefer to speak of a D-group rather than of an individual author, e.g., R. A. Carlson, *David, the Chosen King* (Stockholm: Almqvist & Wiksell, 1964). If by this is meant that the author of the Deuteronomistic History had a community behind him and he was thus not completely alone in his thinking, then this is to be accepted. It is very doubtful that the Deuteronomist wrote as independently as Noth proposed. If the D-group is meant to refer to a group which wrote the history corporately and was able to write it with the same style and with the same theology, then this is probably not too significant. If various people of a group can compose a history in such a unified manner that differences cannot be distinguished, then it becomes essentially irrelevant whether the author was an individual or a group. If, however, the reference to a D-group is meant to imply that different styles of editing can be detected within the history, and that this is due to the fact that different people of the group wrote the different parts, then that is a reference to a multiple-redaction, and it is best to deal with it in this way rather than to speak of a D-group.

[31]Abraham Kuenen, *Historisch-kritische Einleitung in die Bücher des Alten Testaments* (Leipzig: Otto Schulze, 1887-92). Kuenen's views are summarized in Nelson, "Redactional Duality," pp. 5-9.

[32]Wellhausen, *Composition des Hexateuchs*, 297-300.

[33]Two examples are: Rudolf Kittel, *Die Bücher der Könige*, HAT, Abt. 1, Bd. 5 (Göttingen: Vandenhoeck & Ruprecht, 1900) vii-viii; Charles F. Burney, *Notes on the Hebrew Text of the Books of Kings* (Oxford: Clarendon, 1903) xvi-xviii.

suggested that such an adaptation might be valid.[34] A relatively wide-spread acceptance of a two-redaction theory can be found today in OT studies, introductions and commentaries, especially among those on Kings. Robert Pfeiffer,[35] H. H. Rowley,[36] Roland de Vaux,[37] Hans Walter Wolff,[38] Norman Snaith,[39] and John Gray[40] are just a few of the scholars who have indicated their preference for such an analysis.

This position has found new support in recent years through the work of Frank Cross.[41] Cross argues that the Deuteronomistic History was first "written in the era of Josiah as a programmatic document of his reform and of his revival of the Davidic state."[42] This work proclaimed Josiah as the new David and called on all Israel (both Judah and the people of the former North) to turn to Yahweh as directed in the recently found law-book of Deuteronomy. This edition was then brought up to date and revised so that it would speak to the exiles sometime around 550. Cross presents a very attractive setting and explanation for the two editions of

---

[34]Jepsen, *Quellen des Königsbuches.*

[35]Robert Pfeiffer, *Introduction to the Old Testament* (2nd ed.; London: Adam and Charles Black, 1948) 374-412.

[36]H. H. Rowley, *The Growth of the Old Testament* (London: Hutchinson's University Library, 1950) 73.

[37]Roland de Vaux, *Les Livres des Rois,* Vol. 2 Fasc. 4 of *La Sainte Bible,* sous le direction de l'Ecole Biblique de Jerusalem (Paris: Les Edition du Cerf, 1949) 15-17.

[38]Hans Walter Wolff, "The Kerygma of the Deuteronomic Historical Work," in *The Vitality of Old Testament Traditions* by W. Brueggemann & H. Wolff (Atlanta: John Knox, 1975) 83-100.

[39]Norman Snaith, "Introduction to and Exegesis of the First and Second Books of Kings," *IB* (New York: Abingdon, 1955) 3:10-11.

[40]John Gray, *I and II Kings,* OTL (Philadelphia: Westminster, 1964); Gray, *Joshua, Judges and Ruth,* CB (London: Thomas Nelson, 1967).

[41]Frank M. Cross, "The Structure of the Deuteronomic History," in *Perspectives in Jewish Learning,* Vol. 3 (Chicago: Spertus College of Judaica, 1967) 9-24; Cross, *Canaanite Myth and Hebrew Epic* (Cambridge: Harvard, 1973) 274-289.

In this Cross is taking a position earlier taken by his professor, William Foxwell Albright, *The Biblical Period from Abraham to Ezra* (New York: Harper, 1963); and affirmed by a fellow student of Albright's, John Bright, *A History of Israel,* 2nd ed. (Philadelphia: Westminster, 1972).

[42]Cross, *Canaanite Myth and Hebrew Epic,* 287.

the Deuteronomistic History even though he doesn't himself present all the necessary data to support his position.[43]

DtrG - DtrP - DtrN. Some German scholars have recently proposed a new adaptation of Noth's thesis. In 1971 Rudolf Smend wrote an article in which he analyzed a few passages in Joshua and in the introduction of the book of Judges.[44] On the basis of language, of distinctive theology, and of detected breaks in the narrative Smend concluded that Josh 1:7-9; 13:1bβ -6; 23; Judg 2:17, 20-21, 23 had been composed and inserted by a later editor into an already existing Deuteronomistic History. This same editor had also inserted the passage Judg 1:1-2:9 without himself composing it. Since the guiding principle for this later editor was adherence to the law, Smend called him DtrN, N standing for nomistic. Smend believed that this later editor had not only worked in the early traditions of the history but had revised the whole history. As Smend concluded: "Our investigation has pursued the goal of demonstrating the existence of a methodical revision of the Deuteronomistic History, with its major motive being the law."[45] (Translation mine).

Shortly thereafter a student of Smend's, Walter Dietrich, expanded on this and wrote a major, detailed work on the redaction history of the Deuteronomistic History.[46] Whereas Smend had worked with the early traditions Dietrich focussed exclusively upon Kings. In addition to the original Deuteronomist (called DtrG) and the nomistic editor (DtrN) distinguished by Smend, Dietrich found a prophetically inclined redaction (DtrP) as well. Using methods very similar to those of Smend, Dietrich argued that the original DtrG had contained very few prophetic traditions and that most of these had been inserted by DtrP, either by inserting older traditions or by composing his own material. The promise and fulfillment schema in Kings, emphasized by von Rad,[47] was taken to be the

---

[43]Jon D. Levenson, "Who Inserted the Book of the Torah?" *HTR* 68 (1975) 203-33, has accepted Cross's analysis of two Deuteronomistic editors, but has argued that the book of Deuteronomy was only inserted into the history by the second editor rather than by the first.

[44]Rudolf Smend, "Das Gesetz und die Völker," in *Probleme biblischer Theologie* (ed. Hans Walter Wolff; München: Chr. Kaiser, 1971) 494-509.

[45]Ibid., p. 509.

[46]Walter Dietrich, *Prophetie und Geschichte: Eine Redaktionsgeschichtliche Untersuchung zum deuteronomistischen Geschichtswerk,* FRLANT, Nr. 108 (Göttingen: Vandenhoeck & Ruprecht, 1972).

[47]See note 28.

contribution of DtrP. Thus for Dietrich these later two redactions were no minor ones but included rather major additions, both of older traditions and of new compositions. By comparing the language and style of these three redactions with other Israelite literature Dietrich concluded that DtrG had been written around 580 B.C., DtrP about ten years later, and DtrN another ten years later.

Although these proposals by Smend and Dietrich are less than ten years old, already a number of European scholars are following them, or even assuming them in their work. Timo Veijola has written two books in which he begins by assuming Dietrich's proposals, and then modifies them on the basis of his own work.[48] In his *Das Königtum in der Beurteilung der deuteronomistischen Historiographie* he attempts to describe the concept of kingship held by each of these three editions. Tryggve Mettinger begins his work by stating that he considers Dietrich's view to be "basically correct," although he is not quite as convinced that all of these editors worked during the exile.[49] Both Ernst Würthwein,[50] and a student of his, Helmut Hollenstein[51] have written articles in which they suggest that this is the direction Deuteronomistic studies will go, and Kaiser's introduction[52] points in a similar direction. Wolfgang Roth has tried to support the proposal with an analysis of the phrase "Yahweh grants rest to . . ."[53] This rapid acceptance of Dietrich's analysis is quite striking.

---

[48]Timo Veijola, *Die ewige Dynastie. David und die Entstehung seiner Dynastie nach der deuteronomistischen Darstellung,* Suomalaisen Tiedeakatemian Toimituksia Annales Academiae Scientiarum Fennicae, Ser. B, Tom. 193 (Helsinki: Suomalainen Tiedeakatemia, 1975); Veijola, *Das Königtum in der Beurteilung der deuteronomistischen Historiographie. Eine redaktionsgeschichtliche Untersuchung,* Suomalaisen Tiedeakatemian Toimituksia Annales Academiae Scientiarum Fennicae, Ser. B, Tom. 198 (Helsinki: Suomalainen Tiedeakatemia, 1977).

[49]Tryggve N. D. Mettinger, *King and Messiah. The Civil and Sacral Legitimation of the Israelite Kings,* Coniectanea Biblica, OT Ser. 8 (Lund: C. W. K. Gleerup, 1976).

[50]Ernst Würthwein, "Die Josianische Reform und das Deuteronomium," *ZTK* 73 (1976) 395-423. Würthwein also assumes this analysis in his commentary on Kings, Würthwein, *Das erste Buch der Könige. Kapitel 1-16,* ATD, Teilband 11, 1 (Göttingen: Vandenhoeck & Ruprecht, 1977).

[51]Helmut Hollenstein, "Literarkritische Erwägungen zum Bericht über die Reformmassnahmen Josias, 2 Kön. XXIII 4ff," *VT* 27 (1977) 321-36.

[52]Kaiser, *Introduction,* 173-75.

[53]Wolfgang Roth, "The Deuteronomic Rest Theology: A Redaction-Critical Study," *BR* 21 (1976): 5-14.

A RESPONSE TO THE RESEARCH ON
THE COMPOSITION OF THE DEUTERONOMISTIC HISTORY

It is probably correct to say that during the past 35 years Noth's basic thesis has won the day and become one of the "assured results of critical scholarship." The criticism of men like Hölscher and Eissfeldt has not been successful in stemming the tide.[54] The work of Richter[55] and Beyerlin[56] has considerably weakened von Rad's contention that the Deuteronomist's theology of history in Judges is very different from that found in Kings. Despite this basic agreement few are prepared to accept Noth's proposal as he presented it, and there is no consensus among scholars on how it is to be modified. Incongruencies and differences of perspective within the Deuteronomistic History, and especially within Kings, have pushed many, if not most scholars, to argue that the present history is not the product of only one composition, but that further redactions can be detected. Noth had of course recognized that there were a number of

---

[54]One of Eissfeldt's arguments against Noth was that 1 Samuel 7-12 is best explained by seeing it as the combination of parallel strands, and not as the composition of an author adding his anti-kingship comments to the more positively inclined sources, Eissfeldt, "Die Geschichtswerke im AT." Hans Jochen Boecker has responded to such an argument in *Die Beurteilung der Anfänge des Königtums in den deuteronomistischen Abschnitten. Ein Beitrag zum Problem des "deuteronomistischen Geschichtswerks,"* WMANT, BD. 31 (Neukirchen: Neukirchener, 1969). He argues that the Deuteronomistic parts of 1 Samuel 7-12 are not anti-kingship and thus not in conflict with sources used by the Deuteronomist, and so there is no problem in seeing these chapters as the product of a single author.

[55]Wolfgang Richter, *Traditionsgeschichtliche Untersuchungen zum Richterbuch*, BBB, Nr. 18 (Bonn: Peter Hanstein, 1963); Richter, *Die Bearbeitungen des "Retterbuches" in der deuteronomistischen Epoche.* BBB, Nr. 21 (Bonn: Peter Hanstein, 1964).

[56]Walter Beyerlin, "Gattung und Herkunft des Rahmens im Richterbuch," in *Tradition und Situation. Studien zur alttestamentlichen Prophetie* (Göttingen: Vandenhoeck & Ruprecht, 1963) 1-29. Both Richter and Beyerlin argue that the stereotyped frameworks of the individual judge traditions are not the contribution of the Deuteronomist but were already part of a "Retterbuch" which the Deuteronomist incorporated into his history. If they are correct then the cyclical picture of the book of Judges cannot be attributed to the Deuteronomist. This then weakens the conflict between the Deuteronomist's view of history as found in Kings, and as found in Judges, as emphasized by von Rad.

additions which had been made to the Deuteronomistic History at a later point but he never spoke of them as part of a later redaction. Scholars are thus now debating questions like: How many redactions were there? How extensive were they? When and where did they occur? Can the later redaction(s) be separated from the original history?

Walter Dietrich's analysis of the Deuteronomistic history with its answers to these questions[57] has won considerable support in a relatively short period of time. It is our contention, however, that there are some real weaknesses in his analysis. On the one hand, Dietrich (as well as Veijola) places an extremely heavy emphasis on minor differences in word choice, and on a modern concept of what a smoothly flowing passage is. It almost assumes that different editors could not have used the same term for something, or that one editor could not use different terms for an idea. It also assumes that ancient writers never produced material with poor or rough connections between thoughts. On the other hand, Dietrich makes surprisingly little use of form criticism in his analysis. The numerous places in Kings where there is similarly phrased and structured prophetic speech need not necessarily point to the same redactor but may be due to standard forms of prophetic speech which would have been well known to anyone. Any author describing a prophet speaking could then have adopted this form. The fact that similar forms are found in the writings of different classical prophets supports this. In his analysis Dietrich does not recognize the significance of standard forms, and instead places a very heavy emphasis on a linguistic analysis and a type of redaction criticism. What Burke Long says of Veijola in a review of his recent book would apply equally well to Dietrich:

> And yet, the method seems to be too limited and, at the same time, to have been pushed too far. It is now time for the practitioners of classical redaction criticism to confront the growing dissatisfaction with the method itself—its limited assumptions and heavy reliance upon equivocable internal evidence. Words, style, and themes seem so easily restricted to certain groups, as though within the same society separate groups cannot share viewpoints and idioms of language, or express themselves without confusion and ambiguity.[58]

---

[57]Dietrich, *Prophetie und Geschichte*.

[58]Burke Long, review of *Das Königtum in der Beurteilung der deutero-nomistischen Historiographie. Eine redaktionsgeschichtliche Unter-suchung*, 1977, by Timo Veijola, in *JBL* 98 (1979) 120.

The analysis and conclusions of Dietrich (and Veijola) need to be put to a further test. At some point it simply needs to be asked whether the conclusions arrived at make sense, or whether they fit with what is known about Israel's history and history writing. Is there any evidence that the kind of redaction upon redaction which Dietrich suggests ever took place? This is not to imply that OT literature was all produced by individual authors, or that a later editor or redactor could not have added some passages or made some changes in an existing literary work, but this is still far short of the kind of repeated systematic reworking of an earlier history which Dietrich proposes. Further, Dietrich and Veijola argue that these later redactors revised the earlier histories in order to emphasize their distinctive, differing viewpoints. In fact, these different viewpoints are seen as not only reflecting various perspectives, but as directly conflicting. It is questionable whether the evidence supports such an analysis.[59] It also needs to be asked whether the ideology supposedly expressed by the different redactors was really present in Israel at that time. According to Veijola the exilic DtrN revised the text he received on the basis of a rather anti-monarchical viewpoint, whereas Frank Crüsemann has made a strong case for his contention that the only period in Israel's history for which there is any evidence of anti-monarchical sentiment is the time of David and Solomon.[60] Thus both the methods and the conclusions of Dietrich and those following his analysis seem questionable at points. In light of this it is doubtful that this direction of studies will prevail in the future.

This does not mean, however, that the unified exilic authorship

---

[59]In this Dietrich and Veijola are proposing that the Deuteronomist(s) worked exactly as Noth suggested he had in 1 Samuel 7-12. Noth argued that the Deuteronomist added his anti-kingship comments in order to negate or contend against the traditions which were more positively inclined toward kingship. As we argue below, this is also not an acceptable analysis of 1 Samuel 7-12.

[60]Frank Crüsemann, *Der Widerstand gegen das Königtum. Die antiköniglichen Texte des Alten Testamentes und der Kampf um den frühen israelitischen Staat*, WMANT, Bd. 49 (Neukirchen: Neukirchener, 1978).

Karl-Heinz Bernhardt, *Das Problem der altorientalischen Königsideologie im Alten Testament unter besonderer Berücksichtigung der Geschichte der Psalmenexegese dargestellt und kritisch gewürdigt*, VTSup, Vol. 8 (Leiden: E. J. Brill, 1961), had earlier already argued that there was no evidence for an increase in anti-kingship sentiment during the time of the exile.

assumed by Noth will win out. As Kuenen and many others have noted, there are passages in the Deuteronomistic History which appear to be editorial and which are not aware of the exile. 1 Kgs 11:39 expects the division of the kingdom not to be permanent. This would fit well into the time of Josiah's reign when hopes for a reunion of the kingdom were strong.[61] At the same time there are other passages which clearly assume the beginning of the exile. 1 Kgs 8:46-53 and 2 Kgs 21:8ff. are two examples of this. A solution to the redactional question of the Deuteronomistic History must incorporate these two factors. This leads us to some form of the two-redaction theory.

One of the better cases for the two-redaction analysis of the Deuteronomistic History has been made by Richard Nelson.[62] Nelson attempts to support Cross's analysis through a study of the regnal formulae in the history. These stereotyped regnal formulae have long been seen as important for a study of the redaction history of Kings. Various studies of them have been made, but with limited success.[63] Nelson states that if Cross is correct, then "the formulae at the end of the book might be expected to show some subtle change from those of the main redactor, most likely becoming less varied and even more stereotyped than their exemplar."[64] Nelson then proceeds to do a very thorough study of these regnal formulae, and discovers that the formulae for the last four kings of Judah are clearly more wooden and less variable than the formulae for the rest of the kings of Israel and Judah. Helga Weippert's recent study of the regnal formulae of Kings, although on the whole arriving at conclusions that cannot be accepted, also separates the regnal formulae of the last four kings from the rest.[65] Nelson's research thus strongly supports the thesis

---

[61]David C. Greenwood, "On the Jewish Hope for a Restored Northern Kingdom," *ZAW* 88 (1976) 376-85.

[62]Nelson, "Redactional Duality."

[63]Two examples are: Helga Weippert, "Die 'deuteronomistischen' Beurteilungen der Könige von Israel und Juda und das Problem der Redaktion der Königsbücher," *Bib* 53 (1972) 301-39; Shoshana R. Bin-Nun, "Formulas from the Royal Records of Israel and of Judah," *VT* 18 (1968) 414-32.

[64]Nelson, "Redactional Duality," p. 45.

[65]Weippert, "Die 'deuteronomistischen' Beurteilungen der Könige." Nelson, "Redactional Duality," p. 44, says "Weippert's thesis, however, is fatally weakened by the extensive variations within the respective domains of the hypothetical R I and R II, the free variations in other elements of the regnal formulae that cut across Weippert's divisions, and

that the Deuteronomistic History was written some time during the reign of Josiah or shortly thereafter, and that it was then updated by an exilic editor who attempted to copy the style of the original historian.

Once such a thesis is accepted, Cross's proposal regarding a setting and purpose for these two editions of the history becomes quite attractive.[66] The reforms of Josiah had resulted in a new interest in Judah's traditions and history. The role of the Deuteronomic law made it natural that this history would now be interpreted in light of this law. The fact that Josiah had adopted the Deuteronomic law for the land will have made people optimistic that Judah would be able to avoid the fate which fell upon Israel. This history thus proclaimed Josiah as the new David, and called upon the people to turn to Yahweh. The mood of the exilic addition would have been much more somber. It was not without all hope, but it needed to explain the defeat of Judah and Jerusalem. The sins of Manasseh were seen as having been so great that even the reforms of Josiah could not cancel Yahweh's punishment of Judah, 2 Kgs 21:7-15; 23:26-27. With this description Cross has given a possible explanation for how the present Deuteronomistic History came into existence, and has provided a motivation that fits into the historical setting for both the original historian (Dtr[1]) and for the exilic redactor (Dtr[2]).

According to Cross the contribution of Dtr[2] to the history was really quite minor. Dtr[2] is described as having added 2 Kgs 23:28-25:30 in order to bring the history up to date, and some shorter passages within the history itself.[67] Despite the small amount of material added by Dtr[2], Cross considers it possible to distinguish the theology of his Dtr[2] from Dtr[1]. At this point distinctions have perhaps been made too finely.[68] It is also probable that the exilic redactor made more additions than Cross suggested. Nelson already argued for this in his dissertation.[69] We would thus argue that the two-redaction theory is probably the correct one, but

---

the need to postulate an editor vitally interested in cultic centralization a hundred years before the discovery of Deuteronomy."

[66]Cross, *Canaanite Myth and Hebrew Epic*, 278-89.

[67]Cross lists most of the passages which he considers to have been added by Dtr[2] in *Canaanite Myth and Hebrew Epic*, 287.

[68]Cross argues that Dtr[1] accepted the Judaean royal ideology with an emphasis on the unconditional nature of the Davidic covenant, whereas Dtr[2], having experienced the events of 587 B.C., considered the Davidic covenant to have been conditional. It is extremely questionable whether such a distinction can be made.

[69]Nelson, "Redactional Duality."

that the second redactor made more additions in the history than is proposed by Cross.[70] We would question, however, whether the ideology of this exilic redactor was really significantly different from that of the original. His additions were made in order to bring the history up to date, and to explain the events of 587 B.C. within that history, and not in order to correct the message of the first redactor. The reason he added his additions to an already existing history was that that history, although written before the exile, gave the necessary information to interpret the events of 587 B.C. The final form of the history is thus the product of different stages, but reflects a continuity of thought.

A REVIEW OF RESEARCH ON KINGSHIP ACCORDING TO THE DEUTERONOMISTIC HISTORY

In the past, research on the topic of kingship according to the Deuteronomistic History has focussed very largely on the narratives found in 1 Samuel 7-12. This review will therefore also deal largely with studies on this passage.

The Traditional Position

Any review of the way kingship has been seen within the books of Deuteronomy to Kings must begin with the work of Julius Wellhausen. The analysis and conclusions of Wellhausen became the basis of virtually all scholarly work on the subject till at least 1962,[71] and are still accepted by many scholars right till today. At the heart of Wellhausen's analysis rests his concept of the history of Israel. According to Wellhausen the history of Israel reached its highest point in the monarchy. The theocracy of the post-exilic period was then an immense retrogression into a heathen cultus and binding legalism. Wellhausen's view of how the institution of kingship was perceived by Israel at the various stages was then

---

[70]Peter R. Ackroyd presented a lecture at Union Theological Seminary in Virginia in January, 1979, in which he also suggested the existence of a pre-exilic edition of the Deuteronomistic History which had then received a significant redaction during the exile.

[71]1962 marked a turning point of sorts in that one of the first major critiques of the traditional analysis was published then—Artur Weiser, *Samuel: Seine geschichtliche Aufgabe und religiöse Bedeutung. Traditionsgeschichtliche Untersuchungen zu I Samuel 7-12.* FRLANT, hft. 81 (Göttingen: Vandenhoeck & Ruprecht, 1962).

derived from this picture of the history of Israel. Since kingship was seen by Wellhausen as having brought order into the time of the judges,[72] those people experiencing the benefits of the institution must have evaluated it very highly.

> In the eyes of Israel before the exile the monarchy is the culminating point of the history, and the greatest blessing of Jehovah. It was preceded by a period of unrest and affliction, when every man did what was right in his own eyes, and the enemies of Israel accordingly got everything their own way. Under it the people dwell securely and respected by those round about; guarded by the shelter of civil order, the citizen can sit under his own vine and his fig-tree.[73]

Further, he argues "That Hebrew antiquity knew nothing of any hostility or incompatibility between the heavenly and the earthly ruler is plain from the title Anointed of Jehovah, and from the hope of the prophets, whose ideal future would be incomplete without a human king."[74] It is then clear that anti-monarchic sentiment could not have arisen during the time when its benefits were so obvious. Rather, such polemic must have arisen within Judaism after the end of the institution of kingship. As he states, "the idea here before us can only have arisen in an age which had no knowledge of Israel as a people and a state, and which had no experience of the real conditions of existence in these forms; in other words, it is the offspring of exilic or post-exilic Judaism."[75] Wellhausen saw this analysis confirmed by the fact that where kingship is rejected, it is rejected on the basis of Yahweh's kingship, a concept which could only have come into existence after Israel had experienced a human kingship. An emphasis on the exclusiveness of Yahweh's kingship reflects the ideals of the post-exilic theocracy. "At that time, accordingly, the theocracy *existed*, and it is from that time that it is transported in an idealized form to earlier times."[76]

The above picture then provided the assumptions for his analysis of the

---

[72]Crüsemann, *Der Widerstand gegen das Königtum*, 3-10, makes an interesting comparison between Wellhausen's concept of the role of kingship for Israel, and his view of the Kaiser of his day.

[73]Wellhausen, *Prolegomena*, 253.

[74]Ibid., p. 254.

[75]Ibid., p. 255.

[76]Ibid.

extremely important chapters for any understanding of the OT view of kingship, namely 1 Samuel 7-12. Using their opinion of the monarchy as a primary criterion, Wellhausen concluded that these chapters consisted of two series of traditions: a pro-kingship series (9:1-10:16; 11), and an anti-kingship series (7:2-8:22; 10:17-27; 12). The pro-kingship series must have arisen some time during the time of the monarchy and contains some valid historical traditions. The two accounts in this series need not necessarily have been connected with each other originally. The anti-kingship series is obviously totally fictional. It was written by the last redactor of the Former Prophets on the basis of the earlier series, and expresses his negative view of kingship in keeping with the mood of his times. In this way Wellhausen's literary analysis of 1 Samuel 7-12 corresponded perfectly with his understanding of the history of Israel and role of kingship within that history.

Wellhausen's key conclusions could be summarized as follows:

(1) 1 Samuel 7-12 is composed of two series of traditions distinguishable from each other by their evaluation of kingship

(2) The series in 7:2-8:22; 10:17-27; 12 is a literary unity and clearly anti-kingship

(3) The anti-kingship polemic expressed in this series could only have arisen after the end of the monarchy, and is thus much younger and less trustworthy than the pro-kingship series.

These three conclusions of Wellhausen had a tremendous impact upon OT studies. The first two were accepted virtually as Wellhausen presented them, and although many did not accept the exact dating of the third, nor the logic by which he arrived at it, most also accepted his assertion that the anti-kingship series was later and less trust-worthy than the other series. Thus scholars like B. Stade, A. Kuenen, Baudissin, C. Steuernagel and others[77] accepted the existence of an anti-kingship series in 1 Samuel 1-12 and considered it to be a late composition based on reflections on experience with kingship. As O. Plöger stated: "Samuel speaks as though he has known kingship and its defects for a long time, and one would be justified in surmising that this hostile attitude toward kingship would belong to a time which had endured gloomy experiences with royal authority."[78] (Translation mine). Those who practiced source analysis tended to

---

[77]For a summary of the positions taken on this by these and other scholars see Bernhardt, *Königsideologie im AT*, 114-116.

[78]Otto Plöger, *Die Prophetengeschichten der Samuel- und Königsbücher* (Greifswald: J. Adler, 1937). This quotation was cited in Bernhardt, *Königsideologie im AT*, 115.

arrive at similar conclusions. Budde attributed 1 Sam 9:1-10:16; 11 to his J; and the anti-kingship series he assigned to his E, concluding that it was not Deuteronomic, and that it had not been composed on the basis of the earlier pro-kingship traditions but was independent.[79] Hölscher made a similar analysis of these chapters, although he divided the E-strand into two different layers.[80] Eissfeldt also attributed the anti-kingship series to E, and then divided the rest between his L and J.[81] In this way these scholars tended to adopt Wellhausen's conclusions although they argued that the anti-kingship series, while clearly late and younger than the pro-kingship series, need not necessarily have arisen after the end of the monarchy. It is interesting to note that in shifting Wellhausen's conclusions in this way they were making a rather significant change in the understanding of kingship in Israel. Whereas Wellhausen had argued that the anti-kingship polemic could only have arisen at a time when all the positive benefits of kingship had already been forgotten, these scholars now argued that this polemic must have been late since it reflects all the negative experiences which Israel had had with kingship. Despite this significant difference with Wellhausen as to why the anti-kingship series was late, they largely agreed with him on its existence, and on his emphasis that it was much later and much less trustworthy than the pro-kingship series.

Martin Noth was probably the most influential OT scholar to adopt Wellhausen's analysis, fitting it into his own concept of a Deuteronomistic History. In his traditio-historical study of the Deuteronomistic History Noth argued very strongly that the Deuteronomist himself was opposed to the institution of kingship. According to Noth the Deuteronomist was writing an obituary for Israel and at the same time justifying the actions of God. According to the Deuteronomist the end of Israel had been brought about by her kings. Noth detected the Deuteronomist's negative evaluation of kingship in the repeated, almost monotonous negative judgments of the individual kings, as well as in the frequent prophetic condemnations of the kings within that history. Most clearly, however, the Deuteronomist's views were expressed in the narratives recording the origins of the institution in Israel. Noth argued that on the whole the

[79]Karl Budde, *Die Bücher Richter und Samuel. Ihre Quellen und ihr Aufbau* (Giessen: J. Ricker, 1890) 169-88; Budde, *Samuel*, 47-82.
[80]Hölscher, *Geschichtsschreibung in Israel*, 366-67.
[81]Eissfeldt, *Introduction*, 271-80.

Deuteronomist took a rather conservative stance towards his sources, as a rule simply reproducing them as he had received them. Nevertheless, "Dtr has . . . made it totally clear by the way kingship is introduced into the history that it was temporally a secondary, and according to him, even an improper and fundamentally to be rejected adjustment."[82] (Translation mine). At this point the events were too important for the Deuteronomist to leave the received traditions uncorrected. He responded by including the relatively pro-kingship traditions in his history, but also by adding his own interpretation of the events which expressed his negative viewpoint, the anti-kingship series of 7:2-8:22; 10:17-27; 12. In this way the Deuteronomist made his own position clear. As Noth stated in his conclusion, "the negative judgment upon the establishment of kingship, and the characterization of it as a secondary appearance in the history of the people were essential features of his (the Deuteronomist's) entire conception of history."[83] (Translation mine). Noth had thus accepted Wellhausen's analysis of 1 Samuel 7-12, and even supported it by his own study of the Deuteronomistic History as a whole. Anti-kingship sentiment was not only to be found in the anti-kingship series of 1 Samuel 7-12, but was an essential part of the Deuteronomist's understanding of Israel's history.

This traditional position regarding 1 Samuel 7-12 with its implications for the understanding of the Deuteronomist's view of kingship was the standard position of most OT research until a few years ago and is still common in recent monographs, commentaries and articles. Most OT introductions still speak of an "early, pro-monarchic source," and a "late, anti-monarchic source."[84] It is usually implied that the later tradition is then much less valuable as a source for the actual events. There is some disagreement as to who composed the anti-kingship series; some see it as the contribution of the Deuteronomist whereas others consider it to be a separate tradition, although still younger than the pro-kingship series. Hertzberg represents such a position. He finds it difficult to distinguish between his "Mizpah source" and his final "deuteronomistic compiler" in 1 Samuel 8, but then adds "in view of the similarity of the basic position of the final compiler and the material with which he was working, it is at

---

[82]Noth, *ÜgS*, 95.

[83]Ibid., p. 110.

[84]Note: Flanders, Crapps & Smith, *Introduction*, 193-95; Anderson, *Understanding*, 121-34; Norman K. Gottwald, *A Light to the Nations. An Introduction to the Old Testament* (New York: Harper, 1959) 180-84.

the same time not over-important."[85] Aubrey Johnson distinguishes between the two series, and then states that the "later standpoint shows a more critical attitude towards the monarchy, and there is reason to believe that we have here a line of thought issuing in the work of the Deuteronomic school."[86] Despite some of the recent studies which have challenged this position there is apparently still sufficient consensus on this that Joseph Blenkinsopp can say in his article of 1975, "This historical work, written from the perspective of national collapse and dispersion, quite naturally exhibits a starkly negative evaluation of the monarchy. . ."[87] Many other illustrations of this could be given. Wellhausen's analysis of 1 Samuel 7-12, and Noth's understanding of the Deuteronomist's view of kingship quickly became and have largely remained the standard position on the subject.

Recent Alternative Proposals

Although the Wellhausen-Noth analysis of 1 Samuel 7-12 with its understanding of the Deuteronomist's view of kingship became the standard position, it has not gone unchallenged. The issue itself has become especially discussed in the past decade or so as various new proposals have been made. Some of the more significant works will now be summarized.

One of the first major critiques of the Wellhausen-Noth analysis came from Artur Weiser.[88] Weiser contended that in following Wellhausen's analysis of 1 Samuel 7-12 Noth was still bound to the earlier literary critical methods, and that a new tradition-historical ("*traditions-*

[85]Hans Wilhelm Hertzberg, *I & II Samuel*, OTL (Philadelphia: Westminster, 1964) 74.

[86]Aubrey R. Johnson, "Hebrew Conceptions of Kingship," in *Myth, Ritual and Kingship. Essays on the Theory and Practice of Kingship in the Ancient Near East and in Israel* (ed. H. S. Hooke; Oxford: Clarendon, 1958) 204.

[87]Joseph Blenkinsopp, "The Quest of the Historical Saul," in *No Famine in the Land* (eds. J. Flanagan and A. W. Robinson; Missoula, Scholars, 1975) 77.

Note also that the following have both determined that Judges 17-21 was not part of the Deuteronomistic History since its view of kingship clashes with the anti-kingship sentiment of the Deuteronomist: Schulte, *Geschichtsschreibung im Alten Israel*, 103; Gottfried Seitz, *Redaktionsgeschichtliche Studien zum Deuteronomium*, BWANT, hft. 93 (Stuttgart: W. Kohlhammer, 1971) 133.

[88]Weiser, *Samuel*.

geschichtliche") approach was required. To begin with, he considered it
wrong to divide these chapters into two literary series on the basis of
their supposed stance towards kingship. He disagreed with both Wellhausen and Noth when he argued that the so-called anti-kingship series
was not really a literary unity, and was not consistently anti-kingship.
Further, he disagreed with Noth that this series of passages should be
attributed to the Deuteronomist in keeping with his anti-kingship stance.
Such a conclusion, he argued, was not supportable by any linguistic analysis, and was made extremely questionable by the fact "that neither in
Deuteronomy nor in the Deuteronomistic books of Kings is there any
question of a fundamental rejection of kingship."[89] (Translation mine).
Rather, Weiser proposed that the various traditions found in 1 Samuel 7-
12 should be traced back to different sanctuaries where they had been
preserved. According to Weiser the traditions found in 1 Samuel 7-12 are
relatively trustworthy, and all agree upon giving Samuel a central role in
the beginning of kingship. Thus 1 Samuel 7 arose in Mizpah, and relatively
accurately gives a picture of Samuel's role as judge, even though the
account of the victory over the Philistines must be seen as fiction.
1 Samuel 8 was based on the memories of the followers of Samuel in
Ramah and accurately reflects the tensions present at the founding of the
monarchy. Weiser does not see this chapter as totally rejecting kingship,
but argues that the issue here is the kind of kingship which Israel should
have. By incorporating the "ways of the king" based on the practices of
the surrounding nations of that time the author is saying that Israel is not
to have a king like the kings of that time.[90] 1 Samuel 9-12 then continues
the account of how Samuel succeeded in starting a kingship in Israel which
was uniquely Israelite, and which was in keeping with Israel's Yahwistic
faith. The traditions of 1 Samuel 9-12 are also traced back to local sanctuaries. There is then no possibility of dividing 1 Samuel 7-12 into two
strands, one pro-kingship and the other anti-kingship. With his analysis
Weiser rejected all three of Wellhausen's conclusions. By attributing the
traditions to sanctuaries and not to the Deuteronomist he also argued that
1 Samuel 7-12 could not be a major source for discovering the Deuteronomist's view of kingship. Although Weiser's conclusions have not won a

---

[89]Ibid., p. 27.
[90]Ibid., pp. 38-42. On this particular point Weiser has accepted the
conclusions of Isaac Mendelsohn, "Samuel's Denunciation of Kingship in
the Light of Akkadian Documents from Ugarit," *BASOR* 143 (1956) 17-22.

significant following they opened the doors for further critiques of Wellhausen and Noth and the traditional picture.[91]

Writing about the same time as Weiser, Karl-Heinz Bernhardt also presented conclusions different from those of Wellhausen and Noth in a book largely devoted to criticizing the "myth and ritual" approach to kingship in the OT.[92] Bernhardt contended against Wellhausen that the origin of anti-kingship polemic could not be placed in the time of the exile or later. An examination of other writings from this time (e.g. Chronicles, exilic prophets, apocryphal writings) reveals that sentiments against kingship tended not to become harsher during the exile but rather milder. Further, he emphasized that "a fundamental negation of kingship during the exilic and later time fits badly as that was exactly the same epoch in which the eschatological hope for a saving king from the seed of David was at the center of Jewish faith."[93] (Translation mine). Berhardt also argued against Noth that anti-kingship polemic could not have been essentially a Deuteronomistic view.[94] "Deuteronomy and those historical traditions shaped on the basis of its spirit know no fundamental rejection of kingship, but only a critique of individual kings in so far as they did not conform to the positive in the defined royal ideal of the law of the king in Deuteronomy 17."[95] (Translation mine). The Deuteronomist, in keeping with the law of kingship found in Deut 17:14-20, thus criticizes individual kings for not upholding the Deuteronomic law but is in no way basically opposed to the institution of kingship itself. This position was supported by his analysis of 1 Samuel 7-12 in which he concluded that 1 Samuel 12 is Deuteronomistic but not essentially anti-kingship, and 1 Samuel 8 is opposed to kingship but is not Deuteronomistic. Bernhardt placed the origin of anti-kingship sentiment in the nature of pre-state Israel. He

---

[91]It should be noted that Hertzberg, *I & II Samuel,* although in a number of ways still following the traditional position (e.g. 1 Samuel 8 and 12 are clearly anti-kingship, the Deuteronomist is anti-kingship), also traces the traditions of these chapters on the origin of kingship to various old Israelite sanctuaries.

[92]See especially Chapter IV, "Die Ablehnung des Königtums als Charakteristikum der Königsauffassung im Alten Testament," pp. 114-82 in Bernhardt, *Königsideologie im AT.*

[93]Ibid., p. 116.

[94]Although Noth admitted that the anti-kingship views expressed by the Deuteronomist could have already existed much earlier, he seems to have made little allowance for this in his writings.

[95]Bernhardt, *Königsideologie,* 139.

found indications of this in the following texts, all of which he considered to be early: 1 Sam 10:21b β-11:15 (10:27a refers to "worthless fellows" who are opposed to Saul); Judg 9:7-15 (Jotham fable); Judg 8:22-23 (Gideon's rejection of kingship); 1 Sam 8:11-18 (the "ways of the king"). Thus he concluded that the strongest anti-kingship views were found in the earliest traditions, and were based in the nomadic ideal of pre-state Israel, as well as in her amphictyonic Yahwism. Within these traditions the rise of kingship was seen as (1) rebellion against Yahweh, and (2) as tyranny. In this way Bernhardt continued to accept the anti-kingship nature of 1 Samuel 8, but disagreed with Wellhausen's literary analysis of 1 Samuel 7-12, and offered a telling critique of Wellhausen's view that anti-kingship polemic could only have arisen during the exile or later. He was also clearly not satisfied with Noth's emphasis on the anti-kingship nature of the Deuteronomist.[96]

A renewed interest in kingship within OT studies was signalled and perhaps instigated by the work of J. Alberto Soggin.[97] In his major work he traces the institution of kingship from its primitive, democratic origins to its end in 587 B.C. and attempts to place it within its historical setting. In this study he suggests that the traditions contained in 1 Sam 7-8; 10:17-

---

[96]Berhardt's critique of Wellhausen and of some aspects of Noth is quite effective. Despite this, Bernhardt is seldom referred to when the traditional picture is presented or criticized. This is very possibly due to the fact that Bernhardt largely failed in his critique of the "myth and ritual" school. A. R. Johnson points at this when he says in a summary of Bernhardt's book: "To be frank, it is difficult to know what value to place upon a work in which the arguments of so many different authors are wrenched from their contexts and lumped together in such a way as to provide a convenient target for criticism." Johnson, summary of Karl-Heinz Bernhardt, *Das Problem der altorientalischen Königsideologie im Alten Testament unter Berücksichtigung der Geschichte der Psalmenexegese dargestellt und kritisch gewürdigt*, in *A Decade of Bible Bibliography. The Book Lists of the Society for Old Testament Study, 1957-1966* (ed. G. W. Anderson; Oxford: Basil Blackwell, 1967) 352.

[97]J. Alberto Soggin, *Das Königtum in Israel. Ursprünge, Spannungen, Entwicklung*. BZAW, Nr. 104 (Berlin: Alfred Töpelmann, 1967). Note also the following articles: Soggin, "Charisma und Institution im Königtum Sauls," *ZAW* 75 (1963) 54-65; Soggin, "Der offiziel geförderte Synkretismus in Israel während des 10. Jahrhunderts," *ZAW* 78 (1966) 179-203; Soggin, "Der Beitrag des Königtums zur altisraelitischen Religion," in *Studies in the Religion of Ancient Israel*, VTSup, Vol. 23 (Leiden: E. J. Brill, 1972) 9-26.

27; 12; 15, although relatively late and thoroughly Deuteronomistic in their present form, do contain accurate recollections of the tensions present at the origin of kingship in Israel. Opposition to kingship probably had been a major reason why Israel delayed adopting the institution in the first place. This is also reflected in Judg 8:22-23. In fact, anti-kingship feelings suit this early period better than any other later time. Despite speaking of prophetic and Deuteronomistic criticism of kingship, Soggin emphasizes that the Deuteronomist was not opposed to the institution of kingship itself. The Deuteronomist only criticized "non-orthodox" kings, and his negative judgments are clearly theological and not historical. Further, the Deuteronomist highly praised Hezekiah and Josiah indicating that it was possible to be a good king. Although Soggin had been primarily interested in the history of the institution, his work further opened the way for new study of how kingship was treated in the Deuteronomistic History.

Noth had argued that the Deuteronomist himself had composed the so-called anti-kingship series in order to offset the pro-kingship sentiments of the received older traditions. A number of OT scholars had criticized Noth at this point, arguing that the self-contradictory nature of 1 Samuel 7-12 which this produced made the supposition of a single-minded Deuteronomistic historian untenable.[98] Hans Jochen Boecker attempted to defend Noth's theory against such an accusation. He accepts Noth's view that the Deuteronomist himself had composed the series found in 1 Sam 7:2-8:22; 10:17-27; 12, and that it was not based on older traditions. In other words, this series presented the Deuteronomist's own views on kingship. The key question for Boecker then is, however, whether the customary characterization of these Deuteronomistic passages as fundamentally opposed to kingship is correct.[99] Here Boecker disagrees with Noth and says it is not. Boecker argues that there is no real contradiction between the earlier traditions of 1 Sam 9:1-10:16; 11 and the Deuteronomistic parts of 1 Samuel 7-12 since neither series is opposed to the existence of the institution of kingship. Rather, at various points within 1 Samuel 7-12 the Deuteronomist clearly indicated that Yahweh had instituted this new form of government. Samuel is commanded by Yahweh to heed the voice of the people, and it is emphasized that Yahweh had chosen Saul as the first king. "Kingship is in no way 'fundamentally' rejected;

---

[98]Two examples of this would be: Weiser, *Samuel*; Weiser, *Introduction*, 161; and Eissfeldt, "Geschichtswerke im AT," pp. 22-25.
[99]Boecker, *Die Beurteilung der Anfänge des Königtums*.

it goes back to an explicit act (*Setzung*) of Yahweh, and from that it receives its religious dignity"[100] (Translation mine). Because of this Boecker claims that according to the Deuteronomist "In this way kingship is pulled into a sequence with the other great historical acts of Yahweh, the gift of the land, the election of Jerusalem."[101] (Translation mine). In these chapters the Deuteronomist clearly indicates that with the origin of kingship a new era has begun, an era which has the possibility of blessing or curse. "If Israel follows the commands of Yahweh, Yahweh will remain king and helper in battle (12:14), if it resists, he will turn against the people (12:15)."[102] (Translation mine). Boecker recognizes the presence of elements critical of kingship in the Deuteronomistic parts of these chapters, but argues that they were not opposed to the institution itself but only to aspects of it. Kingship was rejected when, in internal policies, it oppressed the people and made slaves of them. Kingship was also wrong, theologically, when the king was seen as replacing Yahweh in Yahweh war. These critical elements were more like warnings to Israel than a rejection of kingship. In this way Boecker accepted Wellhausen's and Noth's literary analysis of 1 Samuel 7-12, but strongly argued that the Deuteronomistic parts of these chapters were not essentially opposed to kingship.

Moshe Weinfeld also makes a number of comments on kingship and the Deuteronomist in his study of Deuteronomy and the Deuteronomic school.[103] According to Weinfeld both Deuteronomy and the Deuteronomistic History were composed by scribes of the Judaean court, heavily influenced by the wisdom tradition. These scribes considered kingship essential for the proper functioning of society, and were clearly not anti-kingship. The time of the judges was seen by them as a time of anarchy and lawlessness; the Deuteronomist agreed fully with the evaluation of this time found in Judg 17:6; 18:1; 21:1; 22:5—"In those days there was no king in Israel; every man did what was right in his own eyes." Weinfeld states that "This extreme, negative assessment of the period of the judges is due to the positive view with which the Deuteronomic authors regarded

---

[100]Ibid., p. 35.

[101]Ibid., p. 77.

[102]Ibid., p. 82.

[103]Moshe Weinfeld, *Deuteronomy and the Deuteronomic School* (Oxford: Clarendon, 1972). Note also his two articles: Weinfeld, "The Period of the Conquest and of the Judges as seen by the Earlier and the Later Sources," *VT* 17 (1967) 93-113; Weinfeld, "Deuteronomy—The Present State of Inquiry," *JBL* (1967) 249-62.

the monarchy. Kaufmann is, therefore, correct in stating that the author of the general introduction 'has darkened the colors and depicted the period black on black . . . *in order to exalt the monarchy.*"[104] The "rest" (מנוחה) towards which Israel strived was only attained once the monarchy was established, and only then could the law of centralization take effect. The Deuteronomist could not conceive of the law of Deuteronomy as being implemented "in the absence of the monarchy or of a quasi-regal figure like Joshua."[105] Weinfeld admits that 1 Samuel 7-12 contains anti-kingship polemic, but together with Weiser, he contrasts this with the rest of the Deuteronomistic History and concludes that these chapters are not Deuteronomistic. He states that "the deuteronomic passages in the book of Kings . . . exhibit no anti-monarchic tendencies. On the contrary, the fact that the Davidic dynasty and its capital, Jerusalem, lie at the core of deuteronomic ideology shows the Deuteronomist's sympathy and esteem for the monarchy, provided that the kings remained faithful to Yahweh's laws."[106] The high role which the Deuteronomist attributed to the kings is also indicated by the fact that during the time of the kingship, in contrast to the time of the judges when the people themselves were held responsible, "it is the actions of the monarchs which determine the fate of the people for good or evil; the righteous kings cast glory on their reigns, while the wicked kings create a shadow over their period and cause their people to sin."[107] By virtually ignoring 1 Samuel 7-12 Weinfeld made a strong case for the pro-kingship tendencies of the Deuteronomist, and raised some serious questions of the traditional position.

A new method in examining 1 Samuel 8-12 is adopted by Dennis J. McCarthy.[108] McCarthy ignores the traditional literary analyses, and focusses on the structure, form and function of the narrative as a whole. He notes that the account of the rise of kingship in Israel is a carefully worked out unit, with an alternation of report and story. The whole is about kingship as a problem. Through a creative use of older traditions the Deuteronomist created an account of the rise of kingship which integrated the new institution into the structure of Israel. It is thus not valid to

---

[104]Weinfeld, "The Period of the Conquest," p. 11. Here Weinfeld quotes from Y. Kaufmann, *The Book of Judges* (Hebrew) (Jerusalem: Kiryat Sepher, 1962) 52.

[105]Weinfeld, *Deuteronomy,* 170.

[106]Ibid., p. 169.

[107]Ibid., p. 171.

[108]Dennis J. McCarthy, "The Inauguration of the Monarchy in Israel," *Int* 27 (1973) 401-12.

divide the present account into an anti-kingship series and a pro-kingship series since in the present text the differing traditions have been united into a whole which clearly does not communicate an anti-kingship message. This whole is then the product of the Deuteronomist.

A recent article by R. E. Clements proposes a still different interpretation.[109] Clements accepts the Deuteronomistic origin of 7:2-8:22; 10:17-27; 12 as proposed by Wellhausen and Noth, and largely agrees with Noth that the Deuteronomist was strongly critical of kingship due to his theocratic ideal. The Deuteronomist was careful to communicate that kingship was not necessary for Israel's salvation, that Yahweh was her true king, and that Israel's request for a king had been rebellion against Yahweh. But there was a further factor which affected the Deuteronomist's view of kingship. "For the Deuteronomists the promise of Yahweh to the house of David has introduced into the kingship a religious factor which overrides its purely institutional function. Yahweh's word is bound up with the Davidic dynasty in a way which is not true of other kings."[110] The Deuteronomist makes a sharp distinction between kings which have been chosen by Yahweh and those who have not, and according to the Deuteronomist only David and his dynasty have received this designation. In 1 Samuel 7-12 the Deuteronomist thus expresses his negative view of the role of kingship as an institution, but because of the Davidic covenant this is applied especially to Saul. The "ways of the king," which had originally been written against Solomon, are now also used against Saul. In this manner Clements interprets 1 Samuel 7-12 in the light of 2 Samuel 7. Yahweh accepts only those kings who have been specially chosen, and since this only fits David and his descendants, Saul (as well as all the kings of the North) as king had to be rejected.

One of the most thorough studies of kingship in Israel ever written was published by Tryggve N. D. Mettinger in 1976.[111] Interestingly, he takes a position relatively close to the traditional one on the attitude of the Deuteronomist towards kingship. He maintains that 1 Samuel 8 and 12 were basically Deuteronomistic, and that the part critical of kingship within 10:17-27, namely vv 18-19a, also came from the Deuteronomist. As he puts it, this framework for the account of the origin of kingship, 1 Samuel 7-8 and 12 "serves to express the negative Dtr attitude to the

---

[109]R. E. Clements, "The Deuteronomistic Interpretation of the Founding of the Monarchy in I Sam. 8," *VT* 24 (1974) 398-410.

[110]Ibid., pp. 405-6.

[111]Mettinger, *King and Messiah*.

events at Mizpah when Saul became king (10:17ff.)."[112] In keeping with this understanding of the Deuteronomist, Mettinger also sees the Deuteronomistic circles as the major force in the conditionalizing of the previously unconditional Davidic covenant. Despite some minor differences, he thus follows Noth fairly closely on this topic, both in terms of literary analysis and in terms of the stance attributed to the Deuteronomist toward kingship.

A rather different analysis is proposed by Bruce C. Birch[113] in his study of 1 Samuel 7-15. Birch accepts the traditional division of 1 Samuel 8-12 into five parts, but attempts to discover the different levels of tradition and composition of each section. He argues for three major levels of material in these chapters. First, there is the old, independent traditions. He argues that these are considerably more extensive than is usually assumed, even in 1 Samuel 8 and 12 where many have allowed virtually no sources. Second, he argues that these traditions have been tied together, redacted and supplemented by a prophetic community with Northern background shortly after the fall of Samaria. Finally, the Deuteronomist has incorporated the prophetic account, and made some additions. In this, Birch attributes much less of the final account to the Deuteronomist than Noth or most others had done. As the result of his literary analysis Birch concludes that according to the Deuteronomist kingship was a concession to reality, and as such, a further temptation to sin even though it was not all bad. In the Deuteronomistic additions the king had no special status and was never referred to as anointed. The Deuteronomist's view could be characterized as not positive about kingship, but not as totally anti-kingship. This stood in contrast to the prophetic edition which considered the king to be the special anointed of Yahweh and the bearer of his spirit. Here the king had special responsibilities and was esteemed very highly. According to Birch the earliest traditions view kingship as "sinful-but-still-of-God." Despite Birch's innovative literary analysis, the Deuteronomist is still seen as, if not anti-kingship, rather critical towards the institution.

In 1977 Tomoo Ishida published his doctoral dissertation on the rise of

---

[112]Ibid., p. 80.

[113]Bruce C. Birch, *The Rise of the Israelite Monarchy: The Growth and Development of I Samuel 7-15*, SBLDS, no. 27 (Missoula: Scholars, 1976). Note also: Birch, "The Choosing of Saul at Mizpah," *CBQ* 37 (1975) 447-57; Birch, "Development of the Tradition on the Anointing of Saul in I Sam. 9:1-10:16," *JBL* 90 (1971) 55-68.

dynastic kingship within Israel.[114] According to Ishida, each narrative in the complex 1 Samuel 7-12 had been "composed independently in the midst of the formation of the early monarchies,"[115] and all were relatively close to the events described, the differences among them having been caused by the different purposes and tendencies of the authors. These narratives then relatively accurately portrayed the opposition of that time to the new institution. In fact, Ishida argues that anti-kingship polemic was limited to that early period, and could not have been the product of a later time, either of the prophet Hosea or of the Deuteronomist. For, once kingship had been accepted, "the monarchy remained the sole system of government in Israel until foreign powers destroyed it. Although the people participated actively in politics from time to time, the monarchy, as a political system, never became a target of criticism, let alone the dynastic principle."[116] Ishida thus clearly rejects the traditional position, both as to its literary analysis of 1 Samuel 7-12, and as to its conclusions on opposition to kingship in Israel. By implication he argues that the Deuteronomist could not have been essentially opposed to the institution of kingship.

A radically new solution to the question was offered by Timo Veijola. Veijola follows the conclusions of W. Dietrich on the redaction of the Deuteronomistic History, and speaks of three distinct editors: DtrG, DtrP and DtrN. In his first book Veijola describes how each of these editors understood King David.[117] In his second book he focusses on how DtrG and DtrN evaluated the institution of kingship.[118] According to Veijola DtrG had a thoroughly positive view of kingship. For Veijola the key to DtrG's view of kingship is to be found in Judges 17-21. Here DtrG attributed all the evil of that time to the fact that "in those days there was no king in Israel" (Judg 17:6; 18:1; 19:1; 21:25). According to DtrG it had been the responsibility of the judge to save Israel from external enemies, but it was up to the king to prevent Israel from committing cultic misdeeds and other crimes internally. From Judges 17-21 Veijola then proceeds to the important narratives on the beginnings of kingship. Again he

---

[114]Tomoo Ishida, *The Royal Dynastics in Ancient Israel. A Study on the Formation and Development of Royal-Dynastic Ideology*, BZAW, Nr. 142 (Berlin: Walter de Gruyter, 1977).

[115]Ibid., p. 30.

[116]Ibid., p. 183.

[117]Veijola, *Die ewige Dynastie.*

[118]Veijola, *Das Königtum.*

discovers that DtrG expressed no criticism of kingship. DtrG's account of these beginnings is a redactional unity, and consists of the following:

8:1-5,22b—the people ask for a king, then go home
(DtrG composition)

9:1-10:16—Samuel, at Yahweh's command, anoints Saul
(older composition)

10:17-18a α,19b-27—Saul's anointing is confirmed
(DtrG composition)

11:1-15—Yahweh's choice of Saul is confirmed by Saul's saving act
(older tradition)

DtrG thus saw kingship as an institution started through a combination of man's initiative and Yahweh's act.

It was DtrN who then thoroughly edited the whole history and gave it its present anti-monarchical slant. He did this primarily by adding considerable material to the account of the origin of kingship. By adding 8:6-22a; 10:18aβγb-19a; and 12 DtrN managed to virtually hide DtrG's positive feelings about kingship. In the book of Judges he inserted 8:22-23 and 9:7-21, both of which also attacked kingship. The basis of DtrN's opposition to kingship was his theocratic ideal. "DtrN was the first, however, to derive from the recognition of Yahweh's kingship the theocratic consequence *that absolutely no human kingship was possible.*"[119] (Translation mine). Veijola considers this to be one of DtrN's most valuable theological contributions. Those passages inserted by DtrN which criticized kingship on the basis of the king's oppressive policies (the "ways of the king," 1 Sam 8:11-17; and the Jotham fable, Judg 9:8-15) had been adopted by DtrN from old Northern anti-monarchical traditions. With this analysis Veijola departs drastically from both the traditional position as well as all of the alternative proposals. A major reason for this is his new literary proposals based on Dietrich. It should be noted, however, that the basis he gave for DtrN's opposition to kingship rather resembles Wellhausen's understanding.

Similar to Birch, Volkmar Fritz proposes that 1 Samuel 8-11 had been

---

[119]Ibid., p. 122.

redacted together before the Deuteronomist incorporated them into his history.[120] He notes that chapters 9-11 present three accounts of the legitimation of Saul. 1 Samuel 12 is then one of the Deuteronomistic speeches placed at key points in the history. After including the three accounts of Saul's legitimation the Deuteronomist officially inaugurated the new era of kingship. Clearly, the Deuteronomist does not reject kingship.

A. D. H. Mayes continues the direction started by McCarthy by emphasizing that the present 1 Samuel 8-12 is a skillfully organized whole which can not be explained on the basis of a gradual growth of tradition.[121] He argues that the literary analysis of Wellhausen and Noth can be largely accepted, but not their theological conclusions derived from it. The Deuteronomist does not condemn kingship in these chapters, but, especially in 1 Samuel 12, solves the theological problem of kingship. Mayes also accepts Boecker's conclusions that in these chapters the Deuteronomist at the same time warns against the dangers of kingship.

Finally, Frank Crüsemann's very fascinating recent work on the phenomenon of opposition to kingship within Israel needs to be mentioned.[122] Crüsemann argues that there are only a very few texts in the OT which are totally opposed to the institution of kingship, these being: (1) parts of 1 Samuel 8-12 (8:1-3, 11-17; 12:3-5 is one series, and 8:7; 12:12 is a second), (2) the Jotham fable, Judg 9:8-15, and (3) Gideon's rejection of kingship, Judg 8:22-23. He warns, however, that the radicality of the opposition expressed in these texts should not be underestimated. The basic questions Crüsemann tries to solve in his book are: (1) who in Israel could have voiced such sentiments, and (2) when could these views have been expressed. He immediately rejects the two answers which have usually been given to the second question: (1) the texts are late, post-Hoseanic or exilic (e.g., Wellhausen, Noth), (2) the texts reflect the opposition to kingship present at the time of its origin (e.g., Weiser, Soggin, Bernhardt, Ishida). Using both, the usual historical-critical methods of exegesis, and the discipline of sociology, Crüsemann paints a picture of Israel into which these texts could be placed. He concludes that the opposition to kingship expressed in these texts must have occurred during

---

[120]Volkmar Fritz, "Die Deutungen des Königtums Sauls in den Uberlieferungen von seiner Entstehung I Sam. 9-11," *ZAW* 88 (1976) 346-62.

[121]A. D. H. Mayes, "The Rise of the Israelite Monarchy," *ZAW* 90 (1978) 1-19.

[122]Crüsemann, *Der Widerstand gegen das Königtum.*

the time between Absalom's rebellion and the division of the kingdom after Solomon's death. Due to the external danger posed by the Philistines Israel had been fairly well united in its request for kingship. Once this danger had been taken care of by David, however, opposition arose against kingship which, in a very short period of time, had become internally oppressive. An analysis of the accounts of Absalom's rebellion, of Sheba's revolt, and of the rejection of Rehoboam by the North leading to the division is used to support this. The major opposition is seen as having been among the rural, land-owning farmers, that segment of society which stood to lose most due to this new form of government. Nabal's statement to David's men (1 Sam 25:10-11) expressed their feelings. The basis for their opposition is thus economic and social rather than religious. Crüsemann sees this as arising out of Israel's pre-kingship organization. Following the sociological model employed by Christian Sigrist in studies in Africa,[123] Crüsemann suggests that the Israel of pre-kingship times had been a "*segmentäre Gesellschaft*," an egalitarian type of society essentially opposed to any form of centralized power. This then explained the delay in Israel's adoption of kingship in the first place, and was also the background for later opposition to it. After the division of the kingdom any real opposition to the institution virtually died out. Once again, external dangers made the need for a centralized form of government clear. Further, kingship itself probably became less oppressive. Crüsemann sees the Succession Narrative, the Jahwistic history, and the Joseph account as strongly against opposition to the institution of kingship, but also opposed to the harsher aspects of the reigns of David and Solomon, and especially against slave labor of the Israelites. After all, Yahweh had freed Israel from this by leading her out of Egypt. These writings had their effect, and the kingship of later times was more moderate with the people (note the role of עַם־הָאָרֶץ) once again having somewhat more power. It is instructive that when the prophets attack the social oppression of their day they do not blame the kings for it. Although individual kings are criticized, as in the Deuteronomistic History, the institution of kingship is fully accepted. With Crüsemann's study a new stage in research has been reached. For the first time a thorough examination has been made of opposition to kingship, and a very probable setting for it has been

---

[123]Ibid., pp. 201-22. Crüsemann here largely depends upon Christian Sigrist, *Regulierte Anarchie. Untersuchungen zum Fehlen und zur Entstehung politischer Herrschaft in segmentären Gesellschaften Afrikas* (Freiburg: Walter, 1967).

proposed. If Crüsemann is correct, then obviously the Deuteronomist would not have been opposed to kingship.

A RESPONSE TO THE RESEARCH ON
KINGSHIP ACCORDING TO THE DEUTERONOMISTIC HISTORY

Earlier we stated that the traditional position quickly became the standard one, and that even today it would probably be the dominant position in most OT introductions and studies. Strikingly, none of the scholars reviewed who have focussed on 1 Samuel 7-12 in the past decade or so have adopted that position as represented by Wellhausen and Noth. Probably Mettinger came the closest. This obviously requires some examination.

Earlier we summarized Wellhausen's position with three points. The socalled traditional position, largely an adaptation of Wellhausen by Noth, could also be summarized in a few points as follows:

(1) 1 Samuel 7-12 consists of two series of traditions distinguishable from each other by their view of kingship

(2) The series in 7:2-8:22; 10:17-27; 12 is clearly anti-kingship

(3) The anti-kingship polemic is late, and historically untrustworthy

(4) The anti-kingship series either came from the Deuteronomist himself, or at least reflects his view. Therefore the Deuteronomist was anti-kingship.[124]

All of these points have been questioned by recent research with varying degrees of success.

First of all, the literary analysis of the traditional position has been attacked. Weiser, one of the first to seriously criticize the traditional approach argued that the chapters could not simply be divided into two opposing series, but should be seen as coming from various sanctuaries. Weiser thus accepted the literary division of 1 Samuel 8-12 into 5 different units, but denied that they formed two series of traditions. Weiser's analysis itself was not accepted very broadly, but he did set the stage for things to come. No one has really challenged the division of these chapters into five sections.[125] There has also not been very much debate

---

[124]This traditional picture differs from Wellhausen's largely in its emphasis on the Deuteronomist, and in its dating of the anti-kingship series.

[125]There is some disagreement as to the exact break between the tradition of chap. 11, and the passage of 10:17-27, but this does not affect the truth of the statement.

about 9:1-10:16; 11. It is usually accepted that these are two older traditions. There is no consensus, however, on the literary analysis of the other
three passages. Soggin, Boecker, Clements and Mettinger, to list some,
continued to see these as the product of the Deuteronomist. Even these
differed among themselves as to how much of these passages was based on
earlier tradition. Other scholars proposed various different analyses of
these passages. Bernhardt separated chapter 8 from chapter 12. Veijola
saw these chapters as the product of different redactors. Ishida did not
connect these passages with each other, and thus they could not be called
a series. These scholars also disagreed considerably among themselves as
to the role of the Deuteronomist in the production of these passages.
Weinfeld, Weiser, and Ishida downplayed his role very much. Birch and
Fritz suggested that the whole account had essentially been put together
by a pre-Deuteronomistic redactor.

As the above paragraph indicates, there is at present no consensus on a
literary analysis of 1 Samuel 7-12. It is striking how frequently the literary decisions were made on the basis of theological judgments. Noth
tended to argue that 7:2-8:22; 10:17-27; 12 were a separate series because
they were anti-kingship whereas the rest was pro-kingship, and that the
former must have come from the Deuteronomist because they reflected
his anti-kingship sentiment. Some of the more recent scholars have argued
that some of these passages are anti-kingship and thus could not have
come from the Deuteronomist because he wasn't anti-kingship. Clearly
more work needs to be done on this.

Although there is no agreement on a literary analysis of 1 Samuel 7-12,
there seems to be a move towards some kind of consensus on some of the
other issues. A number of scholars are emphasizing that the so-called
anti-kingship series is not as totally anti-kingship as Noth argued. This
was already suggested by Weiser, and then defended strongly by Boecker.
It is much more complex than that. This does not deny the presence of
anti-kingship elements in these passages, but suggests that at the very
least, the passages are not one-sidedly opposed to the new institution.
Virtually all the scholars reviewed moved in this direction, either to a
greater or lesser degree.

A number of scholars also questioned the traditional view on the historical trustworthiness of the passages. Both Wellhausen and Noth argued
that the so-called anti-kingship series had been based only on the other
two traditions in the account. Now it is being suggested that older traditions may also stand behind this series. This is being defended both on
literary and historical grounds. Crüsemann and Bernhardt argued the most
strongly that some of the emphases did not fit the later time and must

therefore have been early. Soggin argued that the disputes could very well have reflected the situation present at the rise of kingship. The traditional arguments that anti-kingship views must have been late clearly are no longer accepted.

Finally, none of the scholars reviewed accepted a simple statement that the Deuteronomist was anti-kingship. A few (e.g. Mettinger, Clements, Birch) still argued that the Deuteronomist did not place much value on kingship, or that he was somewhat critical of it, but they were not willing to go as far as Noth. Most of the others rejected the traditional view even more totally.

The scholars reviewed have certainly advanced the study of kingship and of the Deuteronomist. Virtually nothing of the traditional position on kingship in the Deuteronomistic History can be accepted as it was originally proposed. Although these scholars do not represent a consensus on a literary analysis of 1 Samuel 7-12, on the degree of anti-kingship sentiment reflected there, or on the history of anti-kingship polemic in Israel, they largely agree that the narratives of 1 Samuel 7-12 are not sufficient to show that the Deuteronomist was opposed to kingship. It is clear that the Deuteronomist's attitude to this institution has not been sufficiently clarified.

THE PURPOSE OF THIS DISSERTATION

Noth's contention that the Deuteronomist was anti-kingship has been found to be at least inadequately supported, if not completely wrong. Alternative positions arguing that the Deuteronomist was pro-kingship may be more accurate, but they are not too helpful, and have also not been adequately supported and described. *This dissertation will attempt to describe the Deuteronomist's view of kingship as reflected in the whole Deuteronomistic History.* Before we begin, however, a few clarifying statements need to be made.

In describing our purpose we speak of the Deuteronomist. This naturally raises the question of our understanding of the Deuteronomist. According to Noth the Deuteronomist was an individual, separated from the significant groups of the time,[126] who produced the Deuteronomistic History in

---

[126]Noth, *ÜgS,* 109-110. Noth argued that the Deuteronomist could not have been priestly because he displayed little interest in the intricacies of the cult, he could not have been royal because he was opposed to kingship, and he could not have been prophetic because he had no hope for the future.

Palestine following the events of 587 B.C. We would define the Deuteronomist more generally as the *producer*[127] *of the Deuteronomistic History*. It is extremely questionable whether he was as individualistic as
Noth envisioned him. More probably his position was representative of at
least a significant group, or perhaps even of the religious leadership of the
time. The emphasis on a Deuteronomistic school or circle within recent
scholarship is a helpful correction of Noth. As we suggested earlier, this
Deuteronomist probably produced the history before the beginning of the
exile, very possibly as a direct or indirect result of the Josianic reform. If
this is correct, then obviously the last few chapters of the history are a
later addition by an editor who then may have added some passages to the
rest of the history as well. We are not convinced, however, that this later
editor had a significantly different view of kingship than the original
producer, and thus these additions would not have affected the impression
of the whole history. In our work we will point out those passages which
appear to be later additions, but we will not ignore them. We will also try
to be careful not to tie our analysis of the material to any assumption on
the historical origin of the history. Thus although we disagree with those
who argue that the history was first composed during the exile, we believe
that positing such a setting for the history would not affect our analysis
or conclusions on the Deuteronomist's view of kingship. In the dissertation
we are thus attempting to discern how the producer of the Deuteronomistic History viewed the institution of kingship.

As is realized in all disciplines, the success of a venture is frequently
determined by the assumptions of the question asked. We would suggest

---

[127] We use the word "producer" since it most neutrally describes how
the Deuteronomist apparently worked. The amount of material in the
history which appears to be a recording of sources makes it less accurate
to speak of him as "writer" or "author."

Although we are using the term "producer" in the singular, we are not
implying that one individual is responsible for the whole history. The
history may very well have been a group project. We are suggesting,
however, that there is sufficient unity of language and thought within the
history that the singular more accurately reflects the situation. The term
"the Deuteronomist" may thus be hypothetical since it derives its meaning
from the literature or the product. For ease of discussion we will speak of
the Deuteronomist as an individual with a particular viewpoint, realizing
that what we really mean is that individual, group, or even movement
which resulted in, or produced the Deuteronomistic History.

that one reason why past scholarship has failed to describe the Deuteronomist's view of kingship accurately is that it has approached the issue
with the wrong question. Ever since Wellhausen and Noth discussion of the
Deuteronomist and kingship has focussed on whether the Deuteronomist
was anti-kingship or pro-kingship. It was assumed that the Deuteronomist
was either opposed to the institution as such, or he was strongly in favor
of it, and defending it against its opponents. It is very doubtful whether
this is the best question to ask of the Deuteronomist. It is highly unlikely
that whether or not Israel should be ruled by the institution of kingship
was a burning issue at the time of the Deuteronomist.[128] First of all, this
had been the only form of government that Israel had had for at least 400
years. Although it is often stated that Israel, unlike the other nations of
the time, did not see herself as having had kingship from the beginning, by
this time most of her history had been lived under this form of rule.
Second, it should be noted that at that time kingship was the standard
form of statehood for virtually all the surrounding nations. In fact, it is
often said that Israel only became a nation when it became a monarchy.
This fact also would not have encouraged any real discussion of whether
or not Israel should have a king.

This is an important point, and can perhaps be made even more clear
with a modern analogy. The United States just celebrated its bicentennial
as a nation. Recently the U.S. had a president who received unprece-
dented criticism and opposition, eventually leading to his resignation.
Despite all the negative statements made about President Nixon, few, if
any statements were made attacking the U.S. form of government. Criticism of the highest office holder in the U.S. was definitely not criticism
of his office, much less of the form of government which he represented.
In fact, throughout the turmoil there was no significant discussion of
whether the U.S. should adopt a different form of rule, and people were
not divided by the stand they took on the U.S. form of rule. This now
needs to be compared with the situation in Judah toward the end of its
kingship, or even during the exile. Whereas the U.S. has only had this form
of rule for 200 years, Israel had had kingship for 400 years. Whereas the
U.S. could have compared its form of government with various other
forms present in the world today, Israel had no practical alternative as a
model before them. Whereas the U.S. is very aware of how its form of
government was adopted, it is questionable whether the Israel of the 7th

---

[128]This is also supported by the historical conclusions of Crüsemann,
Der Widerstand gegen das Königtum, and Ishida, *The Royal Dynasties.*

and 6th century B.C. was as well informed of the origins of her kingship. This analogy thus suggests that despite all the criticism of the kings found in the Old Testament, or expressed during this time, kingship as an institution or form of government need not have been questioned.

We would thus argue that the Israel of the 7th century B.C., as well as of the exile, simply assumed that kingship was the form of government she should have. The fact that the writings of the exile, although not focussing on kingship, still assume that reconstruction would involve the reinstitution of kingship supports this. In other words, the correct question with which to confront the Deuteronomist with is not whether he was anti-kingship or pro-kingship. Rather, we need to ask what kind of kingship he saw as ideal for Israel, or what role kingship was expected to play for Israel. It is only when the topic is viewed in this way that strides forward in the discussion can be made.

We have so far stated that our task will be to determine how the producer of the Deuteronomistic History viewed kingship. Two further points need to be made on how we plan to do this. As we noted earlier, Noth claimed that the Deuteronomist expressed his anti-kingship views throughout the whole history, but that they were clearest within those passages in 1 Samuel 7-12 which he had himself composed in order to express his own opinion. It is probably accurate to say that Noth interpreted the rest of the history in the light of his understanding of 1 Samuel 7-12. Noth's analysis of 1 Samuel 7-12 was clearly the key to his conclusion that the Deuteronomist was anti-kingship in the whole history. As we observed above, however, recent research has rather convincingly shown that 1 Samuel 7-12 cannot be used as the basis for contention that the Deuteronomist is anti-kingship. First of all, the nature of the critique expressed in these chapters is not totally clear, and second, there is considerable uncertainty regarding the extent of Deuteronomistic involvement in their composition. There is simply no consensus on a literary analysis of these chapters, and it is very questionable methodologically to use as the starting point for a discussion of kingship within the Deuteronomistic History that part of the history which is so fraught with difficulties and uncertainties. Despite this fact, most scholars dealing with kingship in the Deuteronomistic History have focussed largely on these chapters. Wellhausen and Noth set the stage for this, and even those arguing against them on this have tended to accept the ground rules laid down by them.

One scholar who has questioned this approach to the Deuteronomist and kingship is Timo Veijola. Although recognizing the importance of 1 Samuel 7-12 for any full understanding of the Deuteronomist's view, he claims one should begin elsewhere.

> The formation of a judgment concerning the understanding of
> kingship in the Deuteronomistic historiography is above all
> dependent upon a correct interpretation of these chapters
> which take a fundamental position on the foundation of the
> institution. It is not impossible, however, that the fundamen-
> tal estimation of the monarchy is also visible in other Deu-
> teronomistic passages which are not weighted down with as
> many hypotheses as is the report concerning its establish-
> ment. In order to avoid the danger of explaining *obscurum per
> obscurius,* it is worth it to be on the lookout for such pas-
> sages, in the hope, thereafter to be able to approach the
> complicated pieces about the installation of kingship with a
> criterion (*Masstab*).[129] (Translation mine).

Veijola is certainly correct in this attempt. Veijola then suggests that this
criterion for the Deuteronomist's view is found in Judges 17-21. Given
that a majority of OT scholars consider these chapters to be a post-
Deuteronomistic addition to the history, it is questionable whether using
them as a criterion for the Deuteronomist's view of kingship is much of an
improvement. Further, once Veijola has obtained the Deuteronomist's
view of kingship from Judges 17-21, he immediately moves to 1 Samuel 7-
12 and spends the rest of the book analyzing these chapters on the basis of
the found criterion. He totally ignores the rest of the history. Veijola has
the right idea, but first of all he does not choose the most helpful starting
point, and second, he still does not examine the history as a whole. In
order to discover the Deuteronomist's view of kingship a new starting
point needs to be found, and the whole history needs to be examined.

It is our contention that the narratives found in 2 Kings 18-23 would
make such a new starting point. Whether the Deuteronomist wrote during
the exile as is often claimed, or whether he wrote during the latter days
of Judah's kingship, the last major kings which could have had a significant influence upon the Deuteronomist would have been Hezekiah,
Manasseh and Josiah. The producer of the history may very well have
experienced the reigns of Manasseh and Josiah personally, and he would
certainly have heard much about these three kings. It is then likely that
the deeds and ways of these three kings would have most affected the
Deuteronomist's view of kings and kingship, both negatively and posi-

---

[129]Veijola, *Das Königtum,* 13.

tively. The fact that these chapters contain some of the strongest and most categorical statements about kings supports this supposition. It is thus strange that, in light of the proximity of these kings to the Deuteronomist and the statements made about them, very little use has been made of these chapters in trying to discover the Deuteronomist's view of kingship. This dissertation will follow the logic presented and begin with the Deuteronomist's description of the reigns of Hezekiah, Manasseh and Josiah. Once these narratives have been examined, the thesis derived from them will then be tested in the rest of the history.[130]

Finally, a few words need to be said about how we will search for the Deuteronomist's view. Noth argued that the Deuteronomist produced the history by choosing from his sources, by organizing and arranging the sources chosen, by linking the traditions together, and by adding speeches and summary-like passages at key points. If Noth is correct, and we believe he is, then the most accurate way to determine the Deuteronomist's position is to examine the final product. Although the Deuteronomist's thinking would no doubt have come out in those passages which he himself composed, it would not have been limited to them. The Deuteronomist's understanding would also have been reflected in the way he chose or rejected sources, and the way in which the different traditions were bound into a whole. It will thus not be necessary to determine at each point whether a verse was part of his source, or whether the Deuteronomist composed it himself. When it seems helpful to point out that it appears as if the Deuteronomist composed a verse this may be done, but the dissertation will not emphasize the task of separating the Deuteronomist from his sources. The work of McCarthy[131] and Mayes[132] has already moved in this direction with considerable success and we hope to follow their lead.

---

[130]The fact that the way kingship is treated in the rest of the history fits with our thesis derived from 2 Kings 18-23 supports our contention that these chapters are a good starting point for the study.

[131]McCarthy, "The Inauguration of the Monarchy," Cf. McCarthy, "II Samuel 7 and the Structure of the Deuteronomic History," *JBL* 84 (1965) 131-138.

[132]Mayes, "The Rise of the Israelite Monarchy."

2
Kingship in 2 Kings 18–23

KING JOSIAH, 2 KINGS 22-23

2 Kings 22-23 have played an extremely important role in OT studies.[1] The nature of this role, however, has been largely historical. These chapters were used to obtain information on the time of Josiah, and on the events of the reform. The majority of OT scholars concluded on the basis of these chapters that the book of Deuteronomy, or at least its core, was found in the temple during the time of Josiah, and that this book then was a significant factor in the reform. These conclusions were so important since they allowed OT scholars to date Deuteronomy, and then to construct a framework for the history of OT literature. Würthwein[2] and Dietrich[3] have recently challenged this use of these chapters. They argue that it is not valid to use these chapters in order to get at the events of Josiah's time. Instead of downplaying the value of these chapters, however, they both consider them to be important passages reflecting the concerns of the authors who created them. According to Würthwein the author of these chapters composed them to emphasize that the people were bound to the covenant and the law of Deuteronomy. 2 Kings 22-23 are thus meant to point to the book of Deuteronomy, but this is fiction and not history. Clearly a new direction in OT research has begun which could have significant ramifications for a large segment of OT studies.

This new direction is a helpful emphasis. Too often 2 Kings 22-23 have

---

[1]For a review of research on 2 Kings 22-23, see Appendix.

[2]Ernst Würthwein, "Die Josianische Reform."

[3]Walter Dietrich, "Josia und das Gesetzbuch (2 Reg. XXII)," *VT* 27 (1977) 13-35.

A somewhat similar approach is used in Hollenstein, "2 Kön. XXIII 4ff."

been studied primarily for their value in dating the book of Deuteronomy, and the role these chapters played in the presentation of the Deuteronomist has been ignored. We will also approach these chapters with the question of what they say about the Deuteronomist, especially regarding his views on kingship. Whether or not they give an accurate picture of the events of Josiah's reign,[4] and if they do, whether or not the lawbook found in the temple was Deuteronomy,[5] are important questions but not central to our task. What is significant for us is that in these chapters the Deuteronomist expresses some rather strong views of King Josiah. Since the object of this study is the Deuteronomist and not the historical events or even the historical Josiah, we will begin by examining the Deuteronomist's views of Josiah, and then attempt to determine the basis for these views.

The Deuteronomist's Evaluation of King Josiah

The obvious place to begin examining the Deuteronomist's evaluation of King Josiah is in the framework around the account of Josiah's reign. It is within the framework, or the regnal formulae as they are often called, that each king of Israel and Judah is judged.

These formulae have been of interest to scholars for a long time, but this interest has focussed primarily on questions of chronology.[6] Throughout this time it has usually been assumed that these formulae had been produced by the author or compiler of Kings. In fact, the regularity of

---

[4]The fact that we approve of the change of direction in studies of 2 Kings 22-23 represented by Würthwein and Dietrich does not imply that we accept all of their conclusions. Just because these chapters may have been important for the Deuteronomist in presenting his concerns does not exclude the possibility that they could also be historically trustworthy. We are also not convinced of the literary analysis of Würthwein, Dietrich, and Hollenstein. As we stated above, all three divide the Deuteronomistic History into DtrG, DtrP and DtrN, and we rejected such an approach.

[5]The majority of scholars still clearly assume that the lawbook found in the temple was at least the core of the present Deuteronomy. One exception to this is Jack R. Lundbom, "The Lawbook of the Josianic Reform," *CBQ* 38 (1976) 293-302.

[6]Two examples of this are: J. Begrich, *Die Chronologie der Könige von Israel und Juda und die Quellen des Rahmens der Königsbücher,* BHT, Nr. 3 (Tübingen: J. C. B. Mohr [Paul Siebeck], 1929); A. Jepsen, "Zur Chronologie der Könige von Israel und Juda," in *Untersuchungen zur Israelitisch-Jüdischen Chronologie,* BZAW, Nr. 88 (Berlin: Alfred Töpelmann, 1964) 4-47.

these formulae has often been cited as one of the clearest signs of his contribution. Thus in the time before Noth these passages were attributed to some Deuteronomic redactor,[7] and since Noth the Deuteronomistic historian has been seen as having composed them.[8] One scholar who has questioned this is Shoshana Bin-Nun.[9] She bases her conclusion on the many variations present in the formulae, arguing that "it makes little sense to assume that the author created a system in order not to use it."[10] Instead she considers these formulae to have come from king lists which had been prepared independently in Israel and Judah, or in other words, from the Deuteronomist's sources. Even if she is correct, and this is extremely doubtful,[11] the verdicts, or "formulas for the religious estimation of the king" as she calls them could hardly have come from such lists and must have been produced by the editor. Jepsen also considered the formulae to have been part of the source material used by the priestly redactor, but he attributed the verdict part of the framework to the editor himself.[12] On the other side, the success which Nelson has had in determining the redactional history of Kings strictly on the basis of a study of these regnal formulae strongly supports the usual view.[13]

---

[7] Burney, *Kings,* ix-xi; Wellhausen, *Prolegomena,* 282.

[8] Weippert, "Die 'deuteronomistischen' Beurteilungen der Könige"; Nelson, "Redactional Duality."

Fohrer, although not accepting the existence of a Deuteronomistic History as proposed by Noth, states: "Basic to this argument is the framework; unlike the framework of the book of Judges, which was placed around narrative material already extant, the framework of the books of Kings was created at the same time the narrative material of the sources was forged into a whole, so that the author of the framework is none other than the author of the books of Kings" (*Introduction,* 229).

[9] Bin-Nun, "Formulas from the Royal Records."

[10] Ibid., p. 418.

[11] The mere fact of variations cannot be used against the Deuteronomistic authorship of these regnal formulae. It should be noted that these variations also occur in the verdicts, as well as in the synchronizations, both parts of the formulae which hardly could have been in the king lists. It is thus much more likely that the Deuteronomist did create a system, but that he was not slavishly tied to it. Nelson, "Redactional Duality," p. 43.

[12] Jepsen, *Quellen des Königsbuches.*

[13] Nelson, "Redactional Duality." Note that Weippert, "Die 'deuteronomistischen' Beurteilungen der Könige," also attempted to use these regnal formulae as the basis for determining the unity or diversity of the redaction of the Deuteronomistic History.

It thus needs to be realized that when we examine the verdict aspect of the framework we are dealing with that part of Kings which is most universally attributed to the Deuteronomist. It was through these framework passages, and especially through the verdicts he pronounced on each king, that the Deuteronomist changed his sources into a history. The obvious place to begin examining the Deuteronomist's evaluation of King Josiah is thus also the correct place to begin.

The basic structure of these framework passages could be outlined as follows:[14]

Introduction Section
    1. Synchronism (up to 722 B.C.)
    2. Age of King at Accession (for Judah only)
    3. Length of King's Reign
    4. Capital City
    5. Name of Queen Mother (for Judah only)
    6. The Deuteronomist's Verdict of the King
Concluding Section
    1. Source Citation
    2. Death and Burial of King
    3. Notice of Succession

With these framework passages the Deuteronomist gave each account of a king's reign a distinct beginning and end. An integral part of each framework was the Deuteronomist's judgment of the king, being placed at the climax of each introductory passage. This is also the case in the introduction to the reign of King Josiah. After recording that Josiah was the son of Jedidah, the daughter of Adaiah of Bozkath, the Deuteronomist continues with "And he did what was right in the eyes of the Lord, and walked in all the way of David his father, and he did not turn aside to the right hand or to the left." (2 Kgs 22:2). In typically Deuteronomistic language King Josiah is judged to have been one of the good kings.

This verdict now needs to be examined more closely, and put into context. Of Judah's 20 kings,[15] the Deuteronomist roundly condemns 11 of

---

[14]Nelson, "Redactional Duality," pp. 45-46.

[15]The verdicts of the Judaean kings are found in the following texts: (1) Rehoboam—1 Kgs 14:22; (2) Abijam—1 Kgs 15:3; (3) Asa—1 Kgs 15:11, 14; (4) Jehoshaphat—1 Kgs 22:43; (5) Joram—2 Kgs 8:18; (6) Ahaziah— 2 Kgs 8:27; (7) Athaliah—no framework passage, no verdict; (8) Joash (Jehoash)—2 Kgs 12:2-3; (9) Amaziah—2 Kgs 14:3-4; (10) Azariah (Uzziah)

them as having "done evil in the sight of the Lord," or with some other
similarly negative judgment (Rehoboam, Abijam, Joram, Ahaziah, Ahaz,
Manasseh, Amon, Jehoahaz, Jehoiakim, Jehoiachin, Zedekiah).[16] Although
the Deuteronomist gives no verdict upon Athaliah, it is quite clear that he
also totally condemns her. The remaining 8 kings then receive varying
degrees of commendation (Asa, Jehoshaphat, Jehoash, Amaziah, Azariah,
Jotham, Hezekiah, Josiah). The usual phrase used to express this is that
the king "did what was right in the eyes of the Lord." In four of these
cases the Deuteronomist continues and makes a comparison between the
king and David (Asa, Amaziah, Hezekiah, Josiah). In those instances in
which a king followed his father's footsteps positively some mention is
made of the father. The verdict of Josiah fits this pattern perfectly. It is
stated that he "did what was right in the eyes of the Lord," and he is then
compared favorably with King David. Since Josiah's father was judged to
be one of the evil kings it is true to form that he is not mentioned. A first
reading of the verdict then simply places King Josiah within that group of
8 kings who are judged positively by the Deuteronomist.

In contrast to the earlier positive verdicts, however, the Deuteronomist
does not end the positive part of the verdict with a reference to David, or
to the king's father. The Deuteronomist continues by stating that Josiah
"did not turn aside to the right hand or left." This is common Deuteronomistic language, but Josiah is the only king described with it.[17] It is
significant that this same phrase is used in the law of kingship (Deut

---

—2 Kgs 15:3-4; (11) Jotham—2 Kgs 15:34-35; (12) Ahaz—2 Kgs 16:2-4;
(13) Hezekiah—2 Kgs 18:3-6; (14) Manasseh—2 Kgs 21:2; (15) Amon—
2 Kgs 21:20-22; (16) Josiah—2 Kgs 22:2 (23:25); (17) Jehoahaz—2 Kgs
23:32; (18) Jehoiakim—2 Kgs 23:37; (19) Jehoiachin—2 Kgs 24:9;
(20) Zedekiah—24:19.

[16]Of course if a second Deuteronomist added the material after Josiah
then the original Deuteronomist would only have condemned 7 of 16 kings.
If this is correct then less than half of the Judaean kings would have been
condemned giving a rather different picture of the Deuteronomist's
evaluations than is usually assumed.

[17]The combination of "right (hand)" (יָמִין) and/or "left" (שְׂמֹאול) occurs
17 times within the OT, but only 8 times with moral connotations. 7 of
these 8 moral usages are within the Deuteronomistic History (Deut 5:32;
17:11, 20; 28:14; Josh 1:7; 23:6, 2 Kgs 22:2). The one non-Deuteronomistic
occurrence is Prov 4:27.

The verb סָר (to turn) is also part of the Deuteronomistic phrase in that
it is found with it every time whereas the Proverbs phrase uses נָטָה.

17:14-20). Vv 18-20 of this law command the king to study "this law"[18] so
that "he may learn to fear the Lord his God, by keeping all the words of
this law and these statutes, and doing them," and so that "he may not turn
aside from the commandment, either to the right hand or to the left." It is
against this background that the Deuteronomist's verdict of Josiah needs
to be understood. Although there is no direct reference to law or commandment in 2 Kgs 22:2, the emphasis in the Josiah narrative on the
finding of the lawbook and Josiah's actions resulting from this discovery
strongly suggest that the Deuteronomist had Josiah's response to the law
in mind in v 2 already. In his verdict the Deuteronomist thus adopts language from the law of kingship, and states that Josiah did what the law
required of him. With this addition the Deuteronomist has already begun
to take Josiah out of the category of "good kings" and to place him on a
higher plane.

This is also brought out in more ways. In the case of six of the positive
judgments the formal verdict is followed by a restriction usually beginning
with "but" or "nevertheless" (רַק).[19] These six kings received a positive
judgment, but it is restricted by the fact that they did not remove the
high places thus allowing the people to continue to sacrifice and burn
incense there. Only Hezekiah and Josiah receive a total commendation.
Immediately following Hezekiah's verdict the Deuteronomist adds that
Hezekiah "removed the high places, and broke the pillars, and cut down
the Asherah." (2 Kgs 18:4). In the case of Josiah the verdict is followed by
a lengthy narrative describing his reforming acts. Both Hezekiah and
Josiah had not only done what was right in the eyes of the Lord, but they
had also fully obeyed the Deuteronomic law, including its law of centralization. This put these two kings into a category all by themselves.

That the Deuteronomist saw Hezekiah and Josiah in a similar light can
also be seen in that each receives a further formal evaluation beyond the

---

[18]The phrase "this law" is usually taken to be a reference to the code
of law embodied in Deuteronomy. At the heart of this law is the law of
centralization. Thus it is not surprising that the Deuteronomist, in judging
King Josiah who followed this law of centralization more fully than
anyone else, makes use of language from the law of kingship which
commands the king to obey the law of Deuteronomy, including the law of
centralization.

[19]Note the examination of this restriction in W. Boyd Barrick, "On the
'Removal of the "High-Places'" in 1-2 Kings," *Bib* (1974) 257-59.

normal verdict.[20] After a summarizing statement about Josiah's deeds the Deuteronomist states that "Before him there was no king like him, who turned to the Lord with all his heart and with all his soul and with all his might, according to all the law of Moses; nor did any like him arise after him." (2 Kgs 23:25).[21] This immediately reminds us of the conclusion of Hezekiah's verdict, "He trusted in the Lord the God of Israel; so that there was none like him among all the kings of Judah after him, nor among those who were before him." (2 Kgs 18:5).

The obvious question which these two evaluations raise, however, is whether or not they contain a contradiction. A number of scholars have argued that they are contradictory, and then have tried to explain how this came to be. C. F. Burney and Norman Snaith both allowed that in their present form the verses are contradictory, but they argued that this was not the case originally. They both believed that the reference in 18:5 to kings after Hezekiah was a later addition and not part of the Deuteronomist's work. In other words, for the Deuteronomist Hezekiah was the greatest king up to his time, but that Josiah was even greater.[22] Gustav

---

[20]Both 2 Kgs 18:5 and 2 Kgs 23:25 are being treated as part of the Deuteronomist's framework for the reigns of Hezekiah and Josiah. This is fairly clear for 18:5, but not as obvious for 23:25. Still, evidence points in this direction. The parallel between the two is one indication. Deuteronomistic authorship is indicated for 23:25 by the language of the verse, and by the way it evaluates Josiah. Since the verse is clearly part of the Deuteronomist's evaluation of Josiah, and since the Deuteronomist expressed his judgments in the introductory part of the framework, it seems best to treat this verse as a transplanted part of the Deuteronomist's introduction to the reign of Josiah. Perhaps the Deuteronomist placed this verse here since he had no concluding section for the framework as he may have been working during Josiah's lifetime.

[21] The phrase "nor did any like him arise after him" may have been added by a later Deuteronomistic editor. See Snaith, "Kings," p. 326; Cross, *Canaanite Myth and Hebrew Epic*, 286.

[22]Burney, *Kings*, 338; Snaith, "Kings," p. 290.

A number of textual emendations have been suggested for 18:5. First of all, it has been suggested that "all" (כֹל) should be deleted following the LXX. See James A. Montgomery & Henry Snyder Gehman, *A Critical and Exegetical Commentary on the Books of Kings*, ICC (Edinburgh: T & T Clark, 1951). Although this deletion would reduce the impact of the eulogy somewhat, it is really not a significant change.

Second, it has been suggested that "nor among those who were before him" (וַאֲשֶׁר הָיוּ לְפָנָיו) should also be seen as a later addition and not

Hölscher saw the two verses as contradictory, and then explained this by attributing the two verses to different authors, 18:5 to E[1] and 23:25 to Rd.[23] Much more recently J. Robinson also interpreted them as contradictory, but he argued that the reason for this lay in the fact that the Deuteronomist had here used two different sources which disagreed with each other, and that the Deuteronomist had too much respect for his sources to change them.[24] It is really questionable whether any of these explanations is convincing.[25]

A few scholars have suggested more helpfully that the contradiction is only apparent and not real. Unless one emends the text or considers the two verses to reflect the thought of different redactors, one must deal with the fact that both verses occur in the same history, in similar settings, and relatively close together at that. It is doubtful whether the

---

original. Montgomery, *Kings,* 501, calls it an "evident gloss." Gray, *Kings,* 609, also considers it to be a later addition, both because it appears to be awkward and because it appears to forget about King David. In this Montgomery and Gray are following the suggestion of Rudolf Kittel, ed., *Biblia Hebraica,* MT edited by Paul Kahle, 7th edition, with additions and corrections by Albrecht Alt and Otto Eissfeldt (Stuttgart: Württembergische Bibelanstalt, 1951).

Third, it has been suggested that "after him" (אַחֲרָיו) and the "and" (ו) in front of "who" (אֲשֶׁר) should be deleted producing the following: "He trusted in the Lord the God of Israel; so that there was none like him among all the kings of Judah who were before him." Burney, *Kings,* 338 argues for this on the basis that from 1 Kgs 3:12 one would expect the reference back to come first, and that the present text contradicts the Deuteronomist's assessment of King Josiah. Snaith, "Kings," p. 209, also changes the text in this way.

Of these three suggested emendations the first is the most likely as it is the only one with any textual support; it is, however, the least significant. The second and third have no textual support, and it is questionable whether the reasons given for them are sufficiently strong to accept them.

[23]Hölscher, *Geschichtsschreibung in Israel,* 402.

[24]J. Robinson, *The Second Book of Kings,* CBC (Cambridge: Cambridge, 1976) 228.

[25]Hölscher's analysis is based on an unacceptable source division. Robinson's assumes that the Deuteronomist used sources for his judgments. Such an assumption is highly improbable, and would require considerable support before it could be stated as simply as Robinson did. Burney's and Snaith's suggested emendation appears to adapt the text to a particular view.

Deuteronomist considered them to be contradictory, and apparently those who read the history later did not consider them so. Our problem then is to determine how the two verses are related to each other, or how they are to be interpreted. Simon Landersdorfer quite some time ago proposed that in neither case should the phrase be taken literally. In both cases the author is using an expression which is *"formelhaft"* to express his view that the two kings had performed extraordinarily.[26] This is possible, but even more helpful has been the observation of C. F. Keil and Klaus Fricke.[27] Writing almost a century apart, both drew attention to the fact that the basis for the superlative praise in the two passages is different. Whereas there "was none like" Hezekiah in that he "trusted in the Lord the God of Israel," Josiah was incomparable in that he "turned to the Lord . . . according to all the law of Moses." Thus each was the greatest in his own particular way.[28]

This interpretation is supported by the fact that somewhat similar wording is used in 1 Kgs 3:12 where God says to Solomon: "Behold, I give you a wise and discerning mind, so that none like you has been before you and none like you shall arise after you." Again a similar phrase is used, and again it is attached to a specific way in which the king is without equal. Solomon's greatness lay in his incomparable wisdom.

This analysis suggests that rather than focussing on the apparent contradiction between 18:5 and 23:25, it is more helpful and accurate to emphasize that in these verses the Deuteronomist is using a formal phrase which expresses superlative praise. It can be applied to different kings, however, since the basis for their being the greatest differs. This makes it clear that for the Deuteronomist there were three categories of kings of Judah: (1) those kings who were rejected as having done evil, (2) those kings who had basically done what was right, and received conditional praise, (3) Hezekiah and Josiah, both of whom received unconditional praise, and each of whom was in a category all by himself.

The reason given in 23:25 for the Deuteronomist's high praise of Josiah

---

[26]Simon Landersdorfer, *Die Bücher der Könige,* Die Heilige Schrift des Alten Testamentes, 3 Bd., 2 Abt. (Bonn: Peter Hanstein, 1927) 207, 233.

[27]C. F. Keil, *The Books of the Kings* (2nd ed., Clark's Foreign Theological Library, Ser. 4, Vol. 33 Edinburgh: T. & T. Clark, 1877) 432; Fricke, *Das zweite Buch von den Königen,* 335.

[28]The reasons why Hezekiah and Josiah were the greatest will be discussed later. At this point it is sufficient to point out that there is no contradiction between 18:5 and 23:25 because the basis for the praise is different.

is that he "turned (שוב) to the Lord." Hans Walter Wolff has written a
helpful article on the kerygma of the Deuteronomistic History in which he
argues that the central message of the history is a call to its readers to
"turn to the Lord."[29] He observes how this term is used at key junctures
in the account of Israel's history (e.g. 1 Sam 7:3; 1 Kgs 8:33,35,47,48;
2 Kgs 17:13). It is thus significant that Josiah is described with the use of
this term. As Wolff stated, "He is not depicted as the faithful one who
never yielded to apostasy. Neither is he shown as one trusting in a word of
promise. Rather, he is presented precisely, and only, as the one who
returned."[30] Josiah had done what the Deuteronomist called on people to
do. As we shall see, the exact content of this turning to the Lord was
determined by the fact that Josiah was king.

A further interesting feature of 23:25 is the phrase "with all his heart
and with all his soul and with all his might." Although the phrase "with all
your heart and with all your soul" is relatively common within the Deuteronomistic History, the only other occurrence of the phrase with "all his
might" is in Deut 6:5. Deuteronomy 5-11 consists of a series of exhortations to Israel to obey the law of Moses once it has settled in the land
which Yahweh is about to give her. "Singlehearted and devoted loyalty to
God is the primary condition upon which their welfare in the land is
based."[31] Loyalty to Yahweh is the heart of Israel's law, and the rest of
its law is a working out of the implications from this. Lohfink has suggested that when one compares Deuteronomy 5-11 with Deuteronomy 12-
26 one receives the impression that the more fundamental requirements
are presented in chaps. 5-11 whereas chaps. 12-26 present the ramifications of these requirements.[32] These chapters could thus be called the
basic constitution of Israel upon which its laws were based. At the center
of these chapters stands the *Shema* (Deut 6:4-9). The Ten Commandments
had been given, and Israel had been exhorted to follow God's commands.[33]

---

[29] Wolff, "Kerygma."

[30] Ibid., p. 91.

[31] George Ernest Wright, "Introduction and Exegesis of the Book of
Deuteronomy," *IB* (New York: Abingdon, 1953), 2:362.

[32] Norbert Lohfink, *Das Hauptgebot. Eine Untersuchung literarischer
Einleitungsfragen zu Dtn 5-11.* AnBib, Nr. 20 (Romae: E Pontificio Instituto Biblico, 1963) 6.

[33] Deut 5:32—"You shall be careful to do therefore as the Lord your
God has commanded you; you shall not turn aside to the right hand or to
the left." Here again the phrase used in the law of kingship and in 2 Kgs
22:2 is found.

Then came the *Shema* with its statement on the unity of God, followed by
the commandment to "love the Lord your God with all your heart, and
with all your soul, and with all your might." When the Deuteronomist
borrows language from Deut 6:5 to describe King Josiah, he is not using
language which was at the periphery of Israel's faith, but rather language
which came from the very core of Israel's understanding of what God
expected from Israel. God expected Israel to obey the law as summarized
by the command in Deut 6:5 to love the Lord with one's whole being. By
using this phrase the Deuteronomist was giving Josiah the highest marks
possible. King Josiah had obeyed the law of Moses.

That the Deuteronomist held King Josiah in high esteem is obvious and
accepted by all. In our examination of the Deuteronomist's verdict of
Josiah, however, we have gone beyond this. By putting the verdict into
context, and by examining the background to it we have been able to
discern the nature of his evaluation in more detail. Not only was Josiah
one of the eight good kings, but he, together with Hezekiah, received
unconditional praise and was placed in a category by himself. In giving
this praise the Deuteronomist used language from key passages in the
history. Josiah "turned" to the Lord, exactly what the Deuteronomist
asked the people to do. By quoting from the law of kingship and the
Shema, the Deuteronomist implied that Josiah had done what was required
of a king and an Israelite. In Josiah what was required and what was done
have been brought together.

So far we have focussed exclusively upon the Deuteronomist's formal
verdict of King Josiah. The positive view which the Deuteronomist had of
Josiah is also reflected in the rest of the narrative of his reign.[34] But
most of all, there is evidence of this in the make-up of the whole history.
Noth had already drawn attention to the fact that the way in which the
Deuteronomist interpreted Israel's history was largely determined by what
Josiah had done.[35] Noth argued that the significance the Deuteronomist
gave to the Deuteronomic law was due to Josiah's response to it upon
finding it. Further, as has been recognized by many, the Deuteronomist
did not emphasize all aspects of the Deuteronomic law equally but
focussed upon total loyalty to Yahweh as expressed in cultic purity and

---

[34]An example of this is found in 2 Kgs 22:11. Josiah's response to the
words of the lawbook is to rend his clothes in penitence. This is clearly
what the Deuteronomist considered to be the correct and required
response to the contents of the lawbook, and put Josiah in a good light.
[35]Noth, *ÜgS*, 92-95.

cultic centralization. These were also the aspects of the Deuteronomic law which Josiah responded to. And, perhaps for our purposes even more significant, the Deuteronomist interpreted the responsibilities of the king in light of what Josiah had done.[36] Since the Deuteronomist saw the Deuteronomic law largely through the deeds of Josiah, and since the Deuteronomist largely evaluated the different kings on how they responded to this Deuteronomic law, practically this means that Josiah became the norm by which all other kings were judged. Other kings were not judged as much on the basis of their obedience to the whole Deuteronomic law, but rather on the basis of whether or not they followed the ways of Josiah.[37] What higher praise could the Deuteronomist have given

---

[36]Ibid. p. 94—"Noch an einem anderen Punkte wird ganz klar, dass Dtr das 'Gesetz' (Dt) im Lichte der Rolle sieht, die es unter Josia in der Geschichte gespielt hat, nämlich in der Aufgabe, die er dem König hinsichtlich der Durchführung des Gesetzes zuweist. . . . Man kann angesichts dessen wohl fragen, ob Josia wirklich im Sinne des Gesetzes handelte, wenn er nicht nur jenen Bundesschluss vermittelte, der dem gefundenen Gesetz öffentliche Geltung verschaffte, sondern darüber hinaus nun auch seine königliche Machtbefugnis für die Durchführung wenigstens eines Teiles des Gesetzesbestimmungen einsetzte. Jedenfalls aber hat Josia das getan; und Dtr stand unter dem unmittelbaren Eindruck dieser Tatsache, wenn er das unter Josia Geschehene nun sogar zu einer allgemeinen Norm erhob und dem Königtum als solchem die Hauptaufgabe zuwies, für das Einhalten der kultischen Bestimmungen von Dt einzustehen, und wenn er— durchaus abweichend von der Intention dieses Gesetzes selbst—mit dem geschichtlichen Aufkommen des Königtums geradezu die Verantwortung für die vom Gesetze in das Auge gefasste Ordnung des Verhältnisses zwischen Gott und Volk vom Volke auf das Königtum übertrug. Denn dies war in der Tat der Leitgedanke für seine gesamte Darstellung der Königszeit."

[37]This raises the obvious question of the relationship of David to Josiah for the Deuteronomist since the Deuteronomist frequently refers to David as the yardstick by which kings are judged. We would argue that by the time of the Deuteronomist David had become THE king of Israel. David had started a dynasty which had lasted 400 years, and David had given Israel security from its enemies. Now they awaited a new David who would restore the glories of the past. Psalms 89 and 132 give some idea of the role which David continued to play in the royal cult. And there is no evidence that the Deuteronomist rejected this. It was thus natural, if not totally inevitable, that the Deuteronomist compared kings with David. Practically, however, the evidence suggests that the deeds of Josiah influenced him more, and were used as the norm.

King Josiah than to use him as the norm by which all other kings were judged?

The Deuteronomist's description of the history of Israel thus supports the estimation of King Josiah found in the formal verdict. Josiah had done what a king should do and so other kings could be measured by him.

The Basis of the Deuteronomist's Evaluation

The examination of the Deuteronomist's verdict of King Josiah detailed the obvious fact that the Deuteronomist held King Josiah in extremely high esteem. Why was this so? Exactly what did King Josiah do that made the Deuteronomist consider him so highly? What actions or deeds on the part of Josiah determined the Deuteronomist's verdict? And why were these actions so significant for the Deuteronomist? In the formal verdict the Deuteronomist indicated that Josiah had obeyed the Mosaic law, and that he had turned to the Lord. But it is not sufficient to remain with these two statements. After all, 7 other kings are described as having done what was right in the eyes of the Lord. Since most of 2 Kings 22-23 is devoted to describing what Josiah did, it is only logical that here the Deuteronomist recorded the basis for his evaluation. The acts described must be the acts which constituted turning to the Lord for a king, and which put Josiah in a class by himself.

Before the specific actions of King Josiah are examined a few words need to be said about the literary nature of the material on King Josiah, namely 2 Kgs 22:3-23:24. Ever since Oestreicher it has been customary to separate the "Reform Report" (essentially 2 Kgs 23:4-20) from the "Law-book Narrative."[38] The significant differences in style between these two pieces observed by Oestreicher, and the fact that nowhere in the Reform Report is there any reference to the lawbook, whereas it is mentioned frequently in the Lawbook Narrative, support such a separation. The terse

---

[38]Theodor Oestreicher, *Das Deuteronomische Grundgesetz*, BFCT, Bd. 27, hft. 4 (Gütersloh: C. Bertelsmann, 1923) 14. For a more detailed discussion of Oestreicher see the Appendix.

Oestreicher divided the two texts as follows: Reform Report—2 Kgs 23:4-14, 15, 19; Lawbook Narrative—2 Kgs 22:3-23:3, 16-18, 20-24.

Dietrich ("Josia und das Gesetzbuch," p. 32) is one recent scholar who does not accept this distinction. He argues that although presently there may be a difference of style, when the Deuteronomistic additions are taken away the source behind 2 Kgs 22:3-20 resembles the Reform Report. Cf. Würthwein, "Josianische Reform."

style of the Reform Report has suggested to many that it may have been taken from royal annals or some similar source.[39] The Lawbook Narrative, with its more expansive, informal style was then more probably a non-official response to these events.[40] Here the Deuteronomist may have made use of some other source from the time of Josiah, or he may have composed the narrative himself on the basis of personal recollection or received oral tradition. It thus seems likely that the Deuteronomist produced the description of the reign of Josiah by either composing or adapting what is now called the Lawbook Narrative, and then inserting the Reform Report. The exact details of this are really not that important for our purposes, since in any case the Deuteronomist produced an account of the reign of Josiah which depicted Josiah and the events according to the Deuteronomist's interpretation and values. This would be true whether the Deuteronomist composed the narratives himself, or whether he produced them largely by piecing together sources, and it would be true whether the narrative gives a historically accurate picture of the events described as has usually been assumed, or whether the account is highly tendentious with little historical material from the reign of Josiah as has been proposed more recently.[41] In the work of the Deuteronomist the framework

---

[39]Gray, *Kings*, 650; Fricke, *Das zweite Buch von den Königen*, 311. Noth, *ÜgS*, 86, argued that the Deuteronomist here adopted passages from the *Tagebücher* of the king, and Jepsen, *Quellen des Königsbuches* and in "Die Reform des Josia," in *Festschrift für Friedrich Baumgärtel*, ed. Johannes Herrmann & Leonhard Rost, Erlangen Forschungen, Reihe A, Bd. 10 (Erlangen: Universitätsbund, 1959) 97-108, argued that this Reform Report was produced by the levitical redactor, but was based on the royal annals. The complex analyses of Würthwein, "Die Josianische Reform," and Hollenstein, "2 Kön. XXIII 4ff," allow for only a small core which could have been taken from annals.

[40]Gray, *Kings*, 651—"The historical narrative, on the other hand (22.3-23.3, 21-25), is directly from the Deuteronomist, the compiler himself or one of his circle among the Temple personnel." Noth, *ÜgS*, 86, saw the Deuteronomist here using a source which had been composed around the time of the events. The Deuteronomistic language of the chapter he considered to be original, and as having influenced the Deuteronomist rather than as a sign of Deuteronomistic composition. Würthwein, "Josianische Reform," divides the Lawbook Narrative among DtrG, DtrP and post-Dtr additions. Dietrich, "Josia und das Gesetzbuch," divided it among DtrG, DtrP, DtrN and an original report.

[41]Würthwein, "Die Josianische Reform"; Hollenstein, "2 Kön. XXIII 4ff"; Dietrich, "Josia und das Gesetzbuch."

with its verdict and the account of Josiah's reign have become one and
need to be treated as a unit expressing the Deuteronomist's interpretation
of Josiah and his time.

The Discovery of the Lawbook, 2 Kgs 22:3-20. In the narrative of the
lawbook and King Josiah the Deuteronomist essentially provides the
background for chap. 23 which then records Josiah's actions. Although
nothing is directly said about how the lawbook was found, the setting
given for the discovery is the repairing of the temple.[42] The great detail
used to describe this is probably meant to emphasize the importance of
the discovery. The lawbook had not just been lying openly in the temple
but was only discovered during work on the temple. By implications this
states that the lawbook had been there for quite some time. Is the author
suggesting that it had been lost since the time of Joash, the last time
there is record of repairs to the temple and the report of a covenant
renewal ceremony? This may be pushing the evidence, but by giving this
background to the discovery, as well as in the way the lawbook is treated
later, the Deuteronomist indicates that any actions derived from the
lawbook will not be innovations, but based on ancient tradition.

Josiah's immediate response to the lawbook is twofold. First of all it
states that he "rent his clothes."[43] Shaphan and probably Hilkiah had

---

[42]The relationship between 2 Kgs 22:3-7, 9 and 2 Kgs 12:4-16 has been
recognized for a long time. Stade already argued that the 2 Kgs 22
account was based on 2 Kgs 12, and that it was a secondary insertion.
(Bernhard Stade, *Ausgewählte akademische Reden und Abhandlungen.*
Giessen: np, 1899). More recently Montgomery (*Kings,* 524), Würthwein
("Die Josianische Reform," pp. 400-401) and Dietrich ("Josia und das
Gesetzbuch," pp. 18-21) have also argued that these verses are based on 2
Kgs 12. Montgomery simply considers them to be secondary and does not
discuss their authorship. Both Dietrich and Würthwein, however, see these
verses as the product of DtrG. Thus even if 2 Kgs 22:4-7,9 were based on
2 Kgs 12, they still would have been part of the Deuteronomist's account,
and need to be considered in getting at his interpretation. The views of
Würthwein and Dietrich, if true, would have a considerable impact upon
historical reconstruction, however, and most interpretations of Josiah's
reform since Oestreicher would need to be re-evaluated.

[43]Dietrich ("Josia und das Gesetzbuch," p. 25) has proposed that v 11
was a product of DtrP and not part of the original history. The only reason
given for this is that both v 11 and v 12 use the noun "king" as the subject
of the verse. Würthwein ("Die Josianische Reform," pp. 400-402), however, considers it to be original.

already read the lawbook, but Josiah is shown as the first one who truly recognized the significance of its contents. His response was dramatic and sudden. He realized that the book was authoritative and that it required a response. His act of tearing his clothes was the acceptable response of contrition and repentance. That the Deuteronomist considered repentance to be the proper response to a realization that the law had been transgressed can be seen throughout the history.[44] Josiah's first response is thus fully appropriate.

The second stage of Josiah's response to the lawbook is to send a delegation to inquire of the Lord, probably in order to discern what he should now do. In doing this Josiah had already indicated that he is prepared to go beyond repentance to concrete acts. In its present form Huldah's oracle responding to the inquiry contains two messages, vv 16-17 concerning Judah as a people, and vv 18-20 concerning King Josiah himself. In light of the fact that most scholars consider the oracle as now recorded to be at least a reworked form of the original, and very possibly a totally secondary addition, we cannot put too much emphasis on its contents.[45] It should

---

[44]Note the references by Wolff, "Kerygma," to the Deuteronomist's call to Israel to "turn." In the passages referred to the call to "turn" includes both repentance and a new obedience to the law. Josiah's acts in 22:3-20 are thus the first stage in this turning to the Lord referred to in 23:25.

[45]Most scholars argue that at least some of vv 16-20 is secondary. A number of scholars have suggested that the prophecy to Josiah in v 20 could not have been aware of Josiah's violent death, and so vv 18-20 contain at least part of the original oracle. Gray, *Kings*, 661; Montgomery, *Kings*, 526; Cross, *Canaanite Myth and Hebrew Epic*, 286. Jepsen, *Quellen des Königsbuches*, 27 and Würthwein, "Die Josianische Reform," pp. 404-5, have rejected this reasoning, and have argued that vv 18-20 are a later addition by someone who tried to explain why Huldah's prophecy of vv 16-17 was only fulfilled so much later than the prophecy seems to expect.

Dietrich, "Josia und das Gesetzbuch," pp. 26-29, has made an attractive proposal regarding the oracle. He argues that in the original Deuteronomistic History Josiah sent the delegation to inquire of the Lord concerning what his response to the lawbook should be. The original oracle had then authenticated the discovered lawbook, and exhorted him to àct upon its requirements. This helped motivate Josiah to do what is recorded in chap. 23. Dietrich also suggests that the phrase "and for the people, and for all Judah" in v 13 is part of this later reworking which changed the emphasis of the oracle away from Josiah's required response. This rework-

be noted, however, that the part of the oracle dealing with Josiah fits well into the picture of him in the rest of the narrative. Here Josiah is explicitly commended for being penitent and humbling himself before Yahweh when he heard the words of the lawbook. Josiah's first response to the lawbook was thus correct. He had repented, and inquired of the Lord presumably with the intention of acting. Chap. 23 then continues the account by describing how Josiah acted in his role as king in response to the requirements of the lawbook.

The Covenant Renewal Ceremony, 2 Kgs 23:1-3. Chap. 23 now describes Josiah's public response to the newly found lawbook. Josiah's first public act according to the Deuteronomist is to lead Judah in a covenant renewal ceremony. Whether only the elders of Judah gathered together for the occasion as may be suggested by v 1, or whether all parts of Judaean society were represented as is stated in v 2 is not important for our purposes.[46] In either case the passage states that Josiah instigated the event, and that a considerable number of people gathered for it. The fact that he "stood by the pillar" for the ceremony, a place where the king apparently stood at formal public ceremonies, suggests that it was more than a gathering of representatives.[47] Once the people have gathered Josiah reads the "words of the book of the covenant."[48] Although Montgomery has stated that a scribe could have been the actual reader, there is no reason why Josiah could not have done it himself.[49] Once the law has been read Josiah makes a covenant with Yahweh to follow the

---

ing now interpreted the lawbook largely as curses which were then ful-filled in the events of 587 B.C.

[46]In addition to the apparent conflict between v 1 and v 2, v 2 itself contains some problems. Chr 34:30 replaces "the prophets" of v 2 with "the Levites," a reading which is supported by 6 codices as well. The Targums read "the scribes." It is most probable that these variants are attempted corrections rather than original. Even if they were correct, however, the significance of the three verses for our purposes would not be changed.

[47]Note the discussion of הָעַמּוּד in Geo Widengren, "King and Covenant," *JSS* 2 (1957) 3-9.

[48]This is the first time the book discovered in the temple is called "book of the covenant." Norbert Lohfink, "Die Bundesurkunde des König Josias. Eine Frage an die Deuteronomiumsforschung," *Bib* 44 (1963) 261-88, 461-98, argues that the book discovered in the temple was essentially a covenant document, and that this was an early form of Deuteronomy.

[49]Montgomery, *Kings,* 528.

law, and all the people join in.[50] A covenant renewal ceremony takes place.

Artur Weiser and other scholars have argued that Judah had a regular covenant renewal ceremony.[51] The ceremony described in 2 Kgs 23:1-3 should not be used to support such a view. In the present context the covenant renewal ceremony is seen as the direct response to the contents of the lawbook, or book of the covenant found in the temple. Baltzer has argued that covenant renewal ceremonies could be held at significant changes of leadership (e.g. at the death of Joshua, Samuel to Saul, Athaliah to Joash) and in times of crisis.[52] The covenant renewal ceremony of Josiah would be a case of the latter. The contents of the discovered lawbook (as well as the oracle of Huldah if it is original) had proclaimed severe punishment upon the people if they did not obey the law. Baltzer argues that 2 Kgs 22:16 can as well be translated with the perfect tense, suggesting that the punishment had already begun.[53] Even if this is not accepted, 22:13 indicates that Josiah at least recognized the precariousness of Judah's situation: "because our fathers have not obeyed the words of this book, to do according to all that is written concerning us." The ceremony of 22:1-3 can thus not be seen as one of a regularly recurring series of covenant renewal ceremonies, but as a special event instigated by Josiah the king upon the realization that the covenant law had been broken and that Judah was on the road to catastrophe. In the ceremony Josiah and the people then committed themselves to the Sinai covenant as expressed in the lawbook.

The role of Josiah in this covenant renewal ceremony is striking. The text indicates that Josiah both initiated the ceremony, and then led it. Clearly he plays the role of "covenant mediator."[54] Josiah leads the

---

[50]Although the exact meaning of the last phrase in v 3 is disputed, it is generally recognized that it signifies that the people accepted and joined in the covenant. It may be that this was formally indicated by the people rising. Montgomery, *Kings,* 528, points out that in Deut 29:9ff. the people are standing.

[51]Artur Weiser, *The Psalms,* OTL (Philadelphia: Westminster, 1962) 35-51.

[52]Klaus Baltzer, *The Covenant Formulary in Old Testament, Jewish, and Early Christian Writings* (Philadelphia: Fortress, 1971) 39-93.

[53]Ibid., pp. 53-54.

[54]Hans-Joachim Kraus, *Worship in Israel. A Cultic History of the Old Testament* (Oxford: Basil Blackwell, 1966), argues that one of the func-

people in committing themselves to the Mosaic covenant. The term
"covenant" cannot in this passage be interpreted as referring to the
Davidic covenant. The Davidic covenant was essentially one between
Yahweh and the king, and although it obviously had implications for the
people as well, it did not include the people in the way in which this
passage assumes. Since the Davidic covenant had become dominant in
Judah Josiah was here leading a renewal which went back to much earlier
traditions. A lawbook had been found which emphasized the Mosaic covenant and obedience to its requirements, and Josiah instituted it into
Judaean life. The closest parallels to this passage are Exod 24:3-8 and
Joshua 24. In the first case Moses leads Israel in the initial acceptance of
the covenant, and in the second Joshua, the successor of Moses, leads
Israel in a renewal of this covenant. Noth has drawn out the common role
of the covenant mediator in these three texts:

> In *Joshua XXIV*, in the opinion of the narrator, Joshua played
> the same part as Moses in the narrative of *Exod XXIV* 3-8—
> i.e. he staged an act of covenant-making with all that it
> entailed—even though nothing, in this instance, is actually
> said about the act itself. It is obvious that Josiah's covenant
> is to be interpreted in the same way; consequently it must be
> a covenant between God and people. The role of the King was
> to bring about the actual conclusion of the covenant.[55]

It is also striking that both Joshua and Josiah first commit themselves to
the covenant, and then the people follow. Josiah, as the king, the leader
of Judah, and thus its representative, makes the covenant with Yahweh
and the people affirm this. One further somewhat similar passage is 2 Kgs

---

tions of the prophet was to act as "covenant mediator." This view has
been accepted by quite a number of scholars.

When we say that Josiah played the role of "covenant mediator" in
2 Kgs 23:1-3, we are not saying that Josiah played the role of a covenant
mediator as described by Kraus, but rather that in this particular event
Josiah clearly was the one who mediated the covenant. The fact that
Josiah played this role on this occasion, however, suggests that there
probably never was such an office in Israel, and so the prophets never
were formally covenant mediators.

[55]Martin Noth, "The Laws in the Pentateuch: Their Assumption and
Meaning," in *The Laws in the Pentateuch and Other Studies* (Edinburgh:
Oliver and Boyd, 1966) 44.

11:17 where Jehoida the priest leads Judah in a covenant renewal following the reign of the non-Davidide, Athaliah.[56] Moses and Joshua are
evidently the model for the role of King Josiah at this point.[57]

Josiah had now gone beyond repentance, and had acted publicly as king
and leader of Judah. Judah was in a crisis, and Josiah had responded by
taking command and leading Judah in the renewal of the covenant which
had first been mediated by Moses, and now was in obvious need of
renewal.

The Reform of the Cult, 2 Kgs 23:4-20, 24. The only verse in the Lawbook Narrative devoted to Josiah's reform of the cult is 23:24. Here it is
stated that Josiah "put away the mediums and the wizards and the tera-
phim and the idols and all the abominations that were seen in the land of
Judah and in Jerusalem" in order to fulfill the requirements of the lawbook of the temple. This verse should be seen as a summary-like statement of what Josiah did in the area of cultic reform, and not as a specific
listing of the important acts of Josiah in this field. The general nature of
the verse is emphasized by the last line of the first half of the verse. With
it the Deuteronomist concluded the whole account of Josiah's reign, and
so in it the Deuteronomist drew attention to the fact that in addition to
leading Judah in the renewal of the covenant, and commanding a centralized passover, Josiah also intervened in the cult in order to purify it by
eliminating all objectionable rites and practices forbidden in the lawbook.

The Deuteronomist only needed a general summarizing statement at
the end since he had incorporated the Reform Report which described
Josiah's acts in considerable detail. The nature of this report has caused
much critical discussion which fortunately need not deter us.[58]

---

[56]Since Jehoash was only 7 years old at this point, Jehoida the priest
acts for him. For a further discussion of this see below, chapter III.

[57]Note the emphasis in Widengren, "King and Covenant," p. 15: "It is
therefore evident that Joshua in Deuteronomic traditions was seen as a
prototype of the Israelite ruler. From the functions of Joshua as the
maker of the covenant it may for this reason be quite possible to draw
some conclusions as to the action of the Israelite king in this same capac-
ity. Joshua was viewed in Deuteronomic circles of traditionalists as the
great pattern of the Israelite ruler as a covenant maker and possessor of
the law as the basis of the covenant."

[58]The two major issues are: 1) The present text appears to be in an
illogical order. Is this in fact the case, and if so, what caused it? A good

Regardless of the trustworthiness of the report it is valuable for getting at the Deuteronomist's emphases. The proposals of Würthwein and Hollenstein in fact increase the Deuteronomist's role in the production of the report.[59] The Deuteronomist thus not only produced or included the summary-like 23:24, but also included (and may have helped produce) the Reform Report. This must have been an important theme for him. Josiah, the king of Judah, is described as having taken some drastic actions to both purify and centralize the cult. As McKay and Cogan have shown, it is not possible to see these acts as simply part of political rebellion against Assyria.[60] Although this period of time no doubt was also the time when Judah freed herself from Assyrian dominance, the two cannot simply be equated. According to the Deuteronomist a second public response of Josiah to the discovered lawbook was to lead a reform of the cult based on the requirements of the law.[61]

---

example of an attempt to recreate the original order is Jepsen, "Die Reform des Josia." 2) How are vv 16-20 to be treated? Were they originally part of the Reform Report, or are they a later addition? Is there any historical basis for this account of Josiah extending the reform into the North? It is quite common to see these verses as a later addition with no historical basis.

One rather peculiar aspect of the Reform Report is the presence of seven converted perfects. It has been common to see these as indications of late authorship (e.g. Gray, *Kings*, 666), and both Würthwein and Hollenstein separate all lines with them from the rest and treat them as later additions to the Reform Report. It has, however, been argued that this is not necessary in Rudolf Meyer, "Stilistische Bemerkungen zu einem angeblichen Auszug aus der 'Geschichte der Könige von Juda,'" in *Festschrift für Friedrich Baumgärtel*, ed. Herrmann & Rost, Erlangen Forschungen, Reihe A, Bd. 10 (Erlangen: Universitätsbund, 1959) 114-23.

[59] Würthwein, "Die Josianische Reform,"; Hollenstein, "2 Kön. XXIII 4ff."

[60] John McKay, *Religion in Judah under the Assyrians* (SBT, 2, 26 Naperville: Alec R. Allenson, Inc., 1973); Morton Cogan, *Imperialism and Religion, Assyria, Judah and Israel in the Eighth and Seventh Centuries B.C.E.* (SBLMS, 19; Missoula: Scholars, 1974).

[61] The Deuteronomist does not discuss the origin of the law of centralization, but simply considers it to be part of the law. For a discussion of this see: Moshe Weinfeld, "Cult Centralization in Israel in the Light of a Neo-Babylonian Analogy," *JNES* 23 (1964) 202-12; Ernest Nicholson, "The Centralization of the Cult in Deuteronomy," *VT* 13 (1963) 380-89; W. Eugene Claburn, "The Fiscal Basis of Josiah's Reforms," *JBL* 92 (1973) 11-22.

Here again Josiah acts as the leader of all aspects of Judah's life, including the cult. The Deuteronomic law announced curses upon the people if they did not obey the law. It was thus the king's responsibility to purify and centralize the cult in order to protect Judah from these curses. In acting in this way Josiah fulfilled his responsibility as king, and the Deuteronomist clearly approved of Josiah's actions in this reform of the cult.

The Passover Celebration, 2 Kgs 23:21-23. The final event in Josiah's reign described by the Deuteronomist is the passover celebration. In keeping with the lawbook, Josiah commands the people to celebrate the passover in Jerusalem. Unfortunately the narrative contains no information about the passover itself and simply records that it was kept in the eighteenth year of King Josiah.[62] The only descriptive statement made is that "no such passover had been kept since the days of the judges who judged Israel, or during all the days of the kings of Israel or of the kings of Judah;" (v 22).[63] It is usually believed that the newness of Josiah's passover was the fact that until then the passover had been a family or tribal event but now Josiah in response to the requirements of the lawbook, had centralized it and made it a pilgrimage festival.[64] This then assumes that Israel had had a centralized passover during the time of the judges.[65] Josiah thus climaxes the covenant renewal of vv 1-3 with a huge centralized passover celebration.

Again Josiah had acted as the one responsible for the cult. He had observed that Judah's manner of keeping the passover was not consistent with the requirements of the document found in the temple, and he had immediately commanded that this be changed. There is nothing in these

---

[62]Montgomery, *Kings,* 536 considers the dating in v 22 to be secondary. Würthwein, "Die Josianische Reform," pp. 407-408, argues on the basis of this dating that vv 21-23 must be secondary since this event could not have happened in the same year as the covenant renewal.

[63]The LXX does not translate the בְ before הפסח resulting in a translation which implies that the passover had not been kept at all during this time. The implications of the MT are to be accepted at this point.

[64]Gray, *Kings;* Montgomery, *Kings;* etc.

[65]Kraus, *Worship in Israel,* 51, for example argues that the account in 2 Kgs 23:21-23 is correct in that the passover had been centralized in prekingship times.

verses which suggests that the Deuteronomist disapproved of Josiah's action in changing the festal system in this way, and the fact that it was described as part of that narrative which no doubt was meant to explain why Josiah was the model for kings argues that the Deuteronomist considered this action to be proper for Josiah as king of Judah.

Conclusion

According to the Deuteronomist Josiah did what was right in the eyes of the Lord. He and Hezekiah were the only kings of Judah to receive unconditional commendation, and practically Josiah functioned as a model by which all other kings were judged. This description of the Deuteronomist's evaluation is accepted by virtually all.

The basis for the Deuteronomist's evaluation is found in the account of Josiah's reign. When the lawbook was found in the temple Josiah immediately became penitent and inquired of Yahweh as to what he should do. He then proceeded to lead Judah towards obedience of the law. His actions of initiating and mediating a covenant renewal ceremony, of leading Judah in the reform of the cult, and of commanding a new passover were all part of this leadership. Josiah had not only *turned to the Lord* in obeying the law of Moses himself, but he had taken concrete actions as king to establish the law of Moses in the land. Especially important to him, and to the Deuteronomist, was that part of the law which focussed on the purification and centralization of the cult. Again, this analysis of the basis of the Deuteronomist's high evaluation of Josiah would be accepted by most.

Although most scholars would agree that the Deuteronomist evaluated Josiah extremely highly, and that this was because of the acts of Josiah as described in 2 Kgs 22:3-23:24, the logical implications of this are seldom drawn or noticed. Noth's comments on this reflect the common approach. Noth admits that in his actions Josiah adopted a role similar to that which Moses and Joshua had earlier fulfilled. But he then continues: "But Josiah can hardly be considered a charismatic leader of the Israelite tribes, as Moses and Joshua had been; the less so since, in contrast with the monarchy in the former state of Israel, the Davidic monarchy in Judah had never been considered in theory to be a continuation of the old charismatic leadership."[66] He then concludes from this that it was not important who took the initiative in the renewal of the covenant, or in fulfilling

---

[66]Noth, "The Laws in the Pentateuch," p. 46.

the role performed by Josiah as long as it was someone who was part of the "*ʾahal Yahweh*." In this analysis Noth must be rejected. Although Josiah may not have been a charismatic leader exactly like Moses and Joshua, he certainly was seen by the Deuteronomist as a successor to Moses and Joshua. The difference between them in how they became leader is far less significant then the fact that both had been chosen by Yahweh to be leader of his people.[67] Not only could Josiah take the initiative in leading Judah in covenant renewal and reform of the cult, but this was his responsibility as leader of this people. We must thus conclude that the Deuteronomist evaluated Josiah as highly as he did because Josiah fulfilled his responsibilities as king in the acts described. Josiah was not some great personality who arose above his position, but a king who fulfilled his proper role in terms of the law and cult.

KING HEZEKIAH, 2 KINGS 18-20

As was the case with 2 Kings 22-23, so also 2 Kings 18-20 has received very much attention in scholarly research. Montgomery has stated that "no section of Kings has produced more critical debate."[68] In focussing upon 2 Kings 18-20 and 22-23 we are thus dealing with two passages which have definitely not been on the fringe of OT studies.

Although Montgomery's statement is very possibly correct, not all parts of these three chapters have received equal attention. Most of the

---

[67] It should be noted that neither Moses nor Joshua became leader of Israel as is usually considered to be characteristic of charismatic leaders. In other words, both were called to be leader by Yahweh before they led Israel to victory. In this their path to leadership is different from that of the charismatic judges.

It is also questionable whether the contrast assumed by the quote between Israel's and Judah's concept of kingship is valid. It is simply not valid to speak of Northern kingship as charismatic if this term is derived from the charismatic judges. It has even been suggested that it is more valid to speak of Judah's kingship as charismatic in that Yahweh chose the Davidic dynasty to rule in Jerusalem.

We would thus conclude that the charismatic—non-charismatic distinction in terms of Israel's leadership is questionable at best, and even then it must be seen as a modern categorization not really realized in OT times. The Deuteronomist had a certain particular concept of leadership, and certainly Moses, Joshua, and Josiah were leaders in Israel.

[68] Montgomery, *Kings*, 513.

discussion has been devoted to 2 Kgs 18:13-19:37. This passage presents two major historical problems. First of all, the chronology of Hezekiah's reign is exceedingly problematic. According to 2 Kgs 18:1, 9, Hezekiah came to the throne during the reign of King Hoshea in Israel, and so before the end of the Northern Kingdom. On the other hand, 2 Kgs 18:13 introduces Sennacherib's campaign of 701 B.C. by placing it in Hezekiah's 14th year. This would mean that Hezekiah had come to the throne around 715 B.C., well after the fall of the North. Various solutions to this apparent contradiction have been proposed, but so far there is no sign of a consensus on the dating of Hezekiah's reign.[69]

A second, perhaps even more debated, historical dilemma results from trying to coordinate the account in Kings with the events of that time. 2 Kgs 18:13-16 seems to be at least based on a Judaean archival note describing Hezekiah's surrender to Sennacherib in 701 B.C.[70] The Assyrian annals give a strikingly similar description of this event, and so provide a significant extra-Biblical point of contact.[71] This correspondence has been one of the major chronological cross-references between Biblical dates and the dates of the ancient Near East. The problem arises when the remainder of this larger passage is brought into the picture. Does the whole narrative (2 Kgs 18:13-19:37) reflect one major campaign of Sennacherib, with 2 Kgs 18:17-19:37 seeing the events described in 2 Kgs

---

[69]See H. H. Rowley, "Hezekiah's Reform and Rebellion," *BJRL* 44 (1961/62) 395-431. On pp. 409-410 Rowley lists the different dates that have been proposed, and the various scholars who have supported them. John McHugh, "The Date of Hezekiah's Birth," *VT* 14 (1964) 446-53, would be an example of an article dealing specifically with this question.

It should be noted that most, if not all, historical reconstructions of Sennacherib's campaigns into Judah also deal with this question, and make some assumptions regarding Sennacherib's dates.

[70]Gray, *Kings*, 610, simply calls these verses "From the Annals of Judah." Montgomery, *Kings*, 482, speaks of them as having an "annalistic character." Brevard Childs, *Isaiah and the Assyrian Crisis*, SBT, ser. 2, no. 3 (Naperville: Alec R. Allenson, 1967), sees Deuteronomistic style in these verses: "In other words, these verses are narrative prose, typical of the author, and not just a copy from an entry in a state archives." p. 70.

[71]James B. Pritchard, ed., *ANET* (Princeton: Princeton, 1969) 287-88.

See, however, J. B. Geyer, "2 Kings 18:14-16 and the Annals of Sennacherib," *VT* 21 (1971) 604-6, which concludes that "it is not possible to equate 2 Kings xviii 14-16 only with the Annals of Sennacherib in the way that Bright proposes." p. 606.

18:13-16 from a different perspective? Or does the narrative describe different scenes which were still all part of the same campaign? Or were there two different campaigns which lay behind the present narrative, with the one described in 2 Kgs 18:17-19:37 coming either before or after 701 B.C.? These are the major proposals which have been made.[72] At this point none of the proposed reconstructions has won wide-spread support, and Childs has suggested that "in terms of the specific historical problem of 701, it seems unlikely that a satisfactory historical solution will be forthcoming without fresh extra-Biblical evidence."[73] Historians, however, need to attempt to reconstruct the events behind the traditions, and so debate on 2 Kgs 18:13-19:37 will necessarily continue.

Up to this point the historical issues described have dominated all discussion of 2 Kings 18-20. Relatively little attention has been given to the role which these chapters play for the Deuteronomist, or to the theological emphases found within them. To this extent these chapters have been treated similarly to the way 2 Kings 22-23 had been treated before the articles by Würthwein and Dietrich. But whereas Würthwein and Dietrich specifically asked how 2 Kings 22-23 reflected the concerns of the author who produced them, 2 Kings 18-20 have really not been examined to the same extent with this question in mind. This is the case even though it has been assumed that 2 Kgs 18:1-8 do say something about the Deuteronomistic historian. Here the tendency has been to note that the Deuteronomist gives Hezekiah unqualified praise, like Josiah, and to then state that this was because Hezekiah, like Josiah, had centralized the cult as is described in 2 Kgs 18:4. It is interesting that even in these introductory verses the historical background of the bronze serpent called Nehushtan has probably drawn more attention than the question of what the historian was trying to communicate.[74] Thus in the past research on 2 Kings 18-20 has focussed largely on historical issues, and has dealt with other issues on the basis of how they affected the historical questions.

---

[72]The following give extensive bibliographic citations on the issue: L. L. Honor, *Sennacherib's Invasion of Palestine* (New York: Columbia, 1926); Montgomery, *Kings*, 480-518; Rowley, "Hezekiah's Reform and Rebellion;" Childs, *Isaiah and the Assyrian Crisis*.

For a relatively recent, rather innovative proposal see A. K. Jenkins, "Hezekiah's Fourteenth Year. A New Interpretation of 2 Kings xviii 13 - xix 37," *VT* 26 (1976) 84-298.

[73]Childs, *Isaiah and the Assyrian Crisis*, 120.

[74]An example of this is H. H. Rowley, "Zadok and Nehushtan," *JBL* 58 (1939) 113-41.

Since the goal of this study is to discover the Deuteronomist's view of kingship, it is not important for us to attempt to reconstruct the historical events of that time. What is significant is how the Deuteronomist understood his traditions, and how he used them. It is extremely doubtful whether the Deuteronomist intentionally "created" new history, or distorted his traditions, but this does not imply that his understanding was necessarily historically accurate. Fricke summarizes this idea well.

> Despite all attempts, of which there is no lack, to arrange the individual complexes into different historical settings, there remains, nevertheless, no other way than to explain the passage as it now stands, in other words, as a temporal succession of events. After all, the Deuteronomistic historians also understood it that way and not differently.[75]

In other words, the Deuteronomist understood the events described as having taken place consecutively but as part of the same campaign of Sennacherib. This is confirmed by the chronological references in the text. According to 2 Kgs 18:2 Hezekiah reigned for 29 years. In 2 Kgs 18:13 the following events are placed in Hezekiah's 14th year.[76] That the incidents of 2 Kings 20 are still to be placed at this time is attested by 2 Kgs 20:6 which speaks of 15 more years in Hezekiah's reign. Thus the Deuteronomist made clear that everything from 2 Kgs 18:13 till the end of the description was to be seen as having happened in relationship with each other.

John Gray has emphasized how unfortunate it is that the Deuteronomist focussed all of his attention on one series of events in the 29 year-long reign of Hezekiah, and that in doing so much of Hezekiah's reign remains in the dark.[77] For a historian studying the time of Hezekiah this may be so, but for someone studying the Deuteronomist it is not the case. Through his choice of material the Deuteronomist indicated what he

---

[75]Fricke, *Das zweite Buch von den Konigen*, 258.

[76]Rowley's conclusion ("Hezekiah's Reform and Rebellion") that originally there was a "twenty-fourth" in v 13, although possibly helpful in historical reconstruction, is difficult to support, and the relationship between v 13 and 2 Kgs 20:6 argues that the Deuteronomist meant "fourteenth." This, of course, does not exclude the possibility that an original "twenty-fourth" had been changed to "fourteenth" before the time of the Deuteronomist, or even that the Deuteronomist himself made the change.

[77]Gray, *Kings*, 599.

considered to be important, both for his view of Hezekiah as king, and for his view of how the history of Israel was to be interpreted. The fact that the Deuteronomist did spend three chapters on Hezekiah indicates how significant he considered the events described to be, especially when this is compared with the way the reigns of some of the other kings are summarized.

Before the narrative itself is examined one further aspect of it needs to be noticed. The fact that 2 Kgs 18:13-20:19 is virtually identical to Isaiah 36-39 makes it necessary to propose some kind of literary relationship between the two. The general consensus is that the Kings passage takes precedence, and that Isaiah 36-39 was taken from Kings and added to the book of Isaiah at a later point.[78] The different types of arguments that have been used to support this position make this proposal highly likely. This then means that the text in Isaiah may be helpful for determining the original text, but since our goal is the Deuteronomist, the fact that at some time these chapters were added to Isaiah is largely irrelevant. Similarly, the fact that 2 Kgs 18:14-16 is missing from Isaiah is not significant in a study of the Deuteronomist even though it would be in a study of the redactor of the book of Isaiah. In other words, the fact that this passage has been copied from Kings into Isaiah is no doubt significant for some purposes, but it is not that meaningful for our research.

The Deuteronomist's Evaluation of King Hezekiah

The first step in analyzing this narrative is to examine the Deuteronomist's evaluation of King Hezekiah. For this we must again go to the Deuteronomist's introduction to the reign of Hezekiah in which he expresses his formal verdict of the king. As we noted earlier, these verdicts are probably the most definitely Deuteronomistic creations in the history, and the clearest examples of his editing.

The Deuteronomist's evaluation of Hezekiah is found in 2 Kgs 18:3-6, with the stereotyped verdict in v 3, and an expansion of this in vv 4-6. In the formal verdict the Deuteronomist states that Hezekiah had done what was right in the eyes of the Lord, and in this was similar to King David.

---

[78] A few representative examples of this would be: Otto Kaiser, *Isaiah 13-39*, OTL (Philadelphia: Westminster, 1974) 367-68; Gray, *Kings*, 600-601; Otto Kaiser, "Die Verkündigung des Prophet Jesaja im Jahre 701. Von der Menschen Vertrauen und Gottes Hilfe. Eine Studie über II Reg 18 17ff, par Jes 36 1ff," *ZAW* (1969) 304-15.

Since Hezekiah's father, King Ahaz, was one of the evil kings, he is not mentioned in the verdict. With this verse the Deuteronomist simply places Hezekiah in the category of the good kings, those who followed the law.

The immediately following v 4 then describes the reforming measures of King Hezekiah. Although this is not explicitly evaluation, it is undoubtedly meant to be part of it. All six kings who had received positive judgments before Hezekiah had only received a qualified commendation. In each case the positive verdict had been immediately followed by the statement that the king had not, however, eliminated the high places, thus allowing Judah to continue to worship there. Instead of this expected qualification the Deuteronomist continues by stating directly that Hezekiah had removed the high places. This is clearly meant to contrast Hezekiah with the other good kings, and is in this way a strongly positive statement about Hezekiah. Hezekiah had not only followed the law, but he had also led in religious reform. By substituting this verse for the expected qualification the Deuteronomist has made the verse part of his verdict of Hezekiah more than a descriptive verse of the deeds of Hezekiah.

With v 5 the Deuteronomist begins the second part of his evaluation of the king. As was stated earlier, such a second part was only added in the evaluations of Hezekiah and Josiah. According to the Deuteronomist Hezekiah "trusted in the Lord the God of Israel; so that there was none like him among all the kings of Judah after him, nor among those who were before him."[79] The Deuteronomist's high view of King Hezekiah is here strongly affirmed. In fact, Hezekiah is here placed in a category all by himself. It is of course possible that the phrase "there was none like him" could be meant negatively, but the context makes it clear that this is not what was meant here.[80] In this verse Hezekiah is then depicted as one of the great kings of Judah.

Such a view of Hezekiah is also communicated by vv 6-8. V 6, like v 3, emphasizes Hezekiah's obedience to Yahweh. The phrase "he clung to the Lord" is not a common one in the OT, and is used primarily in the

---

[79]For a discussion of some of the textual problems of this verse see footnote 22, p. 51.

[80]A somewhat similar construction is used negatively in 1 Sam 26:15 and 1 Kgs 21:25. This means that the construction itself does not have negative or positive connotations, but is an expression of superlative degree. Its content is then provided by the rest of the sentence or paragraph.

Deuteronomistic History.[81] In various places Israel is challenged to cling to Yahweh. Usually this is stated in connection with obeying the commandments. 2 Kgs 18:6 is the only place in the Bible, however, where it is stated positively about an individual that he did cling to Yahweh. Hezekiah had followed the commandments as was expected of him. Vv 7-8 then describe the results of Hezekiah's obedience. Scholars have often noted that these verses appear to be more theologically motivated than historical. This may be so. According to the Deuteronomist Yahweh blessed the obedient Hezekiah, and thus he prospered militarily. Although the specific events mentioned in these two verses may be accurately recorded, they are not representative of the events throughout Hezekiah's reign, and they have been chosen and placed here in order to emphasize the successful nature of Hezekiah's reign. The Deuteronomist's introduction thus consistently brings out the positive in Hezekiah and his reign.

This positive and sympathetic attitude toward Hezekiah found in the introduction to his reign can also be seen in the narratives which describe what he did. In 2 Kgs 19:1 it is stated that, after hearing the words which the Rabshakeh had spoken, Hezekiah "rent his clothes, and covered himself with sackcloth, and went into the house of the Lord." This reminds us of Josiah's response to the words of the lawbook. This sign of humility and repentance was considered to be the appropriate response, and meant to be seen positively. Further, Childs has argued that the form of the narrative found in 2 Kgs 19:9b-35 is like a prophetic legend, only the center of attention is the king rather than a prophet.[82] The purpose of such a narrative was to highlight the pious and righteous King Hezekiah. Whether the Deuteronomist composed this passage himself, or whether he adopted an already existing tradition, the sentiment of these narratives fits very well with the positive evaluation of Hezekiah already expressed in the introduction.

When this picture of Hezekiah is then put into perspective through comparison with the Deuteronomistic evaluations of the other kings, the following conclusions become clear: First, Hezekiah is one of the eight kings who did what was right, and obeyed the law of Moses. Second, he is one of two kings who received unqualified praise. Whereas the other six

---

[81]This phrase, with the verb "to cling" (דבק), and either the name יהוה or a pronoun referring to him occurs 10 times in the OT. Only two of these are found outside of the Deuteronomistic History: Ps 63:8 and Jer 13:11. The 8 Deuteronomistic texts are: Deut 4:4; 10:20; 11:22; 13:4; 30:20; Josh 22:5; 23:8; 2 Kgs 18:6.

[82]Childs, *Isaiah and the Assyrian Crisis*, 101.

kings who were commended did not eliminate the high places, Hezekiah and Josiah did. Third, he is in a category all by himself. Specifically this means that in some way he is above all the rest, the superlative, the one by whom others could be measured.

It is difficult to try and compare him with King Josiah in order to determine who was greater in the eyes of the Deuteronomist. Clearly, both received total praise, and both are explicitly placed at the top of their class. The fact that the Deuteronomist apparently used Josiah as a model for his examination of the kings suggests that he might have considered Josiah greater than Hezekiah, but this wasn't really the issue at hand. The Deuteronomist was not trying to pick out the greatest king in Israel's history, but was trying to write a history which, given his world view, was naturally theologically determined. The fact that Josiah was nearer to the author in that history may very well have affected his choice of Josiah as a model. If the author had come to his understanding of Israel's history during Josiah's reform, such a procedure would be very possible. In his formal evaluations, however, the Deuteronomist singled out the two kings from all the rest as deserving total praise, and each was further placed in a category all by himself as the greatest in some particular way.

The Basis of the Deuteronomist's Evaluation

That the Deuteronomist had an extremely high regard for King Hezekiah is accepted by virtually all, if not all, OT scholars. It is usually stated that although the Deuteronomist gave varying degrees of praise to a number of kings, unqualified praise was reserved for Hezekiah and Josiah. The above study of the Deuteronomist's evaluation of King Hezekiah is then in keeping with the usual analysis.

Further, it is usually also agreed that the basis for this praise of the Deuteronomist for King Hezekiah was the reforming activities of the king. This has been the tendency in both elementary introductions to the OT as well as in the more scholarly works. Thus Bernhard Anderson states: "In II Kings 18, the Deuteronomic editor gives unqualified approval to his reign, ... This tribute, of course, was based on the Deuteronomic premise that the true worship of Yahweh must be centralized in Jerusalem."[83] Similarly, W. Zimmerli, after noting the historian's high regard of Hezekiah, says: "This is based upon the fact that a reform of the cult can be

---

[83]Anderson, *Understanding*, p. 280.

reported of him."[84] Many more examples could be given. These scholars assume that the Deuteronomist's evaluation of King Hezekiah, especially as found in 18:3 and 5, is based on Hezekiah's reform as described in 18:4. This assumption needs to be questioned.

The significance the Deuteronomist gave to the reign of Hezekiah is indicated at least to some extent by the amount of space devoted to his reign. Even Josiah, the Deuteronomist's model, received only two chapters whereas Hezekiah received three. Uzziah (Azariah), who reigned for 52 years, only received 7 verses of attention. The three chapters devoted to Hezekiah are then quite considerable. This fits well with our observations on the estimation which the Deuteronomist had of Hezekiah. It also, however, raises a question of the usual assumption on the basis of his high regard of Hezekiah. Given that the Deuteronomist considered Hezekiah so highly, is it not striking that in these three chapters the Deuteronomist devotes only one verse (18:4), and one other reference (18:22) to Hezekiah's reform, that which is usually considered to be the basis of his high regard? This suggests rather strongly that the reform may not have been the basis of the Deuteronomist's view. Rather, the basis of the Deuteronomist's view of Hezekiah is more probably to be found in the description of those events in Hezekiah's reign which the Deuteronomist chose to focus upon.

This proposal is supported by the Deuteronomist's word choice in his evaluation of King Hezekiah. 2 Kgs 18:5 states: "He *trusted* (בטח) in the Lord the God of Israel; so that there was none like him among all the kings of Judah after him, nor among those who were before him." (Italics mine.) Whereas Josiah's greatness lay in his turning to the Lord, Hezekiah's was due to his trust of Yahweh. This is a rather significant statement by the Deuteronomist in that בטח is not a common term for him.[85]

---

[84]W. Zimmerli, "Jesaja und Hiskia," in *Wort und Geschichte*, Fs. Karl Elliger (ed. Gese & Rüger, AOAT, No. 18 Neukirchen-Vluyn: Neukirchener, 1973) 205-6.

[85]Childs states: "Although the verb 'to trust' does occur in Isaiah's theology (cf. 30.15) it is a more central term in the theology of the Dtr. historian and serves specifically as the rubric under which Hezekiah is characterized (II Kings 18.5)." (*Isaiah and the Assyrian Crisis*, 85). Childs is no doubt correct when he states that the Deuteronomist has used the verb "to trust" as the rubric under which Hezekiah is characterized. It is questionable, however, whether one can consider the term central in the theology of the Deuteronomist. Outside of this passage the term only occurs 6 times (Deut 28:52; Judg 9:26; 18:7, 10, 27; 20:36) within the

The term occurs 16 times within the whole history, but amazingly, 10 of those usages are to be found right here in the three chapters on Hezekiah. Further, none of the six remaining usages in the history has anything to do with trusting Yahweh. This concept is raised only in 18:5, the Deuteronomist's evaluation, and in the narratives which follow. This is, in fact, the major issue in the Rabshakeh's first speech to Hezekiah's representatives on the wall of Jerusalem where the term בטח is found 7 times within the space of 6 verses. Without question, the Deuteronomist meant the term in the evaluation to point ahead to the narratives which follow in which the issue is discussed. Either the Deuteronomist composed the narratives of the conflict between Assyria and Judah in such a way that the question of ultimate reliance became a central issue, and then affirmed that in this Hezekiah trusted in Yahweh, *or* the Deuteronomist inserted a tradition which already had this issue with the key word בטח at its heart, and then evaluated Hezekiah making use of the thematic term of the tradition. In either case the present connection between the evaluation of 18:5 and the narrative of 18:17-19:37 cannot be avoided. This strongly supports our contention that the Deuteronomist based his evaluation of Hezekiah on the way Hezekiah responded to the Assyrian crisis. The events, and acts of Hezekiah now placed in his fourteenth year must be examined in order to discover the true basis of the Deuteronomist's evaluation of King Hezekiah.[86]

Before the narrative beginning with 18:9 is examined in more detail, the Deuteronomist's introduction to Hezekiah's reign deserves a few more words. If Hezekiah's reform as described in 18:4 is not the basis of the

---

whole history, and all of these are very possibly in source material, and further, none concern trust in God. It thus obviously was not a common Deuteronomistic term. In light of this it seems probable that the traditions which the Deuteronomist incorporated on Hezekiah already contained the emphasis on the term, and the Deuteronomist then took this term from the tradition and adopted it for his evaluation of Hezekiah.

Childs' point that the theological use of the term in the narrative on the Assyrian crisis "reflects a theological schematization" and is thus a sign of a later reworking of a more historically accurate document is still valid. Only, this theological schematization probably did not originate with the Deuteronomist although he apparently accepted it.

[86]Since the Deuteronomist considered all of 18:17-20:19 to have occurred in Hezekiah's fourteenth year, we will use the phrase to describe all these events even though this may very well not be accurate historically.

Deuteronomist's evaluation of Hezekiah, its significance or function needs to be checked. Earlier we noted that this verse was not explicitly evaluation, but did speak to that question. The qualification present in other positive evaluations has here been replaced with a reference to Hezekiah's reforming acts in the removal of the high places. It seems likely that the form of the past verdicts has here determined the form of this verse. In this way the verse becomes more part of the verdict itself than a statement giving the grounds for the verdict. The Deuteronomist is thus saying that not only did Hezekiah do what was right, as David had done, but he also did more in that he removed the high places. As has always been noted, the elimination of the high places and the centralization of the cult were extremely important for the Deuteronomist, and so this additional statement in the verdict is a significant one. The present Deuteronomistic style of v 4a makes it difficult to determine whether his sources described Hezekiah's reforms, or whether the Deuteronomist based this statement largely on the tradition in v 4b.[87] Probably there existed some tradition associating Hezekiah with reform, and the Deuteronomist then described Hezekiah as the reforming king using his own language and added this to the reference on the destruction of Nehustan, the bronze serpent. This all indicates that v 4 should be connected closely with v 3, the two together giving the Deuteronomist's normal verdict of the king. The following v 5 then begins the second part of the Deuteronomist's evaluation in which he draws special attention to Hezekiah's trust in Yahweh, and points ahead to the events of Hezekiah's fourteenth year. The Deuteronomist thus argued

----

[87] The question of the historical nature of Hezekiah's reforms need not detain us here. On the basis of the Kings account alone one could perhaps argue that the only tradition of reform which the Deuteronomist had was the tradition on the destruction of the bronze serpent, but that because of the Deuteronomist's emphasis on cult centralization, and because of his high regard for King Hezekiah, the Deuteronomist produced v 4a so that the great King Hezekiah could not be criticized on this account. The Chronicler's account, however, suggests that somewhere there must have also existed other traditions about Hezekiah's reforming activity. The emphasis on cult centralization in Deuteronomy may also reflect past reform in this area by Hezekiah. It would thus be dangerous to conclude that the Deuteronomist had written v 4a simply so that the picture of Hezekiah would fit his ideal king picture, and that other traditions of Hezekiah's reform were not available. If this were so, then the fact that the Deuteronomist did not record more of this tradition emphasizes that Hezekiah's reforming activity was not the basis of the Deuteronomist's evaluation of Hezekiah.

that the great king Hezekiah also participated in reform, not that King
Hezekiah was great because he participated in reform.

After reaffirming Hezekiah's reliance on Yahweh, and his obedience to
the law of Moses (18:6), the Deuteronomist concludes his introduction
with two verses which detail some of Hezekiah's major accomplishments
as well as describe the results of Hezekiah's policies. V 7a summarizes
these two verses: "And the Lord was with him; wherever he went forth, he
prospered." Vv 7b-8 then state that Hezekiah rebelled against Assyria and
defeated the Philistines, both events which describe what Hezekiah did,
and how Yahweh was with him. Although rebellion against Assyria could
very well have had religious and cultic implications, as is often emphasized, it is questionable whether this, and Hezekiah's reform, is what is
being referred to here. In these two verses Hezekiah's doing what was
right is associated with his deeds in the military and political realm, and
in this way the major events of Hezekiah's fourteenth year are introduced.
It is also difficult to read about Hezekiah's exploits with the Philistines
without being reminded of King David, the king who is also described as
having defeated the Philistines with the help of the Lord (2 Sam 5:17-25).
The Deuteronomist's introduction to the reign of Hezekiah thus emphasizes his greatness, and points ahead to the following narratives which
present the basis of this greatness.

In our treatment of the Deuteronomist's description of the reign of
Hezekiah all of 18:9-20:19 need to be treated together regardless of the
different origin of the traditions incorporated. Even though 18:13-16 most
probably came from a different source than the traditions in 18:17ff, the
Deuteronomist used these different types of material to produce his
account, and the end product is one connected narrative unified by time
and theme.

Introduction, 2 Kgs 18:9-16. The introduction to the main narrative can
be divided into two paragraphs, the first providing background to the
events themselves, and the second introducing the events. Since 2 Kgs
18:9-12 is to be seen as background to the events described, this paragraph needs to be placed here rather than connected to the Deuteronomist's introduction to the reign as a whole. In these verses is recorded the
fall of Samaria in language rather similar to 2 Kings 17. V 12 summarizes
the longer speech of chapter 17 explaining why Samaria fell: "because
they did not obey the voice of the Lord their God but transgressed his
covenant . . ." With this recapitulation the Deuteronomist sets the stage
for the following events. This is a time when the very existence of the
nation is in doubt. The threat to Judah and Jerusalem recorded in 18:13ff.

is very real, and there is the possibility that Assyria will win, capture Jerusalem and deport its inhabitants, and so terminate the Southern Kingdom as it had the Northern. The key to the nation's existence is also given. Israel fell because its people did not obey the law, nor keep the covenant which Yahweh had given her. The unstated implication is that if Israel had obeyed the law, and kept the covenant, she would have continued to exist as a nation on its land. The obvious question which the paragraph raises is whether Judah, and its king, will act differently, or whether it and he will also follow the path of the Northern Kingdom into oblivion.

This opening paragraph setting the scene is then followed by the short passage of 18:13-16. These verses, most probably based on some annalistic source but now set in a Deuteronomistic cloak,[88] describe the first scene in the Assyrian conflict with Judah. The similarity in form between v 13 and the earlier v 9 brings out the seriousness of the threat, and compares it to the events in Samaria just a short time before this. Vv 14-16 then record how Jerusalem managed to survive through the payment of a massive tribute. The costs are huge as the house of the Lord had to be stripped of all its treasures, its silver and gold. On top of this, only Jerusalem was saved as most of the fortified cities of Judah were taken. These verses cannot be taken as describing an event of salvation, but rather, they record at least partial defeat, and certainly great humiliation. This path, or manner of defence, is not the direction that will protect the South from the fate which befell the North. The Deuteronomist's interest in the temple may have contributed to his including this report in his history, but this is not sufficient explanation for the presence of these verses, nor does it explain their function at this point.[89] This function is to provide a contrast to the deliverance which follows. This is stated well by Jenkins and Fricke.

---

[88]Childs, *Isaiah and the Assyrian Crisis*, 69-70.

[89]Often too much is made of the Deuteronomist's interest in the temple. Thus J. Robinson sees the narratives in 2 Kings 18-20 as "one more indication that the main interest of the editors of Kings lay in the history of the temple rather than in the political history of the kingdom." (*Second Kings*, 166). Such an interpretation is extremely questionable. Far too much of Kings, much less the history as a whole, is devoted to the people as a whole and not only to the temple. Even in these chapters deliverance as such, and the king himself, play a more central role than the temple.

The placing of the tribute account before the deliverance
account also emphasized that Jerusalem was saved by
Yahweh alone after attempts at a political solution had
failed. The tribute account thus provided a contrast to the
success which followed when Hezekiah turned to Yahweh in
repentance and trust.[90]

For the Deuteronomist this report would have been a clear
sign that one could not buy freedom with money alone. After
all, what did this high tribute payment finally achieve for
Hezekiah? Nothing! Despite it the Assyrian king sends his
emissaries at the head of the troops to demand of Hezekiah
that he surrender the city. Hezekiah has clearly failed here—
thus it appears in the eyes of the Deuteronomist. The holy
city was not to be saved through money, but through repentance, prayer, and trust in God.[91]

Yahweh's Deliverance of Jerusalem, 2 Kgs 18:17-19:37. This now brings
us to the central piece in the whole, the account of the deliverance of
Jerusalem. Childs has done a very helpful study of this passage in which
he sees this section composed of two parallel accounts of a tradition
about this deliverance. The two accounts (B[1] and B[2]) share a common
stock of this tradition, but are not literally based on each other.[92] In this
Childs follows the analysis of a majority of OT scholars. Thus the Deuteronomist has here inserted, or possibly adapted, two sources which ultimately went back to one tradition or event. Both B[1] and B[2] contain
enough genuine historical recollections to preclude the possibility that
they were simply literary creations, and at the same time, both show
evidence of having been reworked with theological and other interests in
mind. According to Childs it is not possible anymore to divide literarily
between the genuinely historical and the theological reworking. Whether
the Deuteronomist did this reworking of the tradition himself as Childs
suggests, or whether this had already been done by the time the Deuteronomist adopted them, the Deuteronomist used these two sources as the
core of his description of the reign of Hezekiah.

Although Childs is probably correct in seeing B[1] and B[2] as parallel
traditions going back to the same event, the present structure suggests
that the Deuteronomist saw them as consecutive scenes of a series of

---

[90]Jenkins, "Hezekiah's Fourteenth Year," p. 297.

[91]Fricke, *Das zweite Buch von den Königen,* 259.

[92]Childs, *Isaiah and the Assyrian Crisis,* 69-103.

events. In any case, the parallel structure of both is clear. Both begin with
a challenge given by some Assyrian representatives, then continue by
reporting Hezekiah's response to the challenge, followed by a message
from Yahweh via his prophet Isaiah, and then finally conclude with a
summary passage of what happened after the oracle of God. This structure gives us a clue for approaching the material. The Assyrian diplomats
and messengers present the conflict and the key issues. At the center of
each account is King Hezekiah, and the way he responds to the challenge.
The resolution of the conflict is then announced in Isaiah's oracles, and
recorded in the concluding remarks. These different parts of each account
must now be examined one by one.

In both B^1 and B^2 the Assyrian representatives set forth the challenge
in such a way as to point out what the key issue is. Two thematic terms
are used to make the issue especially clear. In the Rabshakeh's first
speech the term "to trust" (בטח) is obviously the key term, occurring 7
times within 6 verses. Hezekiah and the people are challenged to determine on whom they are trusting, and whether their trust is validly placed.
In his speech the Rabshakeh argues that it would be futile to trust Egypt,
or Yahweh, or their own troops. Egypt and their own troops would not be
able to help, and, the Rabshakeh claims, Yahweh whom Judah has
offended is on the side of the Assyrians and so will not help them even if
he might be able to.[93] The second thematic term is "deliver" (נצל). This
term is found 11 times in the three messages from Assyria. It comple-
ments the emphasis on trust, since the issue really is whether, in the final
analysis, Jerusalem can rely on anyone to deliver them from the Assyrian
threat. This is brought together in 18:30: "Do not let Hezekiah make you
rely on the Lord saying, the Lord will surely deliver us," and is again

---

[93]Childs (*Isaiah and the Assyrian Crisis*, 84) considers the Rabshakeh's
claim to have Yahweh's support to be a sure sign of a theological reworking of the historical tradition in that it reflects the theology of Isaiah
(e.g. Isa 10:5ff.). Cogan (*Imperialism and Religion*, 9-21) however, has
argued that such a claim was typically Assyrian. It is thus not necessary
to conclude that this claim has been added by someone borrowing from
Isaiah.

The Rabshakeh's argument is not totally consistent at this point.
Whereas here he claims that Yahweh has commanded Assyria to destroy
Judah, his later arguments compare Yahweh with other gods who were not
able to protect their people from Assyria. As Childs has suggested, such
inconsistency fits with the form of the speech employed, the diplomatic
disputation.

implied in 19:10: "Do not let your God on whom you rely deceive you by promising that Jerusalem will not be given into the hand of the king of Assyria." Through these speeches the representatives of Assyria make the issue confronting the people of Jerusalem and their king very clear. The issue is one of life and death (19:32). According to them the only possible result of trusting in Yahweh, as well as in itself or Egypt, would be death. Yahweh will not or cannot deliver them. The only path to life is to accept the Assyrian ultimatum and to make peace with it, and to then await the deportation which would follow.

The second major part of each account is Hezekiah's response to the challenge presented to him. It should be noted that in both accounts it is Hezekiah the king who is at the center. These are not prophetic legends, as has often been suggested, since they say relatively little about the prophet himself. The focus of attention is on King Hezekiah, and what he does upon receiving the Assyrian ultimatum. Perhaps as significant as what he does is what he does not do. There is no hint of preparing the army for defence, or of sending requests for help to Egypt. This is not the direction in which Hezekiah moves. Hezekiah's response is to put his trust in Yahweh. In B^1 Hezekiah rends his clothes, covers himself with sackcloth, and proceeds to the temple from where he sends a message to Isaiah asking him to pray to Yahweh for help. Perhaps the reference to his mourning in 19:1, and his statement about this being a day of distress, of rebuke and disgrace are to imply repentance for past political moves such as described in 18:13-16.[94] Hezekiah has made his choice, and has met the Assyrian challenge head on—he is relying on Yahweh for deliverance. Although the picture of Hezekiah in B^2 is somewhat different (in B^2 he is more independent as he prays to Yahweh himself, and does not send for Isaiah), his response to the challenge is really the same. Instead of negotiating with Assyria, or sending for help, he turns to Yahweh with a prayer of petition. The form of the prayer is the typical complaint psalm with its elements of invocation, complaint and plea, but the emphasis is not as much on the plea or on the details of the crisis, but on the expression of confidence in Yahweh.[95] Whereas the Assyrians had spoken of the god of Israel as one of the gods of the nations, Hezekiah affirms his trust in the total power of Yahweh: "O Lord the God of Israel, who art enthroned above the cherubim, thou art the God, thou alone, of all the kingdoms of the earth; thou hast made heaven and earth." (19:15). As the only God, the

---

[94]Fricke, *Das zweite Buch von den Königen*, 269.
[95]Childs, *Isaiah and the Assyrian Crisis*, 99.

God who made heaven and earth, Yahweh was surely able to deliver Jerusalem from the Assyrians, and so Hezekiah calls upon Yahweh to "save us, I beseech thee, from his hand, that all the kingdoms of the earth may know that thou, O Lord, art God alone." (19:19). Assyria had mocked Yahweh, and in so doing had questioned his power and existence. Judah's defeat at this point would have communicated to the world that Assur was the powerful God, and that Yahweh was merely one of the local gods whom he had defeated. Hezekiah trusts this will not happen. By implication Hezekiah has also clearly rejected the Rabshakeh's claim that Yahweh had sent Assyria to destroy Jerusalem. His response thus rejects the Assyrian analysis, and affirms that it is upon Yahweh whom he relies for deliverance.

In each case Hezekiah's response is followed by the oracles of Isaiah. These oracles do not play as significant a role in the whole narrative as their extent might suggest. The oracles largely affirm Hezekiah's response in that Yahweh sends a message to confirm that he will deliver Jerusalem, and that Hezekiah's trust is thus valid. Isaiah's first oracle (19:6-7) begins with the phrase typical of the prophetic announcement of success preceding holy war—"Fear Not."[96] This statement of assurance immediately communicates that Yahweh will protect his people. Isaiah's second oracle has been lengthened by the addition of other oracles from Isaiah or the Isianic tradition.[97] Here Assyria's destruction of Judaean cities is interpreted as part of Yahweh's plan and so cannot be seen as a victory of Assur over Yahweh.[98] For the present, however, the message is also one

---

[96]H.-P. Stähli, "ירא jrʾ fürchten," in *Theologisches Handwörterbuch zum Alten Testament* (ed. Jenni and Westermann; München: Chr. Kaiser, 1971) 2:766-778; Gerhard von Rad, *Der Heilige Krieg im alten Israel,* 3 Aufl. (Göttingen: Vandenhoeck & Ruprecht, 1958) 9-10.

[97]2 Kgs 19:21b-28 and possibly 19:29-31 are a later addition to the tradition of 18:17-19:37, as is argued by most. It is possible, however, that this addition was made by the Deuteronomist, and so it is still necessary to include it in our examination. It is not difficult to suggest why these two oracles were added to the narrative. Both fit the context, in that the first proclaims doom upon Assyria, and the second salvation for Jerusalem. The reference to mocking the Lord (19:23) matches the complaint of Hezekiah (19:16). It is not necessary to speak to the question of whether these oracles historically came from Isaiah.

[98]In the narrative of 18:17-19:37 the issue is essentially whether or not Jerusalem will be delivered. 2 Kgs 19:25 speaks of the destruction of Judaean cities noted in 18:13. Perhaps this oracle was originally more closely connected with that tradition. In any case, neither Hezekiah nor

of assurance. Assyria has mocked Yahweh and it will be punished; Jerusalem will be delivered by Yahweh for his own sake and for the sake of David. 2 Kgs 19:9a and 35-37 then narrate that what Isaiah prophesied did come to pass, and that Jerusalem was delivered. Yahweh had defended the city; it had been valid to rely on Yahweh.

The narratives of 18:17-19:37, against the background of 18:13-16, have thus recorded the Assyrian threat, how Hezekiah responded to it, and Yahweh's message to Hezekiah affirming his trust and the deliverance of Jerusalem. At the center of these narratives was King Hezekiah, the pious righteous king who trusted in Yahweh in a time of crisis, and whom history vindicated.

Hezekiah's Illness, 2 Kgs 20:1-11. The lengthy narrative of the deliverance of Jerusalem is followed by two shorter accounts which have literarily been connected with the events of Hezekiah's fourteenth year. In the first this connection is made very clear. The introductory "In those days" immediately associates it with what has just preceded it. This is then confirmed by Isaiah's oracle in 20:6 which places the incident 15 years before Hezekiah's death, and the content of the oracle itself which refers back to 19:34, the oracle announcing Yahweh will defend Jerusalem. Again, in this narrative Hezekiah is pictured as the pious king who turns to Yahweh in the face of a crisis. Isaiah's pronouncement that Hezekiah will die must be seen as also an indictment of Hezekiah in that such a fate would have been seen as punishment for transgression. Hezekiah proclaims his innocence, and asserts that he has done what was good in the sight of Yahweh (cf. the Deuteronomist's formal verdict). The narrative assumes that Hezekiah is right and does not deserve to die, and so Yahweh commands Isaiah to pronounce a new oracle. Isaiah's role in the whole is largely secondary; he brings Yahweh's announcements and signs but does not really affect the events. As in 19:14-19, Hezekiah prays directly to Yahweh and does not need Isaiah to intercede for him. Fricke has stated:

> We can conclude from this that here in this narrative, just as in 19:9bff, the king more than the prophet stands at the center. His trust in God is to be demonstrated, together with the way God does not allow this trust to be in vain, but

---

Isaiah consider Assyria's present threat upon Jerusalem to be supported by Yahweh.

graciously hears the prayer of the trusting one, and even grants him a sign.[99]

This passage does not tell us anything drastically new about Hezekiah, or about the Deuteronomist's understanding of him, but rather confirms what has been said up to this point. Yahweh's change of heart implies the validity of Hezekiah's plea and so supports the Deuteronomist's verdict. The narrative points out that Hezekiah trusted in Yahweh in personal events as well as in military affairs. This was the way a king should act and respond to God in his life.

The Envoys from Babylon, 2 Kgs 20:12-19. The final incident recorded in the Deuteronomist's description of the reign of Hezekiah is the visitation of a delegation from Babylon. In the introduction this visit is connected with Hezekiah's recovery from the illness, and through this to the whole series of events of Hezekiah's fourteenth year. After Hezekiah has shown the envoys the extent of his wealth, Isaiah comes to him and confronts him. As has frequently been noticed, Hezekiah's response avoids Isaiah's first question and appears to be an attempt to put off Isaiah without really dealing with the issue. And this issue is not that Hezekiah had weakened Judah's defence by revealing too much to the envoys, nor that Hezekiah had been too friendly and too proud in his revealing of Judah's wealth, but that the revealing implied the establishment of formal ties with Babylon. Hezekiah had by this act shown that he was in the process of forming or confirming a treaty between Babylon and Judah, probably against Assyria. This fits well with the historical events of ca 710-715 B.C. As Isaiah had done in the past, here too he comes out against such defence pacts and proclaims an oracle of punishment against Hezekiah.[100] The result of such foreign policy

---

[99]Fricke, *Das zweite Buch von den Königen,* 285.

[100]It has been suggested that Isaiah's oracle in 20:17-18 reflects exilic redaction. This would imply that either an earlier oracle has been replaced, or adapted since the tradition is earlier. Although such a suggestion is possible, it cannot simply be assumed.

As is becoming recognized, not all references to an exile need to have had exilic origin. The precedent of the fate of the North, as well as knowledge of Assyrian policies would have made such a possibility real. Further, Eichrodt (*Der Herr der Geschichte. Jesaja 13-23 und 28-39,* BAT, Bd. 17, T. 2 [Stuttgart: Calwer, 1967] 268-270) has argued that the nature of the punishment has in this case been determined by the nature of the

would be defeat and destruction.

Whereas the Hezekiah of 18:17-19:37 had trusted in Yahweh to deliver Judah and Jerusalem from the Assyrians, here he attempts to take Judah's defence into his own hands. In the negotiations with Babylon Hezekiah had placed his trust in armies, and foreign ones at that. In doing this Hezekiah had not fulfilled his responsibility as king. The result of such foreign policy would be defeat and destruction. Isaiah's oracle proclaims a punishment upon the Davidic dynasty which arises directly out of the crime committed. The royal dynasty will be taken into exile in the country which it trusted for its defence.[101] This narrative focusses upon the same issue as 18:17-19:37, but from a negative perspective. The only valid defence of Judah was reliance upon Yahweh.

Hezekiah's response to the prophecy of Isaiah has long troubled scholars. The first part of 20:19 simply seems to accept Isaiah's announcement as valid, but what about the last part? Although it is difficult to state exactly what it meant,[102] it seems likely that it was not considered to be a selfish or improper response to the word of the Lord. There is no indication in the narrative that Hezekiah's statement was a discredit to him. Perhaps one function of the account of Hezekiah's illness was to provide background for this account. In the earlier incident Yahweh had changed his mind after a negative pronouncement, and this possibility must be envisioned at this point as well. Of course in order for this to happen Hezekiah would have had to embark on a foreign policy not dependent upon Babylon. Perhaps the fact that Babylon is not mentioned anywhere else in the Hezekiah narratives implies that the ties with Babylon were

---

crime. Fricke, *Das zweite Buch von den Königen*, 293-94, has argued that the oracle probably was not late in that it conflicted with history since it predicted that Hezekiah's sons would go into exile and this did not happen.

In light of these factors one should not too quickly assign this oracle to exilic times.

[101]Eichrodt, *Jesaja 13-23, 23-39*, 269, has emphasized that the punishment is upon the Davidic dynasty directly and not upon the people of Judah and Jerusalem.

[102]P. R. Ackroyd, "An Interpretation of the Babylonian Exile: A Study of 2 Kings 20, Isaiah 38-39," *SJT* 27 (1974) 329-52 proposes three different possible interpretations of the difficult concluding line, and considers a negative interpretation the least likely. Gray, *Kings*, 639, proposes still a different interpretation. It is significant that neither, although not agreeing with each other on the exact connotations of the phrase, consider the phrase to have been a negative one for the Deuteronomist.

very temporary. 2 Kgs 20:19 is probably meant to depict a Hezekiah who accepted the verdict and submitted himself to God while hoping that the verdict could be taken back as the one spoken to his illness had been taken back.

This last narrative from the reign of Hezekiah, while condemning Hezekiah's act, confirms and strengthens the message of the main event, the deliverance of Jerusalem. The king's responsibility in a time of crisis was to trust in Yahweh to deliver. 2 Kgs 18:17-19:37 records how Yahweh does deliver his people. The attempt at a political alliance is immediately confronted with judgment. The conclusion to the whole account is somewhat unclear, but suggests that Hezekiah recognized the validity of the indictment and acted upon this insight.

Conclusion

In the Deuteronomistic account of 2 Kings 18-20 King Hezekiah has been idealized and virtually placed on a pedestal. This is clear both in the Deuteronomist's more formal evaluation of him, as well as in his description of the events of Hezekiah's fourteenth year. Although the tradition of Hezekiah's reform will have contributed to this idealization, this is not the central focus of these three chapters, and is not the major arena in which this idealization is worked out. The paramount question for Judah in the late 8th century B.C. was whether it would be able to survive as a nation on the land which God had given it, or whether it would perish, like the North had, under the onslaught of the Assyrians. In this crisis period Hezekiah is pictured as acting in the appropriate way in response to this threat. The fact that during his reign Hezekiah also acted in different ways has by now been forgotten, or pushed aside in order to form a more pure picture of Hezekiah. In the present narrative it is stressed over and over again that in this period of crisis Hezekiah trusted in Yahweh. This is stated most explicitly in the account of the deliverance of Jerusalem, and is then brought out again in the two incidents of chapter 20. In the account of the envoys from Babylon Hezekiah is depicted as using an alternative method of defence, the formation of a defence alliance, but this is immediately condemned by Isaiah the prophet, and Hezekiah's piety is brought out in the way he accepts God's word, and places himself under his rule.

Although the Deuteronomist certainly adopted existing traditions in these chapters, the way he has tied them together, and the way in which he has pointed at them with his evaluation indicate that the idealization of Hezekiah in them fits with his view of kingship. In fact, it is very possible that he himself contributed considerably to this idealization and depiction of Hezekiah. In this whole account he then makes clear that in the very important area of defence, the primary responsibility of the king was to trust in Yahweh. Israel as a nation had been chosen by Yahweh, and led out of Egypt through his power. It was also Yahweh's responsibility to protect Israel from its enemies. This did not imply that the king would not be involved in the fighting, or that he would not lead Israel's forces, but in the final analysis his responsibility rested in trusting Yahweh to deliver, and in listening to Yahweh as he speaks to him through his prophets. Hope for the future rested in this form of kingship.

A PROPOSAL: THE ROLE OF THE KING
ACCORDING TO THE DEUTERONOMIST

We have so far examined the Deuteronomist's description of King Hezekiah and King Josiah, the two kings who receive the highest marks in his history. Both kings are depicted as having played a rather significant role in that history, and both had lived relatively close to the author in time. It is very possible and understandable that the style and manner in which these kings fulfilled their position, or the way in which this had been idealized in the time before the Deuteronomist wrote, had strongly affected the Deuteronomist in his understanding of the role of a king for Israel. It is now time to try and tie these two descriptions together and to make a tentative proposal on how the Deuteronomist understood kingship. This proposal will obviously be made largely on the basis of our analysis of 2 Kings 18-20 and 22-23, although some other factors will also need to be included. Once this proposal has been made it will need to be tested on the basis of the remainder of the Deuteronomistic History.

Although kingship played an extremely important role in the history as a whole, the history was not essentially about kingship. Rather, the focus of the history was the people of Israel. The centrality of kingship in the history after 1 Samuel indicates the significance which the author attributed to kingship for the history of the people. Kingship is thus not important in and of itself, but it is of paramount importance for the Deuteronomist because of the role which kingship was expected to fulfill in the history of God's people. In light of this, the Deuteronomist's view of kingship cannot be presented even tentatively totally apart from his understanding of Israel, of Yahweh, and of their relationship to each other. A little space must first be devoted to outlining a few of the major theological emphases or theological assumptions of the Deuteronomistic

History which will then provide the background against which the proposal will be made.

The Deuteronomist's Theology

Recent discussion of the Deuteronomist's theology has focussed largely on his *kerygma*,[103] or his special message. As is the case in so much Deuteronomistic research, an examination of this must begin with Noth's *Überlieferungsgeschichtliche Studien*. In his work he not only emphasized the literary unity of the history, but he also drew attention to its theological nature. Noth had concluded that the history had been writtten during the exile, and he then explained it on this basis. According to Noth this history of Israel had come to an end in the events of 587 B.C. There was no longer any hope for the future. The purpose of his work was to justify the act of God in destroying Israel. The book of Deuteronomy had presented the law which Israel was expected to obey in the land. Israel had continually rebelled against Yahweh and his law and so the tragic end had been inevitable. For Noth the history was an obituary, an explanation of the end of Israel with no hope for a future restoration of any kind.[104]

Although Noth's insights on the theological principles of the Deuteronomistic History have been generally accepted, his view that the history contained no hope for the future has been rejected by most.[105] Two scholars who have argued this case most clearly have been Gerhard von Rad and Hans Walter Wolff. Von Rad agrees with Noth that a central purpose of the history was to explain the events of 587 B.C. on the basis of Israel's rebellion against Yahweh and his law, but this was not the end. The history also contained a countertheme which pointed ahead, and this was the promise to the Davidic dynasty. Both of these themes were based

---

[103]This term was used by Wolff, "Kerygma." See also Walter Brueggemann, "Wolff's Kerygmatic Methodology," in *The Vitality of Old Testament Traditions,* by Brueggemann and Wolff (Atlanta: John Knox, 1975) 29-40.

Note Cross's criticism of the use of this term in *Canaanite Myth and Hebrew Epic,* 277.

[104]Noth, *ÜgS*, especially pp. 100-110.

[105]An example of someone who basically accepted Noth's conclusions regarding the hopeless view of the Deuteronomist is Otto Plöger, "Reden und Gebete im deuteronomistischen und chronistischen Geschichtswerk," in *Festschrift für Günther Dehn,* ed. Schneemelcher (Neukirchen Kreis Moers: Verlag der Buchhandlung der Erziehungsvereins, 1957) 35-49.

on an emphasis on the operative force of the word of God in history, as law with its threats and as promise of salvation. Thus "DtrH did not at all intend only to teach that the exile was a righteous judgment and fulfillment of the threat which Moses and the prophets had proclaimed. Rather, he wanted his readers to expect that beyond that, sometime, the promise made to David of salvation would also be fulfilled."[106]

Wolff also refuses to accept that the history had no hope for the future, but in his view this hope was more muted than von Rad proposed. Israel could not count on the Davidic promise to be fulfilled regardless of what she did. Wolff finds the key to his understanding in the repeated use of the term "to return" (שוב) at key junctures in this history. In its setting in exile Israel is summoned to return to Yahweh, to "listen with her whole heart to the voice of God alone and expect every good from him alone in order that she may become God's agent in the midst of all nations."[107] Returning will not guarantee restoration to the land, but any hope for the future is based on God's goodness, and the assurance that he will accept the return. Walter Brueggemann builds on the work of Wolff, and observes that in addition to "return," "good" (טוב) is also found throughout history, and he sees this as countertheme to the call to repentance motif. Yahweh is good, and his word is good. As history revealed, his promises to the patriarchs had been fulfilled, and so even now the "faithful good word to David" still endures, and provides the basis of hope.[108] In these ways these different scholars have accepted the historical setting which Noth gave to the history, and the basic principles which he saw in the history, but they also saw the historian as looking ahead to the future.

A different interpretation of the themes of the history has been presented by Frank Cross. Cross is representative of many scholars who argue that the Deuteronomistic History was essentially written before the events of 587 B.C., and so obviously its central purpose could not have been to explain why it happened. Cross sees two themes playing back and forth in the history: The first theme is the sin of Jeroboam, going back to the emphases of the old tribal league, and the second theme focusses on the promise to David, coming from the official Judaean royal ideology. "The historian has combined his motifs of the old covenant forms of the

---

[106]Wolff, describing von Rad's position, "Kerygma," p. 85. For von Rad's presentation of his views see von Rad, *OTT*, 1:327-47; von Rad, *Studies in Deuteronomy*, 74-91.

[107]Wolff, "Kerygma," p. 100.

[108]Walter Brueggemann, "The Kerygma of the Deuteronomistic Historian," *Int* 22 (1968) 387-402.

league and of the north, with those taken from the royal theology of the
Davidides to create a complex and eloquent program, or rather, one may
say, he has written a great sermon to rally Israel to the new possibility of
salvation, through obedience to the ancient covenant of Yahweh, and hope
in the new David, King Josiah,"[109] The historian has thus combined the
Mosaic and Davidic covenants.

The above scholars have written about the *kerygma* or special message
of the Deuteronomist. In each case this message was seen as directed at a
particular historical setting, and so the different assumption regarding the
date of composition between Cross on the one hand, and Noth, von Rad,
Wolff and Brueggemann on the other resulted in a rather different understanding of the message. This is only to be expected. When one moves
from the special message of the Deuteronomist to his theological
emphases or assumptions, however, one's conclusions are not as dependent
upon one's views on the historical origin of the history. These can be
agreed upon by both those who see the Deuteronomist as writing before
587 B.C. as well as those who see him working during the exile. These
theological emphases and concerns now need to be examined.

As we stated above, Noth argued that the purpose of the history was to
justify God's acts of 587 B.C.—Judah had been removed from the land
because she had broken covenant. Although Noth's view of the message of
the Deuteronomist has been validly critiqued by von Rad, Wolff and
others, his description of the message focussed on the primary motifs of
the history: *God's people, land* and *covenant*. Yahweh had chosen Israel to
be his holy people. The Deuteronomistic History is a history of this
people. Both von Rad and Cross, by focussing so largely on the role of the
kings in the history, tended to draw attention away from these primary
concerns. It is questionable whether Cross's two themes can really accurately describe the center of the history when neither plays any role
whatsoever in Deuteronomy, Joshua and Judges, and only an anticipatory
role in 1 Samuel. The history as a whole could be described as the drama
of Israel's relationship with its God, Yahweh, and land and covenant were
the decisive issues in this relationship. Any discussion of the Deuteronomist's theological emphases must thus focus on the role of land and covenant with God's people, Israel.

The centrality of the promised land in Deuteronomy has been docu-

---

[109]Cross, *Canaanite Myth and Hebrew Epic*, 274-289.

mented by various scholars.[110] On the one hand, it is emphasized that the land is God's gift to his chosen people. Israel could not claim in any way to have deserved this land, but must recognize that it was a free gift of Yahweh. (e.g. Deut 9:4ff). "Possession of the land and life in it are, therefore, the gift of salvation."[111] Even after having received the land Israel has no real claim to it, but must use it as a gift of grace from God. That Yahweh gives the land to Israel is also brought out in the emphasis that Israel does not defeat the former inhabitants itself, but that this is "the activity of Yahweh. His overthrow of the enemy is the way they and the land are given over to Israel."[112] Deuteronomy is seen as the speech of Moses at the edge of the promised land just before Israel is to receive the gift of life in the land of milk and honey.

On the other hand, the land is not automatically a permanent gift. "But Deuteronomy repeatedly insists that all of this is completely and totally contingent upon the character of Israel's response to her giving Lord, upon her love for Yahweh and obedience to his commandments. Ultimately, therefore, it is not possible to speak of the gift of the land apart from obedience to Yahweh and his laws."[113] The book of Deuteronomy is largely law. This law is both the guideline for good living in the land, and the condition for continued existence on the land. Both aspects of the law are important. Thus the book of Deuteronomy abounds with exhortations to obey the law.

> And now, O Israel, give heed to the statutes and the ordinances which I teach you, and do them; that you may live, and go in and take possession of the land which the Lord the God of your fathers, gives you. Deut 4:1.

> These are the statutes and ordinances which you shall be careful to do in the land which the Lord, the God of your

---

[110]Patrick D. Miller, Jr. "The Gift of God. The Deuteronomic Theology of the Land," *Int* 23 (1969) 451-65; von Rad, "The Promised Land and Yahweh's Land in the Hexateuch," first published in 1943, in *The Problem of the Hexateuch and other essays* (Edinburgh: Oliver & Boyd, 1966) 79-93; von Rad, "There Remains Still a Rest for the People of God: An Investigation of a Biblical Conception," first published in 1933, in *The Problem of the Hexateuch and other essays* (Edinburgh: Oliver & Boyd, 1966) 94-102.

[111]Miller, "The Gift of God," p. 453.

[112]Ibid., p. 455.

[113]Ibid., p. 458.

fathers, has given you to possess, all the days that you live
upon the earth. Deut 12:1.

The law is the constitution for Israel once it is settled in the land.
Miller summarizes both of these aspects of Israel's relationship to the land
as follows: "Israel cannot justify her *original* possession of the land on the
basis of her behavior; she must, however, justify or preserve her *continuing* and *future* possession on the basis of her behavior both in terms of the
worship of God and a proper use of the possession which is her salvation
gift."[114]

The Deuteronomist essentially accepts this Deuteronomic understanding of Israel's relationship to the land, and then writes his history on the
basis of it. This is of course emphasized by placing Deuteronomy at the
head of this history. The key question throughout the history is then
whether Israel will follow the conditions set down for her for continued
existence on the land, or whether Israel will renege upon the covenant it
entered with Yahweh, and forfeit the land. For the Deuteronomist "covenant" is the term used to describe Israel's relationship with Yahweh.[115]
By committing herself to the covenant Israel had committed herself to its
stipulations or requirements. That the term covenant at least included law
and obligation can be observed in 2 Kgs 23:1-3 where book of the law and
book of the covenant are interchangeable. The laws of Deuteronomy are
then the stipulations of the covenant.

The whole structure of the history then follows this theme. It begins
with Israel on the outskirts of the promised land. It is here that Israel
receives the conditions for life and blessing in the land. Deuteronomy 29,
which very possibly was added by the Deuteronomist, points out the
nature of this book—"These are the words of the covenant which the Lord
commanded Moses to make with the people of Israel in the land of Moab,"
(Deut 29:1). At the heart of this law and covenant is Israel's central
obligation of total loyalty to Yahweh. This is emphasized in the first
commandment, "You shall have no other gods before me," (Deut 5:7), in
the *shema,* "Hear, O Israel: The Lord our God is one Lord," (Deut 6:4), in
the law of centralization of Deuteronomy 12, and in innumerable other
places in the history itself. As Noth noted, this is the part of the Deuter-

---

[114]Ibid., p. 461.
[115]Note the emphasis of Lothar Perlitt, *Bundestheologie im Alten
Testament,* WMANT, Bd. 36 (Neukirchen-Vluyn: Neukirchener, 1969).

onomic law which the Deuteronomist focussed upon, and used as his
primary criterion for judging Israel's faithfulness.

> It is because they forsook the covenant of the Lord, the God
> of their fathers, which he made with them when he brought
> them out of the land of Egypt, and went and served other
> gods and worshipped them, gods whom they had not known
> and whom he had not alloted to them; Deut 29:25-26.

> And they forsook the Lord, the God of their fathers, who had
> brought them out of the land of Egypt; and they went after
> other gods, from among the gods of the peoples who were
> round about them, and bowed down to them; and they pro-
> voked the Lord to anger. Judg 2:12.

The history then examines Israel's response to the conditions given her,
and the results of its response for her tenure on the land. The book of
Joshua begins by describing how the promises to the fathers are fulfilled,
and how Israel received the gift of the land under the leadership of
Joshua. It is significant that during his leadership as she received the land,
Israel is described as having served the Lord. After his death this changes,
however, and the book of Judges describes the first results of disobedience of covenant law—oppression by the enemy. Although disobedience
did not immediately result in removal from the land, it did mean the loss
of control, and in this way the possibility of the total loss of the land was
already foreshadowed. With the rise of kingship a new era began, but the
issue was the same. This is confirmed by the covenant renewal ceremony
of 1 Samuel 12. Although Israel now had a king, Israel's life on the land
was still to be determined by her response to the covenant. The disobedience of Solomon resulted in the ten northern tribes being lost to his
dynasty. The relationship between land and covenant obedience was
brought out especially clearly in the Deuteronomist's analysis of the
demise of the North. The actions of the kings caused the people to sin,
and this resulted in exile and the end of the North. This is summarized in
2 Kgs 18:11-12—"The king of Assyria carried the Israelites away . . .
because they did not obey the voice of the Lord their God but transgressed his covenant, even all that Moses the servant of the Lord commanded; they neither listened nor obeyed." This issue then remained
primary right till the end of history. If one argues that the history was
written during the time of Josiah, then the message of it is to call Judah
to follow the conditions of the covenant in order that it not meet the fate
of the North and also lose the land. If one argues that the history was

written after 587 B.C., then the history describes how this loss was also due to Judah's not following the covenant. In either case, the theological assumption and concern is the same: Israel's remaining on the land is dependent upon her observing the covenant, and remaining loyal to Yahweh.

The Role of the King According to the Deuteronomist

The above has emphasized that the focus of the Deuteronomist's history was God's chosen people, Israel, and that the central motifs in the drama of God and his people were land and covenant. Israel's existence as a people is directly related to her life on the land. It is questionable whether the Deuteronomist could have conceived of Israel as a people without land.[116] Yahweh's covenant with Israel then gave Israel the necessary guidelines for a life of blessing on the land, and adherence to it was the condition for continued existence on the land as his people. Although this description of the Deuteronomist's history does not even mention the king, the amount of material in the history immediately suggests that the king had an extremely important role or function in this relationship of God's chosen people with land and covenant. It is thus within this relationship that the Deuteronomist's understanding of the role of the king needs to be sought.

It is our proposal that the Deuteronomist accepted the common understanding of that time regarding the ultimate responsibility and significance of kingship for the people. In other words, the "king was expected to be king."[117] But what was this ultimate responsibility of the king? Henri Frankfort has tried to give the ancient Near Eastern view of kingship.

> The ancient Near East considered kingship the very basis of civilation. Only savages could live without a king. Security,

---

[116]Ibid., p. 453. "The goal and desire of the people of God is life in the land which God gives. Israel's national existence, her existence as a people, depends upon this land and the grace of God."

[117]This phrase, "the king was expected to be king," arose in a discussion of the subject with the writer's doctoral committee, composed of Dr. James L. Mays, Dr. Patrick D. Miller, Jr. and Dr. Sibley Towner (Chairman).

peace and justice could not prevail without a rule to champion them.[118]

Whatever was significant was imbedded in the life of the cosmos, and it was precisely the king's function to maintain the harmony of that integration.[119]

For the truth about their king affected their lives in every, even the most personal, aspect, since, through the king, the harmony between human existence and supernatural order was maintained.[120]

In this way Frankfort has described kingship making use of the mythological worldview common in the ancient Near East. Although Frankfort believed it was possible to describe all of ancient Near Eastern kingship with these statements, he emphasized that the way in which this was worked out varied from civilization to civilization.[121]

---

[118]Henri Frankfort, *Kingship and the Gods. A Study of Ancient Near Eastern Religion as the Integration of Society and Nature* (Chicago: University of Chicago, 1948) 3.

[119]Ibid.

[120]Ibid., p. 12.

[121]Although Frankfort essentially agreed with the so-called myth and ritual school on the ultimate significance of the king for the society, he separated himself from them sharply on the question of how this was worked out.

Aubrey Johnson emphasizes the importance of kingship for Israel. "We have here [2 Sam 21:7] a clear indication that the well-being of the nation as a social unit is bound up with the life of the king," ("The Role of the King in the Jerusalem Cultus," in *The Labyrinth. Further Studies in the Relation between Myth and Ritual in the Ancient World*, ed. S. H. Hooke [London: Society for Promoting Christian Knowledge, 1935] 73). "Four centuries have passed, but the life of the nation as a social unit is still bound up with that of the king—and the House of David." (Ibid., p. 74). With these statements Frankfort probably could have agreed.

But according to scholars like Johnson and Hooke, the king accomplished this through his participation in the cult. Thus Hooke stated "The ritual pattern represents the things which were done to and by the king in order to secure the prosperity of the community in every sense for the coming year." (S. H. Hooke, "The Myth and Ritual Pattern of the Ancient East," in *Myth and Ritual. Essays on the Myth and Ritual of the Hebrews in relation to the Culture Pattern of the Ancient East,* ed. S. H. Hooke [London: Oxford, 1933] 8). This pattern was then also applied to

> This doctrine is valid for the whole of the ancient Near East
> and for many other regions. But, as soon as we want to be
> more specific, we find that a contrast exists between the two
> centers of ancient civilization. Egypt and Mesopotamia held
> very different views as to the nature of their king and the
> temper of the universe in which he functioned.[122]

In the remainder of his work Frankfort then focussed on the implications
of this in Egypt and Mesopotamia. Our contention is that ultimately a
similar understanding of the role of kingship existed in Israel, and was
accepted by the Deuteronomist. This now needs to be explained.

If the above is correct, then kingship for the Deuteronomist was meant
to fulfill the function described above, but this would have been understood in terms of his view of the universe, and Israel within it. The first
implication of this would be in the way in which this function would be
discussed. As was noted above, Frankfort's description adopts the mythological language prevalent at the time. Although Israel certainly also used
mythological language and concepts in her history, as a rule the universe
was understood historically, and this was especially the case for the
Deuteronomist. The function or ultimate responsibility of the king would
then need to be translated into language more suitable to Israel's worldview. In this case the king's function could be described as being to maintain the order of Israel's historical situation. Practically, this meant that
*it was up to the king to insure the continued existence of Israel as a
people and nation on the land which Yahweh had given it.* One cannot have
a king without people, and for Israel her existence as a people was inextricably tied to her life on the land. Walter Brueggeman has given a
definition of kingship which fits this proposal very well—"In the Bible,
'king' refers to those who presided over the organized life of Israel, and so
had responsibility for the land."[123] And so in keeping with the ancient
Near Eastern context, the Deuteronomist also saw the king at the center
of the life of a nation, whose responsibility it was to guarantee the continued life of the people on the land.

The way in which this responsibility was to be carried out in Israel,

---

Israel. At this point Hooke and Johnson have not recognized that the way
in which the ultimate responsibility of the king is worked out can vary
considerably from context to context.

[122]Frankfort, *Kingship and the Gods,* 3.

[123]Walter Brueggemann, *The Land,* Overtures to Biblical Theology
(Philadelphia: Fortress, 1977) 73.

however, was determined by Israel's particular view of herself, of Yahweh, and of her relationship to Yahweh. Israel had been chosen by Yahweh in his own free will, not through merit, and Yahweh had placed this people on the land. Although the land had been given to Israel as a gift, in a sense the land was still Yahweh's and there was always the possibility that Israel would lose the land. It was continually emphasized that the condition which Israel had to follow in order to remain upon the land was to observe the covenant. Whether or not Israel would be able to continue as a nation was wholly dependent on her response to the covenant. This is brought out very clearly in 2 Kgs 17:7-23 and 18:12 where the end of the North is explained simply as resulting from the North's refusal to obey the covenant. This theological understanding of Israel then determined the Deuteronomist's view of the special role of the king in Israel. Since Israel's continued existence as a people on the land was dependent on her obedience to the covenant, and since the king's ultimate responsibility was to insure this continued existence, the king's role was then to make sure that the covenant was observed in Israel. Practically, he could be called the *covenant administrator*.[124]

This is then confirmed by the Deuteronomist's account of the reigns of Hezekiah and Josiah. All of Josiah's acts described would fit under this description. Josiah's dismay upon reading the book of the law/covenant was due to his realization that Judah had not been following the covenant, and he as king had not administered it as he should have. He then turned to the Lord and began to fulfill his responsibilities. His first public act was to lead all of Judah in a covenant renewal ceremony. In this ceremony he and the people of Judah committed themselves to follow the law, to "keep his commandments and his testimonies, . . . to perform the words of this covenant that were written in this book." (2 Kgs 23:3). His reinstitution of the centralized passover was another act arising out of his role. The same would apply to his reforming activities as described in 2 Kgs 23:4-20, 24. As was emphasized above, for the Deuteronomist total loyalty to Yahweh was the central obligation of the covenant. This obviously meant the total rejection of all worship not directed at Yahweh, or borrowed from other nations. And as Deuteronomy 12 brought out, this worship was to be centralized at that place which Yahweh would choose. Josiah's reforming activities were directed at this purifying and centralizing goal. As covenant administrator he was expected to make sure that

---

[124]This phrase ("covenant administrator") should not be seen as a formal title but simply as descriptive of the function.

the covenant was maintained, and the cultic requirements were thus clearly under his responsibility.

Similarly Hezekiah fulfilled this aspect of his kingly role by also removing the high places, by breaking down the pillars, and by cutting down the Asherah. According to the Deuteronomist Yahweh was with Hezekiah so that whenever he went forth he prospered. Hezekiah is depicted as administering the covenant properly, as leading Israel in loyalty to Yahweh, and the result of this is security on the land. Although the reign of Hezekiah was one in which Judah moved to the brink of extinction, the mood communicated by the Deuteronomist's account is one of salvation.

We have not examined the Manasseh narrative in this study, but it would also support this construction. According to the Deuteronomist Manasseh was an evil king, very possibly the worst in Israel's history. This judgment can easily be explained on the basis of the Deuteronomist's description of the reign of Manasseh. Manasseh not only totally failed to administer the covenant, but he also actively participated in leading Israel away from it by bringing in pagan religious influences and by rebuilding the high places which Hezekiah had destroyed. He is thus contrasted sharply with Hezekiah before him and Josiah after him. Such policies must surely lead to the loss of the land, and are thus a complete failure to fulfill the responsibilities of being king.

One further emphasis needs to be brought out at this point. The fact that the king was the administrator of the covenant did not imply that the king stood over the covenant. Rather, for the Deuteronomist the king was clearly also subject to the covenant. The king, like any other Israelite, was expected to obey the law as it was found in Deuteronomy. This is not focussed upon in the narratives we examined but it is assumed. Both evaluations begin by stating that the king did what was right in the eyes of the Lord (18:3;22:2). This must refer to the king's obeying the law. This fact is made even more explicit in 18:6 where it is stated of Hezekiah, "For he held fast to the Lord; he did not depart from following him, but kept the commandments which the Lord commanded Moses." The way in which the term "to turn" (שוב) is used in the rest of the history also indicates that the statement referring to Josiah turning to the Lord implies that he obeyed the law. In these verses the Deuteronomist's assumption on this issue comes out distinctly. This then means that the king was not the lawmaker in that he produced the law, nor could he change the law or circumvent it to suit his purposes. For the Deuteronomist the law had been given to Israel by Yahweh, and all Israelites, including the king, were expected to follow it. In this sense the king's identity as an Israelite was more significant than his identity as king.

So far the proposal has suggested that the king's responsibility was to guarantee Israel's continued existence on the land, and that this responsibility was fulfilled within Israel by being the covenant administrator due to the role of the covenant for Israel's existence on the land. This proposal also has some negative connotations for the role of the king. As has already been emphasized, Israel received the land as a gift, and her continuing on the land was, although dependent upon her obedience to the covenant, ultimately God's decision. God had chosen Israel; God had given Israel the land through conquest; God was responsible for defending Israel. By implication the people were not in a position to defend themselves against their enemies, and the military defence of the nation was then not the king's primary responsibility.

This is brought out most clearly in the Hezekiah narrative. Buying freedom through the payment of tribute, or by depending upon defence alliances are not the way to salvation, i.e. to continued existence on the land. Rather, the role of the king in such a time of crisis, when the enemy threatens, is to trust Yahweh, to pray to Yahweh, and to await his answer. As we noted above, the term "trust" (בטח) is not a very significant term for the Deuteronomist in his history as a whole. It is emphasized in the Hezekiah narrative, however, that this is the required response of the king in such a time. In the OT the term is seldom used positively when speaking of man trusting man. Such trust is generally false, or futile. In contrast to this man is exhorted to trust Yahweh. Man is called to rely totally upon God, and to put his confidence in him. The Assyrians had challenged the validity of this and had referred to Yahweh as one of the gods, but this is rejected since Yahweh is not one of the gods but the only God. Jepsen states that "there is an intimate connection between 'seeking security in God' and 'security' in external and internal life."[125] Jeremiah describes trust in a way which would probably have been accepted by the Deuteronomist as well.

> Cursed is the man who trusts in man
>   and makes flesh his arm,
>   whose heart turns away from the Lord.

---

[125]Alfred Jepsen, "בטח bāṭach," in *Theological Dictionary of the Old Testament*, ed. G. Botterweck and Ringgren, (Grand Rapids: William B. Eerdmans, 1975) 2:93.

> He is like a shrub in the desert,
>   and shall not see any good come.
> He shall dwell in the parched places of the wilderness,
>   in an uninhabited land.
>
> Blessed is the man who trusts in the Lord,
>   whose trust is the Lord.
> He is like a tree planted by the water,
>   that sends out its roots by the stream,
>   and does not fear when heat comes,
>   for its leaves remain green,
>   and is not anxious in the year of drought,
>   for it does not cease to bear fruit." (Jer 17:5-8)

Here again we see the contrast between trusting in Yahweh and trusting in man. Hezekiah is depicted as throwing himself and the people upon Yahweh, and expecting Yahweh to deliver. This does not necessarily imply that the king, or his army, will not be involved in any fighting, although the role of such is often downplayed. But ultimately, Yahweh is the one who delivers, and the king must trust Yahweh to deliver. In the narrative of Hezekiah the king trusted in Yahweh and his faith was vindicated as Yahweh delivered. Hezekiah had fulfilled what was expected of a king in that he had acted as covenant administrator in reforming the cult, and in a time of crisis he did not attempt to deliver Jerusalem through his own means but he trusted in Yahweh to deliver.

This is then our proposal for how the Deuteronomist understood kingship. It could be summarized by saying that the Deuteronomist expected the king to lead Israel by being the covenant administrator; then he could trust Yahweh to deliver. At the heart of this covenant was Israel's obligation to be totally loyal to Yahweh.

3

Kingship in the Remainder
of the Deuteronomistic History

Now that we have made our proposal, we need to test it in the remainder of the Deuteronomistic History. If our proposal is correct, then at the very least it should not be contradicted in the remainder of the History. Further, it is probable that there are other passages which will support it, or which make more sense in light of it. If this proves to be the case, then our proposal on the Deuteronomist's view of kingship has received a strong confirmation.

In this process we can obviously not examine in detail all parts of the Deuteronomistic History. We will thus focus on those passages which have a direct bearing on our proposal, and on those which have been at the center of past discussions on the issue of kingship within the Deuteronomistic History.

DEUT 17:14-20—THE LAW OF KINGSHIP

Preliminary Critical Considerations

It is difficult to know how to make use of passages from Deuteronomy in a study of the Deuteronomistic History. On the one hand, it is usually assumed that the book of Deuteronomy is part of the Deuteronomistic History. This was proposed by Noth in 1943 and has not been seriously contested.[1] On the other hand, it is usually also assumed that the majority

---

[1] Note, however, the recent article by Jon D. Levenson, "Who Inserted the Book of Torah?" Levenson follows the view of Frank Cross and assumes that Dtr[1] produced most of the history before the exile, and that Dtr[2] then brought the history up to date during the exile. His major thesis is that the book of Deuteronomy, although having influenced the Deuter-

of the present book of Deuteronomy was not written by the Deuteronomist himself, but was already an independent document when he did his
work. It is argued that this core, or *Urdeuteronomium,* was the book which
was found in the temple during the time of Josiah, and which played such
a significant role in his reform. This might imply that it would not be too
helpful to examine this book in an attempt to get at the Deuteronomist's
view. A factor which makes it necessary to examine this book in spite of
its coming from a different author and time is that the Deuteronomist
probably included it and placed it at the beginning of the history because
it had rather significantly affected his thinking and so provided a key for
the whole history. In this way Deuteronomy is both a book by itself, and
part of the history. Practically this then means that each passage in
Deuteronomy must be examined separately without assuming that the
views expressed are identical with those of the Deuteronomist. Although
it is probable that in most cases the thinking will be at least similar to
that of the Deuteronomist, this cannot be assumed when the study begins.
We must remember this as we approach Deut 17:14-20, a passage usually
known as the law of kingship.

It is usually agreed that *Urdeuteronomium* consisted of the majority of
the present Deuteronomy 5-26,28. It is then proposed that some later
redactor, probably the Deuteronomist, made some additions and revisions
to this *Urdeuteronomium.* The task then becomes to try and determine
what in these chapters was original, and what was added by the Deuteronomist. One common method of approaching this task is based on the fact
that there is frequent transition within Deuteronomy between plural
address and singular address. This criterion was already used in the last
part of the nineteenth century, and has recently been defended by G.
Minette de Tillesse.[2] According to this approach the singular passages in
Deuteronomy 5-26,28 were part of *Urdeuteronomium,* and the plural

---

onomist, was not part of the first edition of the history, but was only
added by Dtr[2]. He supports his thesis with both lexical and stylistic, and
with theological arguments.

[2]See the summary of the history of this position in E. W. Nicholson,
*Deuteronomy and Tradition. Literary and Historical Problems in the Book
of Deuteronomy* (Philadelphia: Fortress, 1967) 22-34. Nicholson also lists a
number of scholars who support this approach, and a number who do not
accept it.

G. Minette de Tillesse, "Sections 'tu' et sections 'vous' dans le Deutéronome," *VT* 12 (1962) 29-87. According to de Tillesse, Noth himself agreed
with this approach. Ibid, p. 34.

passages were then the later addition. This method has not been accepted by all, however, and many who consider it to be a helpful factor do not follow it slavishly.[3] Nicholson, who largely accepts de Tillesse's thesis still argues that the "attempt to recover *Urdeuteronomium* down to verse and half verse must be abandoned."[4] This may be a good caution, but in exegesis decisions need to be made even while realizing the problem.

That *Urdeuteronomium* contained the law of kingship need not be questioned. Whether all of 17:14-20 was part of the law is debatable. The verses which have been questioned most frequently are vv 18-19. V 18 speaks of the law as being written in a book, a concept which is not found in *Urdeuteronomium* but which is common in those passages which have been added to it. Deuteronomy 29 three times speaks of the law as a book (vv 20,21,27), once using the phrase "this book of the law," (v 21). The importance of the book of law for the Deuteronomist supports the contention that he added this short section on the king and the law. We will thus assume that vv 18-19 were not part of the law of kingship as found in *Urdeuteronomium,* but were added later by the Deuteronomist.[5]

The integrity of vv 16-17, 20 to the original law has also been questioned.[6] De Tillesse's argument for this begins with the plural form in v 16b. This suggests for him that all of v 16 is secondary, having come from the Deuteronomist. The similarity between v 16 and v 17 then implies that v 17 also is not original. V 20 is taken to be secondary because v 20a is an allusion to 1 Sam 8:11, and v 20b supposedly conditionalizes the king's tenure on the throne according to the Deuteronomist's view. De Tillesse also supports his contention that all of vv 16-20 are Deuteronomistic in that they reflect the Deuteronomist's opposition to kingship.[7] It is questionable whether his case is convincing. The plural

---

[3]De Tillesse recognized that there were exceptions to this rule. Ibid, p. 40f.

[4]Nicholson, *Deuteronomy and Tradition,* 34.

[5]That vv 18-19 are secondary to the law is accepted by a majority of scholars. Some representatives of that position are: Kurt Galling, "Das Königsgesetz im Deuteronomium," *TLZ* 76 (1951) 136; Seitz, *Redaktionsgeschichtliche Studien,* 233; Gerhard von Rad, *Deuteronomy,* OTL, from *Das fünfte Buch Mose: Deuteronomium,* 1964 (Philadelphia: Westminster, 1966) 119; de Tillesse, "Sections 'tu' et sections 'vous' dans le Deutéronome," p. 70; G. Ernest Wright, "Deuteronomy," 2:442.

[6]De Tillesse, "Sections 'tu' et sections 'vous' dans le Deutéronome," pp. 47, 69-70.

[7]Here again the clear assumption is that the Deuteronomist was opposed to kingship.

form in v 16b could imply that only it is secondary, and not all of v 16. If that were the case, then the similarity between v 16 and v 17 would not necessarily indicate that v 17 is secondary. The possible relationship between v 20 and the tradition in 1 Samuel 8 is also not sufficient reason to consider v 20 to be secondary.[8] All this indicates that the plural in v 16b might suggest that it is Deuteronomistic, but the evidence given by de Tillesse for considering the rest of vv 16-20 to be secondary is insufficient.

Further, there are indications that the law of kingship did contain vv 16-17,20. First of all, it would be rather undeuteronomic to have the law of kingship end with v 15. A comparison with the other laws, especially those about offices suggests that more detail would be given. Second, Calum Carmichael has drawn some interesting parallels between this law of kingship and Deut 12:20ff.[9] Both laws begin with the reporting of a request by Israel, and continue with Yahweh's giving permission. Both laws use the term שׂים, and after granting the concession, put limiting conditions upon it. In each case these limitations are formally introduced by רק. Finally, both conclude with "similar reward clauses, introduced by למען, that promise life and well-being."[10] This similarity in structures suggests that at least v 16a was part of the original law, and by implication very possibly v 17, and also that v 20 was part of it. In light of this it is safest to assume that in *Urdeuteronomium* the law of kingship consisted of what is now found in Deut 17:14-17,20.[11]

The ultimate origin of this law of kingship has also received some discussion. A number of scholars have argued that the law must be traced back to a Northern origin. Kurt Galling emphasized this in his article on

---

[8]De Tillesse also considers the presence of סר in v 20 to be an indication of Deuteronomistic editing, but admits that the presence of this term in Deut 28:14, a passage which is not clearly Deuteronomistic, weakens the argument. Ibid., p. 57.

[9]Calum M. Carmichael, *The Laws of Deuteronomy* (Ithaca: Cornell, 1974) 104-106.

[10]Ibid., p. 105.

[11]It is of course possible that v 16b is secondary, but it seems rather dangerous to make such a decision only on the basis of the plural form in that part of the verse. Although in exegesis decisions need to be made, it is better to be cautious about dividing up verses too finely unless the evidence is overwhelming. In our analysis, however, we will try to remember that there is some doubt about v 16b.

the passage.[12] The key assumption behind this conclusion is that the North had a charismatic concept of kingship. [13] The reference to Yahweh choosing the king in v 15 is then seen as reflecting this charismatic understanding. Another reason given for considering the law Northern is that the law resembles the opposition given kingship by Northern prophets. Both of these reasons need to be contested. First of all, it is not that obvious that the law expresses anti-kingship sentiment.[14] Second, it is questionable whether Alt's emphasis on the charismatic nature of kingship in the North can be maintained. T. C. G. Thornton has argued that kingship in the North was charismatic neither in the sense that it was non-dynastic, nor in the sense that a unique concept of designation by Yahweh existed in the North.[15] This view has since been supported by others.[16] This is then not a valid starting point for considering the law of kingship to be Northern. Third, it is also questionable whether the phrase "whom the Lord your God will choose" implies a charismatic concept of kingship, at least if charismatic means non-dynastic. Although Saul is described as having been chosen by Yahweh, after him this phrase is reserved for King David, and by implication for his dynasty when it is used of kings (2 Sam 6:21; 1 Kgs 8:16; 11:34).[17] This phrase can simply not be used as a sign of Northern origin. This does not require that the law is Southern, but means that we probably cannot tell from where it comes. Von Rad has correctly said: "No clear answer can be given to the question which constitutional

---

[12]Galling, "Das Königsgesetz."

[13]In this Galling follows the view of Albrecht Alt, "The Formation of the Israelite State in Palestine," first published in 1930, in *Essays on Old Testament History and Religion* (Oxford: Basil Blackwell, 1966) 171-237.

[14]See below.

[15]T. C. G. Thornton, "Charismatic Kingship in Israel and Judah," *JTS* 14 (1963) 1-11.

[16]Tomoo Ishida, *The Royal Dynasties*. This point is especially made on pp. 171-182. Here Ishida discusses reasons why the North had so many dynastic changes compared to the South. In fact, Ishida suggests that it might be more valid to speak of a charismatic kingship in the South with its emphasis on Yahweh's choice of the Davidic line (pp. 178-79).

A similar point is made, although from a different perspective by Giorgio Buccellati, *Cities and Nations of Ancient Syria*, Studi Semitica, n. 26 (Rome: Universita de Roma, 1967).

[17]For a recent good discussion of the term בחר see Byron E. Shafer, "The root *bḥr* and Pre-Exilic Concepts of Chosenness in the Hebrew Bible," *ZAW* 89 (1977) 20-42.

form of kingship can be glimpsed behind this new system, whether it was that of Judah or of Northern Israel."[18]

Finally, the similarity between the law of the king in Deuteronomy, and the so-called anti-kingship sections of 1 Samuel 8-12 (8; 10:17-27; 12) are striking. Both begin with the people requesting a king, and the statement is explicitly made that they want to be like all the nations. Both speak of Yahweh choosing the king, and the limitations placed on the king in Deut 17:16-17 resemble the "ways of the king" of 1 Sam 8:11-17. And both conclude with statements exhorting the king to obedience, with the implication that long life will result. These parallels are too great to be coincidence. The problem is determining what relationship there is between the two passages. If, as is usually assumed, the Deuteronomist produced 1 Sam 8; 10:17-27; 12, then the law of kingship can hardly have been based on the 1 Samuel passages. On the other side, however, the passages in 1 Samuel do not appear to be based on the law of kingship. Our suggestion would be that 1 Sam 8; 10:17-27; 12 were based on earlier traditions on how kingship began in Israel, and that the law of kingship was written on the basis of these same traditions. This would then explain the similarities.[19]

Kingship in the Deuteronomic Law of Kingship

Many scholars have tended to interpret the law of kingship in Deut 17:14-20 as being critical of the institution of kingship. E. W. Nicholson states: "Indeed the law on kingship in Deuteronomy xvii. 14f. makes it quite clear that the authors of the book had little regard for the institution of monarchy."[20] Cross considers the law to have originated out of polemic against kingship,[21] and von Rad says "Hence the one-sidedness of this law concerning the king consists in the fact that Deuteronomy sees in kingship not an office which Yahweh could use for the welfare of his people but only an institution in which the holder must live in a sphere of extreme peril because he is tempted by his harem or his wealth either to

---

[18]Von Rad, *Deuteronomy*, 119.

[19]Note the discussion of the relationship between these two passages in S. R. Driver, *Deuteronomy*, ICC (New York: Charles Scribner's, 1895) 212-13.

[20]E. W. Nicholson, *Deuteronomy and Tradition*, 49.

[21]Cross, *Canaanite Myth and Hebrew Epic*, 231, 240.

turn away from Yahweh or to 'lift up his heart above his brethren.'"[22] If these scholars are correct then there is a conflict, or at least considerable tension between the law of kingship and the way kingship is treated in the Deuteronomistic History according to our proposal. This now needs to be examined more closely.

The law of kingship assumes that it is Israel which initiates the institution of kingship, and not Yahweh.[23] It has been suggested that this picturing of the affair is already a sign of the negative attitude which the author had toward kingship. Not much significance should be given to this fact, however. It is possible that this is simply based on traditions which describe the origin of kingship in Israel. More importantly, Deut 18:16 implies that it was the people who had asked for a prophet, and Deut 12:20 speaks of Israel saying "I will eat flesh," and in neither case is there any hint that this is wrong. The mere fact that kingship was an institution which Israel had requested, or even demanded, is thus not very significant.

The phrase used to describe the request is much more significant. It is stated that Israel requested a king "like all the nations that are round about me." This is meant polemically. In Deuteronomy, as well as in the Deuteronomistic History as a whole, the nations (גוים) are contrasted with Israel and seen as a source of temptation for Israel. The ways of the nations are not the ways of Yahweh, and need to be avoided. This emphasis is expressed forthrightly in Deut 18:9—"When you come into the land which the Lord your God gives you, you shall not learn to follow the abominable practices of those nations." Israel, as Yahweh's holy people, is to be separate from the nations. If Israel follows the ways of the nations, it will also follow the fate of the nations which had been in the promised land before Israel, and will be punished by perishing from the land (Deut 8:20). To ask for a king *like the nations* is then a rejection of Yahweh and his ways.[24]

That Israel's request for a king like the nations was an act of rebellion does not automatically imply that kingship itself is wrong, or that the author of the law was anti-kingship. This fact is made clear by v 15 which states that "you may indeed set as king over you him whom the Lord your God will choose." First of all Israel is given permission to have a king, and

---

[22]Von Rad, *Deuteronomy*, 120.

[23]Cf. 1 Samuel 8.

[24]For a discussion of the "nations" in Deuteronomy see Otto Bächli, *Israel und die Völker. Eine Studie zum Deuteronomium*, ATANT, Nr. 41 (Zürich: Zwingli, 1962).

second, the king receives Yahweh's affirmation by being chosen by him. The concept of Yahweh's choosing is an important one in the OT, especially in Deuteronomy and the Deuteronomistic History. When Yahweh chooses a people, or a place for worship, or a king, he has determined the direction, and given his blessing on the choice.[25] With this phrase kingship is thus immediately placed under Yahweh's rule. On the one hand, it means that Israel cannot appoint just anyone to be king, and on the other hand, that the king, having been chosen by Yahweh has Yahweh's blessing for his particular task or role.

V 14 must now be interpreted in light of v 15a. V 15a makes it clear that kingship as such was not incompatible with Yahwism. Either one must conclude that v 14 conflicts with v 15a, or that v 14 cannot be seen as being opposed to the institution of kingship itself. It is our contention that the latter is the case. In Deuteronomy Israel is not to be like the other nations, and any request by Israel based in an attempt or desire to be like the other nations is considered rebellion. According to v 14 Israel's request for a king was such a request, and was thus to be rejected. It does not necessarily follow however, that kingship itself was to be rejected. The nations surrounding Israel had priests, prophets, and a sacrificial system, and in each case Israel had a parallel institution. If Israel had asked for a prophet "like all the nations round about," the request would no doubt also have been considered negatively. Israel thus had various institutions which were parallel to those of the surrounding nations, but in each case the institution had been reinterpreted or adapted so as to fit into her understanding of Yahweh and his covenant with Israel.[26] It is only logical to expect that this would now need to be done with kingship, and this is exactly what happens in the following verses. Israel is granted permission to have a king, and in fact, in Deuteronomy there is no indication that this even presents a problem. Deut 17:15b-17,20 then continue to describe what form this institution would need to take within Israel.

The required form of kingship in Israel is delineated largely in terms of limitations. These limitations are as follows:

---

[25]There is considerable disagreement as to the historical growth of the concept of Yahweh's choosing in Israel's history. See Shafer, "The root *bḥr*." Whether one accepts Shafer's view, or the view of Wildberger whom he criticizes is not that significant at this point in that both would accept that the term is theologically important in Deuteronomy.

[26]This does not speak to the question whether in fact Israel always did adapt borrowed institutions to Yahwism, but affirms that for the author of Deuteronomy this was seen as necessary.

a) The king must be a brother—Various scholars have wondered why this was in the law, and whether it was directed at certain attempts to place a foreigner on the throne, or specifically against the kingship of Abimelech.[27] It is questionable whether some historical situation needs to be seen behind this directive. Rather, the motivation for this requirement was religious. If Israel was to have a king, then the king should be a brother, someone who was also under the covenant. This requirement was really basic to all the other limitations. Only someone who recognized the true nature of Israel's existence could be expected to fulfill the royal functions within Israel. The king was thus a brother to all other Israelites, and was expected to act as a brother even when king.

b) He must not multiply horses—The major value of horses was for an army. The central role of the king was not to focus on preparing a strong standing army which could defend Israel against its enemies. It should be noted that Holy War had not required such an army. Deuteronomy 20 gives directives for Holy War; Israel is told not to be afraid of enemies who have horses and chariots for Yahweh who brought them out of Egypt is on their side.

c) He must not cause the people to return to Egypt—This prohibition probably refers to the selling of Israelites as slaves to Egypt in return for horses. This would be wrong both because it would not be treating fellow Israelites as brothers, and because it would again be an act in which the king tried to take control of the defence of the nation.[28] It is also significant that the result of this act is the reversal of Yahweh's salvation given in the exodus.

d) He shall not multiply wives—It has often been noted that political marriages were a common method of sealing international treaties or alliances, and that this prohibition speaks against such defence arrangements. Although such covenants with foreign nations are specifically denied elsewhere in Deuteronomy (7:2), they are probably not the point of this prohibition. It is explicitly stated that this should not be done "lest his heart turn away." Foreign wives were dangerous because they might turn the king away from his primary allegiance to Yahweh to other gods. This is strong Deuteronomic emphasis throughout, and it is only natural that it is referred to here as well.

---

[27] Note David Daube, "'One from among your brethren shall you set king over you,'" *JBL* 90 (1971) 480-81.

[28] Remember that this prohibition is found in v 16b, a verse which has been considered secondary.

e) He shall not greatly multiply silver and gold—The king, as a brother, could not be too different from other brothers. Israel was not to have a class distinction in which the king was raised above all the rest. V 20a may be a continuation of this prohibition which explains it by saying that his heart should not be lifted above his brothers.

f) He may not turn aside from the commandment—This last requirement brings us back to the first statement made, the king was able to be a brother. All Israelite brothers were under the covenant, and so here it is explicitly stated that this means that the king also must obey the commandments which Yahweh has given.[29] Notice that this verse (20) includes a promise of a long reign if the king obeys the commandments.

This examination of the law of kingship can now be summarized. To begin with, it is clearly not possible to say that the law is anti-kingship. Although the language used to describe Israel's request for a king indicates that the author considered the request to be at the least inappropriate, and more probably a rejection of Yahweh, kingship itself is not seen as being incompatible with true Yahwism. It is true that the kingship of the nations needed to be changed somewhat in order to be incorporated into Israel's covenant faith, but this would have been true also of other institutions borrowed. At the heart of this transformation was the fact that the king was to be a brother, someone who was also under the covenant, and had to follow its commandments.

To say that the law of kingship is not anti-kingship is not the same as saying that the law of kingship has the same view of kingship as the Deuteronomist. The examination shows that on the one hand, the two views are not contradictory and even agree on basic points, on the other hand the emphasis is different. Both the law of kingship and the Deuteronomist assume that Israel will have a king, that Yahweh supports the institution of kingship, and that the king is under the covenant law. Both also continue to see Yahweh as the one responsible for Israel's defence thus implying that this is not central for the king. If Deut 17:18-19 is the contribution of the Deuteronomist, however, then the law of kingship does not give the king any positive role to fulfill. The emphasis in the law of kingship is largely on prohibitions. There is no hint in the law of kingship of the very significant role given to the king by the Deuteronomist in the area of administrating the covenant. Of course the law of the king does

---

[29]We observed above that in 2 Kgs 22:2 Josiah is described as not having turned "aside to the right hand or to the left" just as Deut 17:20 required.

not prohibit such a role, but one does not get the impression from the law that kings were expected to fulfill such a role. Our quotation from von Rad at the beginning of this study of Deut 17:14-20 is thus not totally wrong. If it is correct, as some suppose, that Deuteronomy was written during the time of Manasseh, then this difference could be explained historically. A major concern at that time was to make sure that the king did not abuse his position. The Deuteronomist, however, writing during or after the time of Josiah would have been more optimistic about the possibilities of a king fulfilling a leading role in administering the covenant.

Kingship in the Deuteronomistic Addition to the Law of Kingship

As we indicated above, the evidence suggests that vv 18-19 were added to the law of kingship by the Deuteronomist. It is frequently assumed that the emphasis of these two verses is rather similar to that of the rest of the law.[30] The king is required to study the law in order to prevent him from falling prey to the temptations of kingship prohibited in the rest of the law. If the rest of the law is critical of kingship, then so are vv 18-19. In this way these two verses are seen as simply confirming and strengthening the message of the rest of the law: the king is under the law and so has to obey it like everyone else.

Otto Bächli has suggested a rather different interpretation of these two verses in his *Israel und die Völker*.[31] According to Bächli the reading of the law commanded in these verses is not a private reading for personal meditation, but a public reading of the law before the people. For Bächli

---

[30]Helmut Lamparter, *Der Aufruf zum Gehorsam. Das fünfte Buch Mose*, BAT, Bd.9 (Stuttgart: Calwer, 1977) 93; Peter C. Cragie, *The Book of Deuteronomy*, NICOT (Grand Rapids: William B. Eerdmans, 1976) 256-57; Nicholson, *Deuteronomy and Tradition*, 93.

This is also the conclusion of Larry Miller, "An Exegetical Study of Deuteronomy 17:14-20," Elkhart, 1974 (mimeographed), pp. 23-27. Miller concludes his study of these two verses as follows: "What we have here is a call to royal obedience: the king is to fear and obey Yahweh. It is an explicit statement that the king is to be under covenant law like all the other brothers. So what we have in vv 18 and 19 reinforces what we had already seen in vv 14-17. That being the case, the possible secondary nature of these verses is of secondary importance."

[31]Bächli, *Israel und die Völker*, 88-92.

the king is the "Speaker of the Law" (*Gesetzessprecher*) in Israel. Through his reading of the law the king becomes the "Keeper" (*Hüter*) and "Administrator" (*Verwalter*) of the law. As Bächli says, "The king is not only bound to the law of Yahweh, but he also guarantees its existence and takes care of its preservation."[32] Deut 17:18-19 is thus seen as giving the king a very significant function in Israel. Bächli draws attention to Josiah as an example of the king fulfilling this function. If Bächli is correct, then the Deuteronomistic addition to the law of kingship supports our proposal on the role which the Deuteronomist gives kingship very well.

Bächli's view has been sharply criticized, however. The key question is whether the reading of v 19 is to be public or private. Moran, in a review of Bächli's book, has argued that the reading commanded in the verse is a private reading. He states that when the term קרא implies a public reading, it is used with the phrase "in the ears of . . ." (בְּאָזְנֵי)[33] It has also been questioned whether historically the king ever fulfilled such a function.[34] Thus Bächli's view has gone virtually unaccepted.[35]

It needs to be admitted that seeing Deut 17:18-19 as commanding a public reading of the law by the king as *Gesetzessprecher* or as covenant mediator seems to be pushing the evidence somewhat, much as this would suit our thesis. Linguistically it would probably be possible to interpret קרא as referring to a public reading, but Moran is correct in that as a rule when such a public reading is meant by the term an additional phrase such as "in the ears/hearing of . . ." is usually added. More significantly, however, the text of vv 18-19 needs to be taken seriously. According to v 19 this reading is to be done so "that he may learn to fear the Lord his God, by keeping all the words of this law and these statutes, and doing them."

---

[32]Ibid., p. 90.

[33]W. L. Moran, review of *Israel und die Völker* by Otto Bächli, 1962, in *Bib* 44 (1963) 375-77. Nicholson, *Deuteronomy and Tradition*, 93 accepts Moran's argument at this point.
Note, however, that in Jer 36:8 קרא is used of a public reading without any such accompanying phrase.

[34]Miller, "An Exegetical Study of Deuteronomy 17:14-20," p. 26. Geo Widengren, "King and Covenant," has argued, however, that the king did fulfill the function of covenant mediator, and that this included the regular reading of the law. Widengren uses both vv 18-19 of the law of kingship, and the incident of Josiah of 2 Kgs 23:1-3 to support his case.

[35]Bächli himself notes that his interpretation goes against the view of A. Caquot, "Remarques sur la 'loi royale' du Deutéronome (17:14-20)," *Sem* 9 (1959) 31.

Here the immediate reason for the reading is given. It is thus not possible to make a case for the king as reader of the law on the basis of these verses. But an examination of Deut 17:18-19 cannot end with this conclusion. If these verses were added by the Deuteronomist, then it is necessary to interpret them in light of what the Deuteronomist says at other points. Here the connection between these verses and Josh 1:7-8 is significant. In Josh 1:7-8 Joshua is commanded as follows:

> Only be strong and very courageous, being careful to do according to all the law which Moses my servant commanded you; turn not from it to the right hand or to the left, that you may have good success wherever you go. This book of the law shall not depart out of your mouth, but you shall meditate on it day and night, that you may be careful to do according to all that is written in it.

Both passages command the person to study the law thoroughly in order that (לְמַעַן) he may learn to obey the law. Josh 1:7-8 speaks of a private reading leading to personal obedience. But both Joshua and the king are public officials with public responsibilities; in fact, each is the supreme leader of Israel of the time, and the major reason it is so important for them to read the law and to follow its commands is that their way of fulfilling their public responsibility is determined by their obedience to the law. Thus the Joshua who is commanded in 1:7-8 to study the law in order that he will obey it is pictured in Joshua 23 as exhorting Israel to obey the covenant.[36] Joshua is the leader of Israel at this point, and it is up to him to make sure that Israel remains true to Yahweh. According to the Deuteronomist he fulfilled his function properly, and so the Deuteronomist summarizes this time in Israel's history as one in which the people served the Lord (Judg 2:7). The private reading of the law, with the purpose of his obeying the law, is the necessary background to his fulfilling his responsibility as the leader of Israel, the successor of Moses. It is

---

[36]Joshua 24 pictures Joshua as a covenant mediator even more clearly, but this chapter is usually considered to have been added to the Deuteronomistic History at a later date even though it contains old tradition. If it were part of the history it would support our point very well, but since it has been questioned, it was not used here.

Notice, however, that Rudolf Smend ("Das Gesetz und die Völker") considers Joshua 24 to be part of the original Deuteronomistic History.

perhaps also not a coincidence that Josiah is first pictured as hearing the law himself, and inquiring of the Lord what this means for him, and only later reading the law to the people and leading them in covenant renewal. This now gives us the needed background to interpret the Deuteronomistic addition to the law of kingship. The two verses themselves only speak of a private reading of the law. In light of the connections between them and Josh 1:7-8, and in light of Josiah's acts in 2 Kings 22-23, however, more can be said. As the supreme leader and covenant administrator, the king obviously was required to know the law well. The addition to the law of kingship emphasizes this fact. The addition does not assign a specific role to the king, but it makes most sense when it is realized that the Deuteronomist gave the king a very important function in the life of Israel. By adding these two verses the Deuteronomist directed the king to study the law, with the assumption that only then could he fully obey and fulfill his royal responsibility within Yahwistic Israel. This addition thus fits perfectly with our proposal on the role of kingship according to the Deuteronomist.[37]

JOSHUA

Past examinations of kingship in the Deuteronomistic History have paid very little attention to the way in which Joshua has been depicted in that History. This is still the case even though a number of different studies have shown how he is described as a royal figure in the narratives.[38] We

---

[37] We would thus accept Bächli's statement ("Der König ist nicht nur an das Gesetz Jahves gebunden, sondern er garantiert auch seinen Bestand und sorgt für seine Erhaltung." Bächli, *Israel und die Völker*, p. 90) as an accurate description of the Deuteronomist's understanding of kingship, but not as a position that can be arrived at on the basis of the law of kingship alone.

Further, we would not accept Bächli's title of *Gesetzessprecher*, or Geo Widengren's title of "mediator of the covenant" as accurate for the king if by them is implied a formal office. Neither Joshua's role in Joshua 24, nor Josiah's in 2 Kgs 23:1-3 is sufficient evidence to conclude that there was a formal office which each was fulfilling at the time. Rather, both were the supreme leaders of the Israel of the time, and both acted as "covenant administrator" (this is meant descriptively, and not as the name of an office) in the way appropriate for the occasion.

[38] Geo Widengren, "King and Covenant," J. R. Porter, *Moses and Monarchy. A Study in the Biblical Tradition of Moses* (Oxford: Basil Blackwell, 1963); Porter, "The Succession of Joshua," in *Proclamation and*

have already noted the connection between the directive given the king in the law of kingship (Deut 17:18-19) and the exhortation given Joshua in Josh 1:7-8. This picture of Joshua as a forerunner of the kings, with its implications, now needs to be examined.

First we need to take a brief look at the case that has been made for seeing Joshua as a royal figure. Geo Widengren stated: "It is therefore evident that Joshua in Deuteronomic traditions was seen as a prototype of the Israelite ruler."[39] He based his conclusion largely on his view that both Joshua and the kings fulfilled the office of covenant mediator. We would, however, question whether this is a good starting point since the evidence is not that clear that this was ever seen as a formal position. E. M. Good has listed a number of other parallels between the picture given of Joshua, and the role of kings in Israel.[40]

> The figure of Joshua has also been invested with a certain royal aura. He is described as having the "spirit" (Num 27:18; Deut 34:9; cf. 1 Sam 10:10; 16:13; Isa 11:2). He is called the "servant of Yahweh" (Josh 24:29). He calls the people together for the making of a covenant (Josh 24:1; cf. 2 Sam 5:3). His name is said to have been changed from Hoshea to

---

Presence, Essays in Honor of G. Henton Davies, ed. J. I. Durham & J. R. Porter (London: SCM, 1970) 102-132; E. M. Good, "Joshua Son of Nun," in *IDB,* 2:995-96; Gunnar Östborn, *tora in the Old Testament* (Lund: Hakan Ohlssons Boktryckeri, 1945).

The following emphasize how the picture of Joshua is related to that of Josiah: Thomas W. Mann, *Divine Presence and Guidance in Israelite Traditions: The Typology of Exaltation,* The Johns Hopkins Near Eastern Studies (Baltimore: The Johns Hopkins, 1977) 196-206; J. A. Soggin, "Gilgal, Passah and Landnahme. Eine neue Untersuchung des kultischen Zusammenhangs der Kap. iii-vi des Josuabuches," in *Volume du Congrès. Genève, 1965,* VTSup, no. 15 (Leiden: E. J. Brill, 1966) 263-77.

See also Dennis J. McCarthy, "The Theology of Leadership in Joshua 1-9," *Bib* 52 (1971) 165-75.

[39]Widengren, "King and Covenant," p. 15.

[40]We are not arguing that the historical Joshua acted as a king, or that he was looked at as a king. It has long been recognized that the OT picture of Joshua has received considerable reworking before it was incorporated into the Biblical texts. It would be difficult at this point to reconstruct the exact role that Joshua had, or what his relationship to Moses was. In any case, our discussion is focussing not on this historical Joshua, but on the way in which Joshua is pictured in the OT, and especially in the Deuteronomistic narratives of him.

Joshua (Num 13:16); recalling the common royal practice of
assuming regnal name. His division of the land is parallel to
the king's erection of administrative districts (1 Kgs 4:7-19).
Likewise, Joshua is called upon to decide claims (cf. Josh
14:6-15; 17:14, 14-18), a function of the judge which also fell
to the king (cf. Isa 11:3b-4).[41]

In this list Good uses material from throughout the OT, but a strong case
can also be made relying more strictly on Deuteronomistic material.

One of the clearest examples of this picturing of Joshua as a royal
figure is found in the Deuteronomistic account of Joshua's succession to
Moses. Norbert Lohfink has argued that Josh 1:1-9 is not simply an exhortation given to Joshua, but represents a regular pattern for the installation of a person into a specific office.[42] In other words, Josh 1:1-9
records the formal accession of Joshua into an office. Clearly, he is seen
as succeeding Moses. Porter has argued convincingly that this pattern of
installation is not a literary creation, but was taken from a practice
within Israel, namely the enthronement of a new king.[43] The succession
from Moses to Joshua is thus seen through the practice of one king succeeding another.

The very fact that we have a narrative about Joshua entering his new
position contrasts him to the later judges. The account of his succession,
as well as the role later attributed to him, place him in the line of kings
and not as one of the pre-kingship charismatic judges. Judges did not
succeed each other upon death, but arose in response to a crisis. The
Joshua narrative, however, assumes that Joshua became leader immediately upon the death of Moses. There appears to be concern that there not
be a time when Israel is without a leader. This danger is avoided in a
manner at home within dynastic succession. It is also interesting that pre-
leadership conquests are not emphasized for Joshua. Joshua does receive
the spirit, but this does not happen immediately preceding a mighty act of
Joshua, but rather through the laying of Moses' hands on Joshua. This

---

[41]Good, "Joshua Son of Nun," p. 996.

[42]Norbert Lohfink "Die deuteronomistische Darstellung des Übergangs
der Führung Israels von Moses auf Josue," *Scholastik* 37 (1962) 32-44.
According to Lohfink this pattern had three main parts:
  1) Encouragement of the person addressed,
  2) Statement of a task or function,
  3) Assurance of divine presence and help.
[43]Porter, "The Succession of Joshua."

implies that the spirit came upon Joshua as he was installed into the office of leader of Israel, the successor of Moses. Although Joshua was not the son of Moses, he is depicted as succeeding Moses as a son succeeds his father within the normal dynastic succession of the Davidic monarchy.

The above is sufficient to show that in the Deuteronomistic History Joshua is seen as a royal figure, as a forerunner to the kings and not as one of the charismatic judges.[44] Our proposal suggested that ultimately the king was responsible for ensuring Israel's continued existence on the land, and that the major method of accomplishing this was to make sure the covenant was followed. Joshua fits into this proposal very well. First of all, his responsibility for the land is very clear. After all, it was Joshua who was Israel's leader when God gave Israel the land. He is also described as dividing this inheritance among the tribes. According to Brueggemann a king had responsibility for the land;[45] if this is accurate, then there is justification for calling Joshua the first king.[46]

---

[44]Although this picture is clearest within Deuteronomistic passages it is probably not the creation of the Deuteronomist. The account of his succession in Numbers also reflects this picture. Very possibly, however, the Deuteronomist emphasized this since it fit his understanding of the role of a king, or leader so well. Note the work of Thomas Mann who emphasizes how the Deuteronomist exalted Yahweh's representative before Israel, Thomas Mann, *Divine Presence and Guidance*, 196-206.

[45]Brueggemann, *The Land*, 73.

[46]D. Daube, *Studies in Biblical Law* (Cambridge: University, 1947) 25-39, has argued that Moses' ascent of the mountain to see the land is based on an ancient tradition of property transfer. A formal viewing of the land sealed the transfer or sale. On this basis Porter states: "We seem justified in assuming then that Joshua's succeeding Moses implied his inheriting the right of full ownership of the Promised Land which his great predecessor has not been able to exercise. But such an absolute right was something that belonged only to the Israelite king, in sharp contrast to the older type of charismatic leader, as such a verse as 1 Sam 8:14 makes clear." ("The Succession of Joshua," pp. 125-26). Although the role of Joshua in terms of the land is more that of the king than that of the judges, it is questionable whether it is proper to speak of "full ownership of the Promised Land." Although the king may have been seen as owner of the land in some ancient Near Eastern countries, this was not the case in Israel, and definitely not the case for the Deuteronomist. Israel's stay on the land was always conditional as it was Yahweh's land, and the king was responsible for ensuring that these conditions were met and that Israel could thus continue on the land. The king thus had a very important role with regard to the land, but he was not the owner.

Even more clearly, Joshua is depicted as relating to the covenant and law as our proposal suggested a king was expected to act. This becomes evident again and again, especially in passages which have been judged to be creations of the Deuteronomist. Thus in Josh 1:1-9 Joshua is exhorted to obey the law. Just as in the law of kingship, Joshua is to study and meditate upon the "book of the law." Joshua's success as a leader is seen as being dependent upon his obedience to the law. If he obeys, Yahweh will be with him.[47] Porter has argued that such an exhortation was a feature of royal installations, and only of such installations.[48] This passage says nothing about Joshua's public role in connection with the law, but the picture given here would be necessary before a public role would be possible. This passage then needs to be seen together with those which speak of a public role.

Josh 8:30-35, another Deuteronomistic passage, is also interesting in this regard. Here Joshua leads Israel in a covenant renewal ceremony. Joshua is obviously the leader in the ceremony. The basis of the ceremony is "the book of the law of Moses." V 32 then reads: "And there, in the presence of the people of Israel, he wrote upon the stones a copy of the law of Moses, which he had written."[49] Joshua is clearly responsible for the law. Further, it has been suggested that "the law of Moses which he had written" may be a reference to a copy of the law which he had supposedly written earlier in his leadership.[50] This can obviously not be pushed very hard, but it is striking that according to the law of kingship, when a king came to the throne he was to "write for himself in a book a copy of this law." After this, Joshua reads the book of law to all the people assembled. Regardless of the origin of this tradition, now it is in a Deuteronomistic robe, and it describes how Joshua read the law publicly and led Israel in a renewal of the covenant. The similarity between Joshua here, and Josiah in 2 Kgs 23:1-3 cannot be missed.[51]

---

[47]Note the similarity between this and the Deuteronomist's description of the reign of Hezekiah. 2 Kgs 18:6 states that Hezekiah kept the commandments which the Lord commanded Moses, and 18:7 states that Yahweh was with him, and that wherever he went, he prospered.

[48]Porter, "The Succession of Joshua," p. 118.

[49]The last phrase, "which he had written" is sometimes considered a gloss on the basis of the LXX.

[50]Ibid, p. 115.

[51]In fact, it has been suggested that the picture of Joshua has been considerably affected by the ideal Josiah, see Soggin, "Gilgal, Passah und Landnahme," p. 276; and Mann, *Divine Presence and Guidance*, 205-206.

This role of Joshua comes out again in Joshua 23. Joshua, the leader of Israel, gathers Israel together for his final statement. In v 6 he exhorts Israel to "be very steadfast to keep and do all that is written in the book of the law of Moses, turning aside from it neither to the right hand nor to the left." Joshua is acting as the one responsible for enforcing the covenant. In v 8 he challenges Israel to "cleave to the Lord your God."[52] The chapter concludes with a warning that if Israel transgresses the covenant, she will perish from the land. Joshua, acting as a leader should, exhorts Israel to keep the law in order that she may remain on the land. The Joshua of Joshua 24 fits this picture very well also, but since Noth and others have argued that it was not part of the original Deuteronomistic History, it will not be focussed on at this point.[53] But again, Joshua acts as the one responsible for the covenant as he leads Israel in making a covenant with Yahweh. Note especially vv 25-26: "So Joshua made a covenant with the people that day, and many statutes and ordinances for them at Shechem. And Joshua wrote these words in the book of the law of God. . ."

The above picture of Joshua fits perfectly with our proposal on the Deuteronomist's view of kingship. Joshua was not the king, but he was a forerunner of the later kings. He fulfilled those functions which the kings were later expected to do. Porter's statement at the conclusion of his work is fitting:

> It would then be no accident that the succession of Joshua to the office of Moses is most strongly emphasized, and its royal features most clearly discernible, in the scheme of the 'Deuteronomistic historical work', with its central pre-occupation with the responsibility of the Israelite king for the maintenance of the Covenant and thus for the whole religious and social wellbeing of the nation.[54]

So far, however, we, as well as the studies mentioned have focussed on

---

Mann states: "Moreover, the emphasis on Joshua himself is most naturally to be understood as reflecting the deuteronomistic ideal of Josiah. . . . We would thus understand the import of Joshua's exaltation as an implicit message to the contemporaries of the deuteronomistic redactor: they are to fear and obey Josiah as their ancestors had Joshua, and indeed, as they had Moses." (pp. 205-6).

[52]Similar language was used of Hezekiah in 2 Kgs 18:6—"For he held fast (דבק, as in Josh 23:8) to the Lord."

[53]Noth, *ÜgS*, 87.

[54]Porter, "The Succession of Joshua," p. 132.

only one aspect of our proposal: the king's role in terms of the law. Our proposal stated that ultimately the king was responsible for the land, but that since existence on the land was dependent upon Israel's obedience to the law, the king's responsibility in the area of defence was also the administration of the covenant. Yahweh was ultimately responsible for Israel's defence against its enemies, and the king and the people were to trust Yahweh to fulfill this task. In Joshua 1-9 Joshua leads Israel militarily as a king should. The two major examples of this are the battles against Jericho and Ai. In the conquest of Jericho Joshua is not a great military commander, but he is Yahweh's representative who trusts Yahweh to give Jericho into his hand (Josh 6:2), and then follows Yahweh's directions in detail. Here is the ideal of Holy War with Yahweh presenting the enemy to a trusting Israel. The relationship between the law and land comes out in the account of Israel's battles with Ai. The first attack of Ai is rebuffed because Achan has been disobedient. Already we have a foretaste of later times when disobedience will lead to the loss of land. Joshua's role in defeating Ai is then *not primarily in plotting military strategy, but in determining where disobedience had occurred, and then taking care of it.* Ai was only captured once obedience was again the case.[55] And so in the Deuteronomistic account of the conquest of Palestine Joshua acts as a king should act in the realm of defence: he trusts Yahweh to deliver the enemies into his hand, and he administers the covenant. As McCarthy has said of Josh 1-9, "There is the familiar lesson of the holy war: total trust in Yahweh."[56]

Our examination of the Deuteronomistic account of Joshua has found that Joshua, the royal figure and leader of Israel is seen as acting exactly as we proposed the Deuteronomist expected the king to act. To this extent this examination supports our thesis very well. It does, however, raise one suggestion. Perhaps our proposal does not describe the Deuteronomist's view of kingship as much as the Deuteronomist's understanding of real leadership in Israel. McCarthy has said of Joshua 1-9: "If you will, this is a theology of legitimate leadership, and the problem of leadership is one which will confront the deuteronomistic historian throughout the story."[57] If this is the case, we could simply adapt our proposal as follows.

---

[55]Was the account of the covenant renewal of Josh 8:30-35 perhaps placed immediately following the narrative of the capture of Ai because it was felt that the covenant needed renewing after the sin of Achan?

[56]McCarthy, "The Theology of Leadership in Joshua 1-9," p. 175.

[57]Ibid.

According to the Deuteronomist the leader of Israel was primarily responsible for ensuring or guaranteeing the covenant. This was the way Israel's continued existence on the land was assured. In order to defend itself from enemies Israel was to obey the law and trust in Yahweh. The kings, as Israel's officially recognized leaders, were then expected to fulfill this role of covenant administrator. Earlier this role had been fulfilled by Joshua, and before him by Moses, and now this was the responsibility of the kings.

JUDGES

The first discussion of kingship in the Deuteronomistic History after the law of kingship of Deuteronomy appears in Judg 8:22-23, and in the account of Abimelech's kingship with its use of the Jotham fable. These passages are frequently seen as confirming the position that the Deuteronomist was opposed to the institution of kingship. It is thus necessary to examine them. Is it really correct to say that they support the contention that the Deuteronomist was anti-monarchical? Judges 17-21 have not received quite as much attention in past discussion of the Deuteronomist, but considering how directly these chapters speak of kingship, they will also be looked at.

Gideon and Kingship, Judg 8:22-23

Judg 8:22-23 records how the "men of Israel" ask Gideon and his descendents to rule over them. The term "king" (מֶלֶךְ) or the related verb "to rule" (מָלַךְ) are not used in the passage but it is clear that the issue is one of kingship.[58] Here is the earliest record of this issue being raised in Israel's history[59] and so this passage needs to be examined.

---

[58]Hans Wilhelm Hertzberg, *Die Bücher Josua, Richter, Ruth*, ATD, Teilband 9 (Göttingen: Vandenhoeck & Ruprecht, 1959) 199; James D. Martin, *The Book of Judges*, CBC (Cambridge: Cambridge, 1975) 108; Gray, *Joshua, Judges and Ruth*, 313; etc. The fact that the verse speaks of Gideon's sons also ruling after him has usually been taken to mean that Gideon was offered dynastic kingship.

The similarity between Gideon's reason for rejecting the offer, and some of the language in 1 Sam 8 also confirms that the issue in Judg 8:22-23 is one of kingship.

[59]Even if the historical Gideon was never offered kingship, and these verses are a literary creation, they would still be significant since they would be the first discussion of the issue for the historian.

These two verses have received considerable attention in OT research, and many different analyses have resulted. The conclusions reached on this passage have tended to center around three questions: (1) Did Gideon become king after this incident? Largely on the basis of some so-called royal features in the text following v 23 a number of scholars, especially in times past, have argued that Gideon accepted the offer and became a king in Israel before the time of Saul, even though this kingship would obviously not have been over all of Israel.[60] This position has been rejected by many others, especially in more recent studies.[61]

(2) What does Gideon's answer to the offer mean? As a rule it has been assumed that 8:23 is a clear rejection of the offer of kingship.[62] Those who argue that in fact Gideon did become king assume that v 23 was not originally connected with the offer in v 22, and possibly even replaced an earlier tradition which described how Gideon accepted the offer.[63] Recently G. Henton Davies has proposed that v 23 is not a refusal of the offer but a politely worded acceptance.[64] With this form of acceptance Gideon is seen as committing himself to a just rule in which there will be no tyrannical element, and in which ultimately Yahweh will be ruling.

---

[60]Julius Wellhausen, *Prolegomena*, 239; Bernhard Stade, *Geschichte des Volkes Israel*, Allgemeine Geschichte in Einzeldarstellungen, 1 Hptabt., 6 T. (Berlin: G. Grote'sche Verlagsbuchhandlung Separat-Tonto, 1886), 190; Eduard Nielsen, *Shechem. A Tradition-Historical Investigation* (Copenhagen: G. E. C. Gad, 1955), 143; G. Henton Davies, "Judges VIII 22-23," *VT* 13 (1963) 151-57. Many more could be listed.

[61]A few examples are: John Bright, *History*, 173; Martin Buber, *Kingship of God*, trans. Richard Sheimann, from 3rd edition of *Königtum Gottes*, 1st published in 1932 (New York: Harper & Row, 1967) 59-65; Robert Boling, *Judges*, AB (Garden City: Doubleday, 1975) 161.

A number of scholars suggest that Gideon refused the title of king but accepted a position of leadership which gave him virtually the same power as that of a king, only without the name.

Various others do not speak to the question specifically, but by their discussion indicate that they assume that Gideon refused the offer and thus did not become king.

[62]This is the case both among those who believe that Gideon did not become king in Israel, and among those who argue the contrary.

[63]An example of this is Stade, *Geschichte des Volkes Israel*, 190.

[64]Davies, "Judges VIII 22-23."

Arthur E. Cundall, in "Antecedents of the Monarchy in Ancient Israel," in *Vox Evangelica III* (London: Epworth, 1964) 48, considers Davies' proposal to be a "reasonable interpretation of the incident."

(3) What is the origin of the view in v 23? Davies, who sees the verse as a pious acceptance, naturally sees the verse as simply going back to the time of Gideon.[65] Conclusions have differed among those who interpreted v 23 as a refusal. In the past a majority of scholars saw v 23 as a late, theocratically determined, interpolation into an earlier tradition. The exclusive alternative assumed by the verse (either Yahweh is king or a person is king, but not both), and the anti-kingship element assumed by this were seen as arising out of negative experiences with the monarchy, probably between the time of Jeroboam II and the fall of the North.[66] Others have argued that v 23, if not expressing Gideon's response, at least accurately reflects the sentiments of some in the period before the rise of kingship.[67]

This brief summary of the conclusions of scholars on these two verses reveals that at present there is still very little consensus on an analysis of Judg 8:22-23. It also shows that attention has been largely focussed on historical issues (did Gideon become king?) and traditio-historical questions (what is the origin of the sentiment expressed in v 23?). Much less attention has been given to the verses as part of the Gideon narrative as a whole, or as part of the Deuteronomistic History. When connections have been made between 8:22-23 and the Deuteronomistic History the tendency has been to note that the anti-kingship bias of these two verses fits well with the views of the Deuteronomist,[68] or even that the verses may be a product of his views.[69] This is obviously unsatisfactory, and so further

---

[65]Davies, "Judges VIII 22-23."

[66]George Foot Moore, *Judges*, ICC (New York: Charles Scribner's, 1903) 230; Wellhausen, *Prolegomena*, 239; Gray, *Joshua, Judges and Ruth*, 313; C. F. Burney, *The Book of Judges* (London: Rivingtons, 1918) 235; Barnabas Lindars, "Gideon and Kingship," *JTS* 16 (1965) 315-26.

[67]Buber, *Kingship of God*, 59-65; Bright, *History*, 173; Martin Noth, *The History of Israel* (New York: Harper & Row, 1960) 165; Soggin, *Das Königtum*, 15-20; etc.

Crüsemann (*Der Widerstand gegen das Königtum*, 42-54) has very recently argued against both those who see the sentiment of v 23 as premonarchic, and those who see it as a product of late prophetic theology. Crüsemann places it in the early years of kingship, arguing that it could not be late, but that it could not have been stated before experience with kingship.

[68]Gray, *Joshua, Judges and Ruth*, 313.

[69]W. Beyerlin, "Geschichte und Heilsgeschichtliche Traditions-bildung im Alten Testament. Ein Beitrag zur Traditionsgeschichte von Richter VI-VIII," *VT* 13 (1963) 20, cites H. Gressmann as one who argues that Judg 8:23 was the product of Deuteronomistic thought.

examination is needed.

The redactional history of the book of Judges is a truly complex one. At the very least, it is usually agreed, the material in the book of Judges had three stages: the independent existence of different stories, a book of saviour judges, and the book of Judges as part of the Deuteronomistic History. The same holds for the Gideon narratives. Unfortunately there is considerable disagreement among scholars as to the literary analysis of this section.[70] Since no major post-Deuteronomistic additions have been proposed for the section, for our purposes it is probably the most helpful to simply accept the text as is in order to arrive at what the Deuteronomist considered this passage to say.

That Judg 8:22-23 reflects anti-kingship sentiments needs to be admitted.[71] Despite the suggestion by Davies,[72] it is difficult to interpret Gideon's answer in any other way. Gideon's answer assumes that Yahweh, and man as king cannot both rule at the same time. Since Israel affirms that Yahweh rules, there is no place for a king. As different scholars from Buber to Soggin[73] have suggested, it is very possible that Judg 8:23 contains memories of opposition to kingship from the time of judges. Kingship was an institution which Israel did not adopt immediately upon settling in the land, probably for a number of different reasons.[74] As Cundall suggests, at least one of these reasons will probably have been religious. Whether this was the major reason is here irrelevant. Regardless of the role which theology played in this early rejection of kingship, it is very likely that Israel's traditions would have emphasized the theological reason for the opposition. There is thus no reason to deny that very early, probably already before the time of kingship, and certainly during the

---

[70]See Richter, *Traditionsgeschichtliche Untersuchungen*, 112-246; Beyerlin, "Richter VI-VIII,"; Boecker, *Die Beurteilung des Anfänge des Königtums*, 20-23; Crüsemann, *Der Widerstand gegen das Königtum*, 42-54.

[71]Crüsemann, *Der Widerstand gegen das Königtum*, considers it to be one of the four anti-kingship passages in the whole OT.

[72]Davies, "Judges VIII 22-23."

[73]Buber, *Kingship of God*, 59-65; Soggin, *Das Königtum*, 15-20.

[74]Cundall, "Antecedents of the Monarchy," 44-45, gives the following reasons for the delay:
 a) Israel's love of independence
 b) Israel's tribal structure
 c) Israel's conception of Yahweh.

early days of the new institution, there were those who argued that Israel's allegiance to Yahweh precluded the possibility of a human king. Judg 8:22-23 contains memories of such opposition to kingship.[75]

In its present context, however, the message of 8:22-23 is not that kingship is incompatible with Yahwism. Walter Beyerlin drew attention to the significance of the reason given in v 22 for Israel's asking Gideon to be king.[76] According to v 22 the men of Israel want Gideon to be king because "you have delivered us out of the hand of Midian." Hans Jochen Boecker pursues this direction further in his study of the passage.[77] In v 23 the issue clearly is who will rule over Israel. The verse assumes that it is not possible for both Gideon and Yahweh to rule at the same time. Boecker suggests that the natural question which this raises is in what way does human kingship conflict with the rule of Yahweh, since this is by no means obvious. Boecker argues that the answer to this question is pointed at by the motivation given for the offer in v 22. The key word in this statement of motivation is "to save" (ישׁע). But this is a central term not only in 8:22-23, but in the whole Gideon narrative, as well as for the Deuteronomistic History as a whole. The term "to save" (ישׁע) is used six further times in the Gideon narrative. In Judg 6:14-15 Gideon responds to his call by saying "how can I deliver Israel?"[78] In 6:36-37 there are two, virtually identical references, to Yahweh delivering Israel by Gideon's hand. In 7:2-7 the issue at hand is made very clear. Here Yahweh says to Gideon: "The people with you are too many for me to give the Midianites into their hand, lest Israel vaunt themselves against me, saying, 'My own hand has delivered.'" (Judg 7:2). The danger is that Israel will fail to give Yahweh credit for the deliverance. Thus in 7:7 Yahweh again says "With the three hundred men that lapped I will deliver you." In this way the narratives have emphasized over and over that it is Yahweh who delivers, and not Israel or Gideon. In the present text the men's offer to Gideon

---

[75]This could be the case whether one accepts the view of those who hold that this was the nature of the opposition in pre-kingship times, or whether one follows Crüsemann (*Der Widerstand gegen das Königtum*) who maintains that such opposition could not have arisen before practical experience with kingship, but that it did arise early in the monarchy.

[76]Beyerlin, "Richter VI-VIII," p. 21.

[77]Boecker, *Die Beurteilung der Anfänge des Königtums,* 20-22.

[78]It needs to be admitted that not too much emphasis can be placed on the use of the term here since this may be part of the formulaic call narrative, as Boecker realizes (Ibid, p. 21). It does, however, contribute to the cumulative effect.

must be seen against this background. As Beyerlin says: "After everything Israel's men *can* not say to their leader: Rule over us, for *you* have delivered us out of the hand of the Midianites! This offer—and even more the basis given for it—is a priori untenable and absurd, since not Gideon but Yahweh had delivered."[79] (Translation mine). The men's offer to Gideon was a failure to recognize Yahweh's role, and had to be rejected.[80]

Regardless of whether or not Judg 8:22-23 originally was a separate tradition, now it must be interpreted within the context of the whole Gideon narrative. Our analysis has done this, and also shown how well the passage then fits the Deuteronomist's emphases in other parts of the history. Yahweh is Israel's deliverer, and this Israel must not forget. Kingship is wrong whenever it usurps Yahweh's role in this area. Although 8:22-23 very possibly had an anti-kingship background, in its present context it contributes to a different message.[81] Yahweh is Israel's ruler in

---

[79]Beyerlin, "Richter VI-VIII," p. 21.

[80]Crüsemann (*Der Widerstand gegen das Königtum*, 46-47) rejects Boecker's analysis largely on the basis of his own literary conclusion that Judg 6:36-40; 7:2-8 do not belong to the same redactional level as Judg 8:22-23. He then considers it improper to interpret 8:22-23, as well as 6:14-15, in light of these later passages.

If Crüsemann is correct in his literary analysis, and this is possible, then Boecker's analysis would not be valid for that stage of the text. Boecker has, however, already anticipated such criticism: "Der im jetzigen Text vorliegende Komplex der Gideongeschichte ist wohl ursprünglich keine einheitliche Grösse. Auf die verwickelte traditionsgeschichtliche Problematik brauchen wir hier nicht einzugehen, da es hier lediglich um die letzte Ausgestaltung der Gideongeschichte geht." (*Die Beurteilung der Anfänge des Königtums*, 21). Boecker, like we are, was trying to get at the meaning for the Deuteronomist. Although at some point in the past 8:22-23 may have had no connection with 6:36-40 and 7:2-8, in the present text they do and the relationships cannot be avoided. Since this was most probably the case already before the Deuteronomist incorporated the narratives of Gideon (even Crüsemann does not deny that) into his history, they need to be treated together when studying the Deuteronomist. Crüsemann's analysis of 8:22-23 may thus be correct for the past stage, but for the Deuteronomist 8:22 with its use of the catch word ישע will have pointed at 6:36-37 and 7:2-8, and must be interpreted in light of them. It is of course possible that 8:22-23 were even changed when 6:36-40 and 7:2-8 were added so as to point at them more directly; if so this would only confirm our view.

[81]Is it possible that when the text of 8:22-23 was used to express opposition to kingship that the term "king" (מֶלֶךְ) was used, and that it was

that he delivers Israel from the hands of her enemies. This is emphasized
in the Gideon narratives as a whole, and 8:22-23 contributes to this message. The chapters on the rise of kingship in 1 Samuel 8-12 are already
being prepared for.

Jotham's Fable and the Story of Abimelech, Judges 9

Martin Buber has said the following about the Jotham fable:

> The Jotham fable, the strongest anti-monarchical poem of
> world literature, is the counterpart of the Gideon passage.
> . . . The kingship, so teaches the poem . . . is not a productive
> calling. It is vain, but also bewildering and seditious, that men
> rule over men. Every one is to pursue his own proper business,
> and the manifold fruitfulness will constitute a community
> over which, in order that it endure, no one needs rule—[82]

This assessment, although perhaps a little more extreme, basically
describes how the Jotham fable has been viewed by most scholars. Yet
this fable is in the Deuteronomistic History. How is this to be explained?
Whether or not its presence in the history challenges or undermines our
thesis about the Deuteronomist's view of kingship needs to be examined.

While Buber's position no doubt represents the dominant one, this view
has not gone unchallenged. Eugene Maly has argued that the moral of the
fable is that if responsible people in the community do not take upon
themselves the burden of leadership, then one who is not responsible will
become the leader to the great detriment of the community. "The meaning of the original fable, therefore, was clearly not directed against
kingship itself, but against those who refused, for insufficient reasons, the
burden of leadership."[83] Barnabas Lindars has accepted Maly's proposal,
and has also suggested a possible origin for the fable. Since, he argues, the
fable presupposes the institution of kingship, it could not have arisen in
response to the Abimelech incident. Further, Abimelech was not the last
resort. "But such a situation is perhaps conceivable in a Canaanite city-

---

eliminated from the text as the meaning changed so as to avoid an anti-
kingship interpretation, and to make sure that the issue was seen as one of
rule (מׁשל) and deliverance (יׁשע)?

[82]Buber, *Kingship of God*, 75.

[83]Eugene Maly, "The Jotham Fable—Anti-monarchical?" *CBQ* 22 (1960)
303.

state of the conquest period, in circumstances where local cohesion is disintegrating, and the landowners are more concerned to protect their own estates than to take responsibility for territorial claims which can no longer be maintained."[84] These two together have thus presented a significant challenge to the traditional position that the fable is antimonarchical and primarily makes fun of the institution of kingship.

Crüsemann, however, has totally rejected the challenge of Maly and Lindars.[85] He emphasizes that no conceivable context can be given which could give rise to a fable with the message which Maly suggests.[86] After comparing the fable to other fables about kingship of that time he concludes with the traditional picture—"Kingship is unproductive, it gives no fruit, and the protective function, which it takes for itself, it cannot fulfill."[87] (Translation mine). He concludes from this that since this picture of kingship is so drastically different from that of any other society where there is usually competition for the position, the fable must have originated within Israel.

This is then the debate which has arisen regarding the original intention of the Jotham fable. Although the arguments which Maly and Lindars have produced make one a little more cautious about stating the position too strongly, the traditional view still seems to be stronger. If the fable originally arose within Israel, either in pre-kingship times or during the early years of the monarchy, as is likely, then it is difficult to read it in any other way than as a denigration of kingship. As has already been suggested earlier, the fact that Israel delayed as long as it did before adopting the institution makes it very likely that there was some kind of opposition to the introduction of kingship at the time. Such opposition could very conceivably have given rise to such a fable. One must thus conclude that the Jotham fable most probably arose in early Israel as an expression of those who saw kingship as an institution with no positive function.

To conclude that the original intention of the fable was to denigrate the institution of kingship is not the same, however, as to say that in the

---

[84]Barnabas Lindars, "Jotham's Fable—A New Form-critical Analysis," *JTS* 24 (1973) 365.

[85]Crüsemann, *Der Widerstand gegen das Königtum*, 28-29.

[86]Ibid, p. 28. Crüsemann states this in spite of the fact that Lindars has attempted to suggest a possible context for the origin of the fable. It must be admitted, however, that Lindars' suggestion is very hypothetical, and probably rather unlikely.

[87]Ibid, p. 29.

present context the fable expresses anti-kingship polemic. It is usually agreed that the present story of Abimelech is a compilation of various originally independent traditions,[88] and that these traditions were tied together by a pre-Deuteronomistic narrator.[89] More specifically, it is then also usually assumed that the fable was not originally composed for the Abimelech incident but was only later literarily added to the account.[90] In other words, some pre-Deuteronomistic editor probably made use of an already existing fable, and incorporated and adapted it into his account of Abimelech. This narrator may have just produced the Gideon/Jerubbaal—Abimelech cycle, or he may have produced the whole pre-Deuteronomistic book of saviour judges. If this is correct, then it is much more relevant for our purposes to determine how the fable was used in the Abimelech story as a whole, and how the Deuteronomist is likely to have understood it.

When Judges 9 is examined as a whole, it is quickly clear that within this chapter the Jotham fable is not used in order to attack the institution of kingship as such, but to indict Abimelech and the citizens of Shechem. As Lindars says, "It is sufficient that the fable gives the lead for the one thing that is essential for the narrator's purpose, and that is the curse of Jotham."[91] The tone for the chapter is set by v 15, the second part of which is probably an addition by the narrator as he adapted the fable to the Abimelech story[92]—"If in good faith you are anointing me king over

---

[88]Lindars, "Jotham's Fable," p. 355, states: "Commentators are generally agreed that the main narrative of verses 22-49 is made up of two different accounts of the action, or even of two entirely separate actions, one in verses 22-5 and 43-9, the other in verses 26-41. The ending of the first also seems to be composed of two variant accounts, 43-5 and 46-9. Further, the latter shows signs of connection with the opening account of the *coup* of Abimelech (verses 1-6). The final episode appears independent of the rest."

[89]One exception to this is Gray, *Joshua, Judges and Ruth*, 229-30. Gray sees the Deuteronomist here using the traditions to express his criticism of kingship. Again this understanding of the Deuteronomist is seen.

[90]One exception to this is: Moore, *Judges*, 245.

[91]Lindars, "Jotham's Fable," p. 358.

[92]Lindars, "Jotham's Fable," p. 361, considers all of v 15 to be the product of the narrator. Maly, "The Jotham Fable," p. 303; and Crüsemann, *Der Widerstand gegen das Königtum*, 19, both argue that v 15b is secondary. One strong argument in favor of this is that whereas in v 15a it is the bramble that is speaking, in v 15b the bramble is spoken of in the third person.

you, then come and take refuge in my shade; but if not, let fire come out
of the bramble and devour the cedars of Lebanon." In the story itself the
first option is not considered to be a real one. This then leaves the second
option, and the rest of the account then describes how this takes place.
The motif of fire has been introduced here, and is again brought up in v 20
where the threat now applies to both the citizens of Shechem, and to
Abimelech—"but if not, let fire come out from Abimelech and devour the
citizens of Shechem and Beth-millo; and let fire come out from the citizens of Shechem, and Beth-millo, and devour Abimelech." The last two
verses of the chapter, also probably added by the narrator, then tie it all
together, and give an explanation for the events:

> Thus God requited the crime of Abimelech, which he com-
> mitted against his father in killing his seventy brothers; and
> God also made all the wickedness of the men of Shechem fall
> back upon their heads, and upon them came the curse of
> Jotham the son of Jerubbaal. (Judg 9:56-57).

Justice had been accomplished, and sin and rebellion had been punished.

The striking fact is, however, that nowhere is there any hint that
Abimelech's sin was that he became king. Nor is it suggested that
Shechem's crime was that they made Abimelech king. Rather, it is explicitly stated that Abimelech's crime was killing his brothers (9:24,56), and
that Shechem's crime was helping him to kill his brothers (9:24). The
verses immediately following the fable focus on the question of whether
or not the citizens of Shechem had acted in good faith in making Abimelech king, but here also there is no criticism implied of the mere making
of someone king. Thus above all the chapter describes the results of
murder and complicity with murder—death.

Since Abimelech becomes king through his crimes, it must be admitted
that the chapter cannot be separated from the question of leadership. But
even then the message of the chapter is still not that kingship is a crime,
but that when kingship is based on crime and the abuse of force, especially against ones brothers, then the inevitable outcome of such a kingship will be destruction. Crüsemann speaks of the chapter as emphasizing
the necessary connection between act and result (*Tun—Ergehen*), especially with regard to the foundation of kingship.[93] The story of Abimelech
would thus be an example of the proverb of the one living by the sword

---

[93]Ibid, p. 40.

also dying by the sword. Such a message would of course fit very well with the Deuteronomist's view of kingship.

When the Abimelech cycle is looked at within the larger context, the contrast between Gideon/Jerubbaal and Abimelech cannot be missed. Although Gideon is described as refusing the offered kingship, both are clearly seen by the Deuteronomist as leaders of Israel. As we noticed earlier, for the Deuteronomist the kings are the leaders of Israel, and the issues of kingship and leadership are integrally related with each other if not totally interchangeable. This contrast between the two is evident in at least three areas. First of all, whereas Abimelech came to his position of leadership as the result of his own initiative, through the use of intrigue, force, and bloodshed, Gideon came to his position after being called by Yahweh. This fits well with the law of kingship which allowed Israel to make king "him whom the Lord your God will choose." Immediately one can conclude that Gideon's rule was legitimate, and Abimelech's not. This contrast between the two is also evident within their rule. Thus second, whereas Abimelech continued to use the force of his troops to protect his people, Gideon was Yahweh's representative in holy war and allowed Yahweh to be Israel's protector. When Gideon was offered the kingship on the basis of a misunderstanding of Yahweh's role, Gideon had to refuse. Israel's security could not be guaranteed by political restructuring. Finally, the difference between Gideon and Abimelech is also evident when the impact of their rule upon the internal affairs of Israel is examined. Judg 9:33-35 states that Israel began to play the harlot after Gideon's death. This implies that during his time of his leadership Israel did remain loyal to Yahweh. Obviously Gideon is seen as having led Israel in this, and so having fulfilled his role as leader during this time. He may not have been king, but in the eyes of the Deuteronomist he led Israel in covenant obedience just as the kings were expected to do. According to the Deuteronomist Abimelech was the leader of Israel following Gideon, and his reign is depicted as a time of sin, as is suggested in Judg 8:33-35, and as is brought out by the description of Abimelech's life. Abimelech clearly did not lead Israel in any covenant obedience and is obviously to be condemned.

The Deuteronomist's understanding of legitimate leadership is thus also reflected by his accounts of Gideon and Abimelech. Gideon was chosen by Yahweh, and fulfilled his proper function, both in holy war as the executor of Yahweh's commands, and internally as the one who led Israel in loyalty to Yahweh. Abimelech failed on all accounts. Once kingship arose in Israel, the kings were expected to fulfill this leadership function. Within the book of Judges the time of Gideon is probably more the exception

than the rule. During the time of the judges Israel is described as continually falling into sin and rebellion against Yahweh. The Abimelech story,
placed right at the center of the book, typifies this time. This is reinforced by Judges 17-21, and the whole then provides the background for
the rise of kingship, that institution which was expected to lead Israel in
covenant obedience and loyalty to Yahweh.

Judges 17-21

The last five chapters of the book of Judges record two incidents which
took place among the tribes of Israel before the rise of kingship.[94] Judges
17-18 describes the migration of the tribe of Dan to the north, and its
establishing a sanctuary there, and Judges 19-21 relates the tale of what
happened to a Levite and his concubine in Gibeah, and the revenge which
the rest of Israel took against the tribe of Benjamin for the outrage
committed. There has been considerable discussion among scholars on a
number of critical questions in these chapters—What is the relationship
between chapters 17-18 and 19-21? Are chapters 17-18 the product of a
compilation of two different narratives? When did the narratives originate? What was the original function of the narratives? There is one issue
upon which there has been virtual consensus, however. It is usually agreed
that in their present form and location Judges 17-21 prepare the way for
the rise of kingship by emphasizing the anarchy present during the time of
judges and thus demonstrating the need for kingship.[95]

---

[94]Although the view has been questioned, it is usually agreed that the
two accounts contain a historical basis some time in the period before
kingship.

[95]George Mendenhall seems to interpret the key phrase in Judges 17-21
positively when he speaks of the goal of early Israel's revolution as
follows: "Indeed, the purpose of the revolution was the creation of a
condition of peace in which every man could sit under his own fig tree and
under his own grapevine, doing 'what was right in his own eyes'—a description of self-determination and freedom from interference or harassment
by the king's bureaucrats or military aristocracy." (*The Tenth Generation.
The Origins of the Biblical Tradition.* Baltimore: Johns Hopkins, [1973]
27). It is difficult to see how he associates the phrase in Judges 17-21 with
the language in 1 Kgs 4:24 about the fig tree and grapevine. It is also
difficult to see how he can arrive at a positive implication for the key
phrase in the context of Judges 17-21.

Note also the suggestion by Shemaryahu Talmon that the term מלך in
the key phrase does not necessarily mean "king" in the usual sense but

Martin Noth: Elsewhere in the entire Old Testament there is hardly a passage which assumes such an absolutely positive attitude toward the institution of historical kingship.[96]

Moshe Weinfeld: The formula 'In those days there was no king in Israel', etc. serves the same uniform purpose throughout chs. 17-21 to discredit the period of the judges and demonstrate Israel's essential need for a monarchy.[97]

Martin Buber: One cannot say more plainly: 'That which you pass off as theocracy has become anarchy,' and: 'Only since this people, as is fitting for human beings, took unto itself a human king, has it known order and civilization.'[98]

The editor emphasized this point by adding the phrase, "In those days there was no king in Israel; every man did what was right in his own eyes," or a shortened version thereof, four times (17:6; 18:1; 19:1; 21:25) to the two accounts of lawlessness and rebellion. Regardless of the original intention of these narratives, now they function to demonstrate the dire straits into which Israel had fallen, and to show the need for a king to bring order into this situation of anarchy.[99]

As Judges 17-21 have been described so far they would fit very well into our thesis about the Deuteronomist. There is one major problem, however. Ever since Budde the tendency has been to see these five chapters as appendices added to the book of Judges after the contribution of the Deuteronomistic editor, or after the Deuteronomistic History had

---

should be seen as meaning something similar to "judge" (שׁפט). Talmon then interprets Judges 17-21 as attacking those periods before kingship when no judges ruled. Historically this would have been between the time of Joshua and the rise of the charismatic judges. Shemaryahu Talmon, "In Those Days There Was No King in Israel," in *Proceedings of the 5th World Congress of Jewish Studies, August, 1959* (Jerusalem: World Union of Jewish Studies, 1969), Hebrew: I:135-44, English abstract: 1:242-43.

[96]Martin Noth, "The Background of Judges 17-18," in *Israel's Prophetic Heritage* (New York: Harper, 1962) 80.

[97]Moshe Weinfeld, *Deuteronomy and the Deuteronomic School,* 169.

[98]Buber, *Kingship of God,* 78.

[99]Note the different conclusions arrived at on the original intention of Judges 17-18 by Noth, "The Background of Judges 17-18," and by Crüsemann, *Der Widerstand gegen das Königtum,* 164-65.

been produced.[100] Noth reinforced this position in his *Überlieferungs-geschichtliche Studien,*[101] and most commentaries and introductions have assumed this. If this is correct, then these chapters cannot be used in our study of the Deuteronomist's view of kingship.

While the majority of scholars have viewed Judges 17-21 as appendices to the book of Judges, this verdict has not been unanimous,[102] and so the issue deserves some further examination. The arguments which have been used to support the contention that these chapters are later additions can be summarized as follows:

(1) Judges 17-21 do not fit the Deuteronomist's schema for the time of the judges. They do not fit into his chronological framework, they do not contain a major judge or personality, and they do not contain the Deuteronomist's cycle of sin, punishment, and deliverance.

(2) Judges 17-21 do not agree with the Deuteronomist's ideology. Whereas the Deuteronomist is seen as being critical of kingship, Judges 17-21 are pro-kingship. As Soggin says,

> In general the phrase 'In those days there was no king in Israel
> . . .' (17.6; 18.1; 19.1) is seen as a criticism of the political
> situation obtaining under the tribal alliance, a situation which
> is seen as one of open disorder. The Deuteronomistic history
> work, on the other hand, tends to exalt these times and the
> mode of government then prevailing;[103]

The validity of these arguments now needs to be tested.

As the first argument maintains, there is something different about Judges 17-21 which sets it apart from the rest of the book of Judges. This does not prove, however, that Judges 17-21 was not part of the original Deuteronomistic History. 1 Samuel 1-6 also do not fit into the Deuteronomist's schema very well, and still they are clearly part of the history. Further, this difference may be due to the nature of the source material. This becomes an even better possibility when the Deuteronomist is seen

---

[100]Budde, *Richter,* 110.

[101]Noth really does not defend this position but simply states, "Ri. 17-21 hat anerkanntermassen nicht zum Werke von Dtr gehört, sondern ist später eingefügt worden." (*ÜgS, 54*).

[102]Veijola, *Das Königtum,* 27, lists the following as having questioned or disagreed with the traditional position: Bentzen, Hertzberg, Schunck, Eissfeld, Weinfeld and Täubler.

[103]Soggin, *Introduction,* 180.

not as producing the book of Judges by compiling separate independent traditions, but as building the book around an earlier existing book of saviour judges. If this is the case, then the Deuteronomist's contribution in terms of the so-called schema is not as great as was often thought, and then the addition by the Deuteronomist of traditions which do not fit the schema is more easily imagined. The first argument, although raising some valid questions, is thus not conclusive. The second argument, especially when used apart from the first, cannot be accepted. As we have already shown, it is not possible to simply state that the Deuteronomist was anti-kingship.[104] Approaching the issue from the other side, Timo Veijola has attempted to show that not only was Judges 17-21 part of the Deuteronomistic History, but that it shows signs of Deuteronomistic redaction. First of all he draws attention to the key phrase, "In those days . . ." He suggests that the second part of the phrase needs to be seen as formulaic, and then notes that the only other occurrence of this exact phrase in the OT is in Deut 12:8, right at the heart of the Deuteronomic law of centralization, and in a verse which has been considered a Deuteronomistic addition to the law.[105] The similarity between the phrase and the very common Deuteronomistic evaluative phrase "and did what was right/what was evil in the eyes of the Lord" should not be missed. After having looked at this key phrase, Veijola examines the rest of Judges 17-21 and finds a number of other connections between it and the Deuteron-

---

[104]Two scholars who have explicitly separated Judges 17-21 from the Deuteronomistic History because of the supposed different views of kingship are Hannelis Schulte and Gottfried Seitz.

Hannelis Schulte, *Geschichtsschreibung im Alten Israel,* 103: "Da das Königtum als positive Antwort auf eine negative Zustandsschilderung erwartet wird, kann die Komposition nicht der deuteronomistischen Schule entstammen, die dem Königtum ablehnend oder mindestens zurückhaltend gegnüberstand."

Seitz, *Redaktionsgeschichtliche Studien,* 133: "Wenn er in Ri 17,6; 21,25 als Leitmotive für die Schilderung der "königslosen, der schrecklichen Zeit" erscheint, dann steht dahinter eine hohe Einschätzung des Königtums, so dass der Verfasser dieser Kapitel nicht der Verfasser des dtr Geschichtswerkes sein kann."

[105]Veijola, *Das Königtum,* 16 states that R. Smend has shown this. Note that Minette de Tillesse, "Sections 'tu' et sections 'vous' dans le Deuteronome," p. 39, also considers Deut 12:8 to be a Deuteronomistic addition to the law.

omistic History.[106] He thus concludes that Judges 17-21 was part of the original Deuteronomistic History, and then goes on to use the estimation of kingship found in these chapters as a rule (*Massstab*) for describing his DtrG's view of kingship.

The above discussion has shown that the case for seeing Judges 17-21 as a later addition to the Deuteronomistic History is at best weak, and more probably not valid. Although it would be dangerous to use these chapters as a starting point for getting at the Deuteronomist's view of kingship, as Veijola does, it should be possible to use them as supporting evidence for a position grounded on firmer parts of the history. In light of the commonly held view that these chapters are secondary, we would not emphasize them too much, but it does seem probable and fitting that they were part of the history, and that they do represent the Deuteronomist's view of the time preceding kingship.

The Deuteronomist and the Time of the Judges

Earlier we quoted Soggin where he said "The Deuteronomistic history work, on the other hand, tends to exalt these times and the mode of government then prevailing."[107] This view needs to be contested. It is questionable whether any evidence can be found which would indicate that the Deuteronomist idealized this period of time in any way. The book of Judges, both the main body of the book in chapters 2-12(16), and the so-called appendices in chapters 17-21, suggests rather that the period of the judges was seen as a time of sin, of rebellion and apostasy.

The tone for this period is already revealed in the Deuteronomist's description of the death of Joshua. According to the Deuteronomist the time of Joshua and the conquest was a glorious time, a time when "the people served the Lord." (Judg 2:7). But upon the death of Joshua and those elders who had served with him and had seen what Yahweh had done, this all changed. After this time there arose a generation "who did not know the Lord or the work which he had done for Israel." (Judg 2:10). The period of the judges was thus distinguished from the time of Joshua preceding it in that now the people no longer followed Yahweh. The immediately following verses give a good description of the time as a whole.

---

[106]Veijola, Ibid, pp. 17-27.
[107]Soggin, *Introduction*, 180.

> And the people of Israel did what was evil in the sight of the
> Lord and served the Baals; and they forsook the Lord, the God
> of their fathers, who had brought them out of the land of
> Egypt; they went after other gods. (Judg 2:11-12).

It is true that Yahweh raised judges to save Israel from oppression
during this time, and that these judges are considered very highly in the
book of Judges. There are also suggestions that when some of these judges
"judged" that Israel did follow Yahweh.[108] But the periods of apostasy
certainly receive more attention in the narratives, and dominate the
picture of the time. Whether Weinfeld is correct or not when he states
that for the Deuteronomist Israel did not repent during this time,[109] this
is not the prevailing picture. The judges were Yahweh's instruments during
this period, but they did not succeed in leading Israel in covenant faithfulness.

This has led Veijola to suggest that for the Deuteronomist the judges
were primarily saviours or deliverers (*Retter*),[110] whose function was to
deliver Israel from its enemies. He argues that the fact that both Samson
and Samuel were also forced into this role in order to qualify as such
judges supports this. The judges were thus not expected to become
involved in the internal or cultic affairs of the people, or to lead them in
following the covenant. This would become the responsibility of the kings.
Although this is perhaps an oversimplification, it does draw attention to a
valid point. The judges are pictured as being Yahweh's representatives in
holy war, and in this they are successors of Joshua, but there is no hint of
them fulfilling the role which Joshua played with regard to the covenant.[111] To this extent they are not leaders like Joshua. In terms of the
question of legitimate leadership as we discussed it with regard to Joshua,
Joshua is succeeded by the kings and not by the judges.

This all tends to support the view that Judges 17-21 were part of the
Deuteronomistic History. In them are recorded two incidents which typify

---

[108]See Judg 2:19; 8:33.

[109]Moshe Weinfeld, "The Period of the Conquest," pp. 106-107.
Weinfeld argues that there is a significant difference between the statement that Israel cried to the Lord, and the statement that Israel repented
in that crying to the Lord does not imply repentance. It is questionable
whether this distinction is as clear as he suggests.

[110]Veijola, *Das Königtum*, 29.

[111]Gideon would, at least to some extent, be an exception to this.

this time. Order will only come once Israel has legitimate leadership. The kings at least have the possibility of fulfilling this role.

THE RISE OF KINGSHIP

Preliminary Critical Concerns

We have now arrived at that passage which has stood at the center of all debate on kingship and the Deuteronomistic History. In fact, as was noted above,[112] much of the debate has focussed almost exclusively on this passage. Clearly this is an important part of the History, and deserves careful attention.

The literary analysis of 1 Samuel 8-12 has played an important role in the debate. The starting point in most attempts at getting at the Deuteronomist's view of kingship has usually been to try and determine what part of 1 Samuel 8-12 the Deuteronomist himself wrote. Although it is often admitted that the Deuteronomist may very well have used some sources in his writing of these parts, it has still usually been assumed that these passages would express the Deuteronomist's sentiments most clearly. This procedure was already initiated by Noth in his study of the Deuteronomistic History. Following the analysis of Wellhausen, he proposed that the Deuteronomist had composed 1 Sam 7:2-8:22; 10:17-27; 12 largely on the basis of the material now found in 1 Sam 9:1-10:16; 11 without the use of any other traditions.[113] Noth then found the Deuteronomist's thinking in those passages which he had himself composed. In fact, he argued that the Deuteronomist wrote these parts in order to offset the relatively positive attitude toward kingship reflected in the two traditions which he adopted. In other words, 1 Samuel 8-12 was seen as containing two conflicting attitudes toward kingship, and the Deuteronomist's view was naturally present in those passages which he had himself composed. Noth's conclusions have recently been rejected by quite a number of scholars, but his methodology is still usually followed. Those who claim that the Deuteronomist is not anti-kingship tend to either argue that 7:2-8:22; 10:17-27; 12 are Deuteronomistic but not anti-kingship, or that they are anti-kingship but not Deuteronomistic. Thus Boecker focussed exclusively upon the

---

[112]See above, pp. 26-53.

Also note that because of this correlation, a discussion of the history of research on 1 Samuel 8-12 was presented at that point.

[113]Noth, *ÜgS*, 54-60.

passages which Noth had considered to be Deuteronomistic and tried to show that they were not essentially opposed to kingship.[114] Birch, concluding that the basic form of the story of 1 Samuel 7-15 had been produced by a pre-Deuteronomistic prophetic editor, assigned much less material than most to the Deuteronomist, but he still arrived at his description of the Deuteronomist's view of kingship almost totally on the basis of those verses which he attributed to him. [115] In this way Noth's methodology has remained dominant.

There are, however, two problems with using this methodology in the study of the accounts of the rise of kingship. First of all, there is a practical problem which arises due to the nature of this particular passage of scripture. At the present time there is no hint of consensus among scholars on a literary analysis of 1 Samuel 8-12. Some follow Noth and consider the Deuteronomist to be the author of the so-called anti-kingship series. Others accept the literary division of Noth, but consider this series to be pre-Deuteronomistic and simply adopted by him. Others reject the traditional literary division completely, and make various alternative proposals.[116] The traditional methodology employed thus tends to produce conclusions dependent upon a particular literary analysis, and given the present state of affairs, this means that the conclusions need to be relatively tentative, and even then can only be accepted by those who follow that particular literary analysis.

The second problem is more inherent in the method itself. It was Noth's thesis that the Deuteronomist was an author (*Verfasser*) who produced a history with a particular perspective and message. The Deuteronomist did this through the judicious use and redaction of traditions available to him, through composing his own additions, either speeches or summarizing material, and through organizing this into a purposeful whole. In this process the Deuteronomist no doubt adopted some traditions, rejected others, and adapted still others. In other words, the history as a whole

---

[114]Boecker, *Die Beurteilung der Anfänge des Königtums*.

[115]Birch, *The Rise of the Israelite Monarchy*.

[116]Note some of the proposals made by the following:

Bernhardt, *Königsideologie im AT*, 147-54, proposes that 1 Samuel 8 is not Deuteronomistic, but 1 Samuel 12 is.

Weiser, *Samuel*; and Hertzberg, *I & II Samuel*, 64-134, see 1 Samuel 8-12 as a series of traditions coming from different cultic centers.

Fritz, "I Sam 9-11," suggests that 1 Samuel 8-11 were redacted together before they were incorporated by the Deuteronomist, and that 1 Samuel 12 was then added by him.

should be seen as the production of the Deuteronomist, and not only those passages which he himself obviously composed. In terms of 1 Samuel 8-12 this means that not only the Deuteronomistically composed passages need to be examined to arrive at the Deuteronomist's thinking, but the final product as a whole. Although it is not impossible, it is improbable that Noth's Deuteronomist would have included the traditions of 1 Sam 9:1-10:16; 11 in his history if they sharply disagree with his ideology, and then written 1 Sam 7:2-8:22; 10:17-27; 12 in order to contradict them producing an account with a rather two-sided nature.[117] Rather, it is more probable that the Deuteronomist adopted and adapted his sources, and combined them with his own writing in such a way that the final product reflected his own thinking. This means that not only his own composition can be used for arriving at the Deuteronomist's view, but those parts of the tradition which he incorporated are also important. This also suggests that for the Deuteronomist there was more of a unity in 1 Samuel 8-12 than Noth saw, and than is frequently proposed.

The above is not meant to imply that literary analysis is not extremely important in Old Testament study, or even in research on 1 Samuel 8-12. It is impossible to try to reconstruct the events of the rise of kingship in Israel without doing source analysis and an analysis of the history of traditions. This is also the only way of trying to determine the thinking within Israel at the various stages between the events themselves, and the final text. But our concern is the Deuteronomist, the producer of the final form of the material, and here literary analysis may not be as important as is often thought. In light of the disagreement among scholars on their literary analysis, we can only be thankful for this. We will thus approach 1 Samuel 8-12 as the Deuteronomist's account of the rise of kingship. In producing this account he no doubt made use of various traditions, and it is probable that in 9:1-10:16; 11 he largely adopted extensive sources, whereas in the remainder of the material he contributed somewhat more himself although not without the use of other traditions.[118]

---

[117]At this point Eissfeldt's critique of Noth is valid ("Die Geschichtswerke im AT"). Noth's proposal that the Deuteronomistic History was written by a purposeful author does not fit well with his analysis of 1 Samuel 7-12 as a composition reflecting both anti-and pro-kingship sentiment. Noth's mistake, however, was not in proposing a Deuteronomistic historian, as Eissfeldt argued, but in his analysis of 1 Samuel 7-12.

[118]The method suggested here is already used by McCarthy, "The Inauguration of the Monarchy," and by Mayes, "The Rise of the Israelite Monarchy."

1 Samuel 8-12 and Anti-Kingship Rhetoric

Ever since Wellhausen the tendency has been to say that 1 Sam 7:2-8:22; 10:17-27; 12 are anti-kingship. In fact, frequently source analysis has been done largely on the basis of supposed different attitudes toward kingship in 1 Samuel 8-12. As we have just indicated, however, it is necessary to treat 1 Samuel 8-12 as a whole. Even if the passages picked out by Wellhausen as anti-kingship were truly so disposed, it would still not necessarily be valid to conclude from this that 1 Samuel 8-12 is anti-kingship. Given the fact that 1 Samuel 8-12 includes 9:1-10:16; 11, and that there is no criticism of the positive way in which kingship is treated here in the rest of the narrative, one obviously cannot consider the whole of 1 Samuel 8-12 as anti-kingship.

But even further, it is questionable whether anti-kingship is an accurate description of those passages picked out by Wellhausen. Numerous scholars have already drawn attention to this. In 1 Samuel 8 Yahweh three times tells Samuel to heed the voice of the people and to grant them their request of a king. In 1 Sam 10:17-27 Saul is chosen by lot. In this the passage emphasizes that it is not the people who have selected Saul, but that he has been designated king by Yahweh. This is made explicit by 10:24 where Samuel says: "Do you see him whom the Lord has chosen?" Yahweh has been integrally involved in the selection of the first king, and has himself chosen Saul. In 1 Samuel 12 Saul is twice spoken of as Yahweh's "anointed." This again implies Yahweh's choice and blessing. Then in 12:13 Samuel states: "the Lord has set a king over you." Further, 1 Samuel 12 as a whole may be seen as pointing to a covenant renewal ceremony which was to place the new order under Yahweh's reign. This is enough to show that those parts of 1 Samuel 8-12 which have usually been designated as anti-kingship are not one-sidedly opposed to the institution of kingship. To call them anti-kingship is at best a gross over-simplification, and more probably simply inaccurate.

How is one then to explain those verses within 1 Samuel 8-12 which appear to be anti-kingship? Crüsemann has stated that although there is not nearly as much anti-kingship rhetoric in the OT as is sometimes thought, one must be careful not to weaken or ignore those passages which express such sentiment.[119] Some of these verses are in 1 Samuel 8-12 and need to be recognized as such. Veijola has argued that DtrG composed a history which was very positively inclined towards kingship, but

---

[119]Crüsemann, *Der Widerstand gegen das Königtum*, 1-18.

that at a later point DtrN edited this history and added those verses which express anti-kingship sentiment, and in so doing changed the mood and emphasis of the whole passage.[120] This solution cannot be accepted, however. Crüsemann has argued that there is no indication of any essential opposition to the institution of kingship after the time of Solomon.[121] Before this the conflict over this new institution was very real. The rise of kingship in Israel caused considerable change within Israel, and it is inconceivable that such major upheaval of the status quo could have occurred without opposition or heated debate. Whether or not Crüsemann is correct in his view that such conflict was not present at the time of the origin of kingship itself, but only arose later, he is correct in placing the most serious conflict during the early years of kingship. It is thus much more likely that 1 Samuel 8-12 contains reflections of this early conflict, than that these verses are later additions to an otherwise pro-kingship text as Veijola suggests. Such a conclusion is, if not directly supported, made much more possible by criticisms of those arguments which had formerly been used to argue for a late setting for anti-kingship rhetoric. Cross and others have shown that the concept of the kingship of Yahweh could very well have been early, and so the use of it in 1 Sam 8:7; 12:12 is no proof of a late origin.[122] Further, criticism of kingship from the stance that it would abuse its power, and make slaves of the people, could also have been early, either from pre-kingship or early kingship times.[123] There is thus no good reason to deny an early origin for the anti-kingship sentiment reflected in 1 Samuel 8-12. We must then conclude that these

---

[120]Veijola, *Das Königtum.*

[121]Crüsemann, *Der Widerstand gegen das Königtum.*

Note also the effective arguments of Bernhardt, *Königsideologie im AT,* 116-36, against an exilic origin for anti-kingship rhetoric.

[122]Cross, *Canaanite Myth and Hebrew Epic.*

See also: Georg Fohrer, *History of Israelite Religion* (Nashville: Abingdon, 1972) 166; Buber, *Kingship of God.*

[123]Note I. Mendelsohn, "Samuel's Denunciation of Kingship." Mendelsohn argues that 1 Sam 8:11-17 reflects the Canaanite city states of the last part of the second millennium BC, and thus needs to be placed in that period. It is questionable whether Mendelsohn's thesis can be accepted as presented. As has been noted by others, 1 Sam 8:11-17 could fit most autocratic monarchies. In other words, it cannot be placed historically on the basis of the analogy noted by Mendelsohn. His study confirms, however, that it is not possible to say that it could not have been early. There is no reason why Israel would have had to experience kingship before it could have been aware of possible royal abuses of power.

chapters contain remnants or reflections of the early debate over the new institution of kingship.

It should be noted, however, that *within 1 Samuel 8-12* these verses or remnants are not used to make a case for the rejection of kingship. In 1 Samuel 8-12 there is no larger unit which implies that kingship is totally wrong, or needs to be eliminated. Rather, within 1 Samuel 8-12 it is not the institution of kingship which is evil, but Israel's request for the institution. In their request Israel had demonstrated a total lack of faith in Yahweh's ability to successfully lead them in battle. In this they had rejected Yahweh's kingship over them in the crucial area of defence. They now wanted a king to go out before them in battle whereas this was the responsibility of Yahweh. Thus in 1 Sam 10:19 Yahweh is described as the one who saves Israel from its distresses, and it is this king whom Israel is depicted as rejecting. Arthur E. Cundall says of these verses: "These verses need not be interpreted as indicating that the monarchy was outside the will of Yahweh for Israel. . . . The point is that the attitude of the people in their demand for a king was wrong, it was in spirit a rejection of Yahweh."[124] In the present text remnants of an earlier opposition to kingship have been adapted into an account which is not opposed to kingship itself, but which interprets the original request for kingship as a rejection of Yahweh and so an act of rebellion and sin. In this Israel's request is in keeping with Israel's response to God after the death of Joshua—Israel did not know the Lord or the work he had done (Judg 2:10), and thus did what was evil in the eyes of the Lord. (1 Sam 8:8).

The Function of 1 Samuel 8-12 in the Deuteronomistic History

Since we consider the Deuteronomistic History to be the product of a purposeful historian/theologian it is valid to ask what function 1 Samuel 8-12 play in this whole. It is true that on one level these chapters simply account for the events which resulted in the rise of kingship in Israel, but they certainly have a significance beyond this as well. As McCarthy has shown, this is a carefully constructed whole[125] in which the Deuteronomist gives his explanation of the events. Within the History this explanation of the rise of kingship has two different functions. 1) 1 Samuel 8-12 warns Israel of the dangers of the new institution. Those traditions which had expressed opposition to kingship were especially helpful in communi-

---

[124]Cundall, "Antecedents of the Monarchy," p. 50.
[125]McCarthy, "The Inauguration of the Monarchy."

cating this warning. 2) 1 Samuel 8-12 integrates the institution of kingship theologically into the structure and history of Israel. Israel had not had kingship before this during her formative period. Kingship was an institution of the nations around Israel. This raised the question whether kingship could be integrated with Yahwism, and become part of Israel's covenant-based existence, and if so, how. 1 Samuel 8-12 answers these two questions.

1 Samuel 8-12 Warns of the Dangers of Kingship. As we have stated at a number of points, it is our contention that the Deuteronomist was not opposed to the institution of kingship. This does not imply, however, that he simply accepted or affirmed kingship without realizing its weaknesses or potential pitfalls. As the Deuteronomistic evaluations of the different kings indicate, most kings did not fulfill the position adequately according to the Deuteronomist's standards. One reason for this lay in the very nature of the institution. Before kingship could be adopted in Israel it had to be adapted to fit into Israel's particular relationship with Yahweh. Since the kingship of the Canaanites and other surrounding peoples was somewhat different from this adapted form, there was always the temptation that kingship in Israel would become like that of the other nations. This was a temptation not only for the kings, but also for the people. The Deuteronomist uses these accounts of the origin of kingship to warn the people of the dangers of the new institution.

Hans Jochen Boecker has made a very helpful study in this regard of those passages in 1 Samuel 8-12 which have often been called anti-kingship. Following Noth he considers them to be Deuteronomistic. He then argues that these passages are not anti-kingship, but that they warn Israel of the temptations which kingship would face, and which historically it frequently succumbed to. According to Boecker the Deuteronomist warns Israel of the danger of kingship in two major areas: 1) Its internal policies could become oppressive, 2) It could undermine Israel's understanding of Yahweh as their protector. Mayes summarizes these two as follows: "firstly, that it might itself be a cause of injustice within Israel because of the burdens which it will lay on the people, and, secondly, that the king, rather than Yahweh, will come to be seen as Israel's deliverer in war."[126] Boecker's analysis can largely be accepted, and is the basis of the following.[127]

---

[126]Mayes, "The Rise of the Israelite Monarchy," p. 11.
[127]Boecker, *Die Beurteilung der Anfänge des Königtums.*

First of all, there is the obvious danger that kingship will be a burden upon the people of Israel, and itself perpetrate injustice even though a significant role of the king is to insure justice within Israel. This role of kingship is pointed at in the setting given to the request for kingship. Samuel's sons are described as not following the ways of Samuel and so the people ask for a king to govern them. But the danger is that the king will be no better than Samuel's sons, and very possibly worse.

This theme is especially brought out in chapter 8. 1 Sam 8:11-17 describes a kingship which has fallen prey to this temptation.[128] These "ways of the king" describe how the king will take their sons, their daughters, the produce of their fields, their servants, and the best of their flocks; through the policies of the king the people will lose their freedom and become slaves of the king. But this was what Yahweh had delivered them from in the exodus from Egypt. The danger is that a king could return them to such status even while in the promised land. The key term in the "ways of the king" is the verb "to take" (לקח). When the king governs like the kings of the other nations, he will forget that in Israel all are under the covenant and thus brothers, and that he does not have the right to take anything he pleases.

This danger is again hinted at in chapter 12. In 12:1-5 Samuel claims to be innocent of any wrong-doing during his time as judge. Yahweh and the new king witness to the fact that he is innocent. Nothing can be found in his hand which does not belong there. The natural question which this raises is whether the new king who has just been installed will also act as fairly as Samuel has, or perhaps whether he will follow in the ways of

---

[128]Much has been written about the possible origin of 1 Sam 8:11-17. Boecker (Ibid, pp. 18-19) argues that here the Deuteronomist has adopted a piece of non-Israelite writing since at no point in Israel's history was the situation as bad as depicted by the "ways of the king." Mendelsohn ("Samuel's Denunciation of Kingship"), followed by various scholars, (e.g. Weiser, *Samuel*) sees here an early Israelite criticism of kingship.

We would conclude that Mendelsohn has shown that these verses could be early, but not that they need to have been early. Further, Boecker's view that they could not be Israelite because the situation never was so bad in Israel cannot be accepted. Indications are that under Solomon at least the North lost much of her freedom, and it is very possible that these verses reflect criticism of the extremes of Solomon's reign. The Deuteronomist has thus probably made use of an early tradition attacking the excesses of kingship as a means to warn Israel of this danger. (cf. Crüsemann, *Der Widerstand gegen das Königtum*.)

Samuel's sons. Again the focus is on internal issues. It is predicted that kings will be tempted to abuse the power which their position naturally has, and oppress the people.

The assumption behind this warning is that the king, although the supreme leader of Israel, is still subject to the covenant and its law, and in this respect on equal footing with all other Israelites. That the king also needs to follow the law is brought out clearly in 12:14. As we earlier noted, this is also central to the law of the king of Deuteronomy 17. There the king was told to study the law so that he would obey it. The same point was made by emphasizing that the king was to be a brother (i.e. not a foreigner who was outside of Israel's law). The specific prohibitions given in the law of the kingship also fit well with the warning given in 1 Samuel 8-12. The view of kingship reflected in the Deuteronomist's warning of possible abuses in the area of internal policies is thus totally consistent with the law of kingship of Deuteronomy, and the picture of the role and responsibilities of the king derived from 2 Kings 18-23.

Second, the Deuteronomist warns that the king, and Israel, will be tempted to see the king as replacing Yahweh as Israel's protector and ultimate defender. In fact, Israel has already fallen prey to this temptation in its request for the king. The Deuteronomist's condemnation of the way in which Israel asked for the king is a warning to Israel not to allow this to happen again. This comes through over and over again within 1 Samuel 8-12.

In 1 Sam 8:7 Israel's request is interpreted as a rejection of Yahweh. The assumption behind this is that either Yahweh is and remains king, or a man steps into his place. This cannot be a rejection of all leaders so one must ask in what way kingship could mean a rejection of Yahweh. Here the above analysis of Judg 8:22-23 is helpful. It is Yahweh who saves and delivers Israel, and human kingship displaces Yahweh when Yahweh is no longer seen as being responsible for Israel's defence. That this is what Israel was doing in their request is confirmed by 1 Sam 8:20. Israel has asked for a king who will "go out before us and fight our battles." But this is the very language used of Yahweh in his role as the defender of Israel. Judg 4:14 and 2 Sam 5:24 speak of Yahweh going out before the people in battle, and in the important chapter 23 of Joshua, it is affirmed twice that it is Yahweh who has fought on behalf of Israel (vv 3, 10; cf. Josh 10:14, 42). But now Israel wants a king to lead them in battle, and to do their fighting for them. This point is again made in 1 Sam 10:19 where Samuel says "But you have this day rejected your God, who saves you from all your calamities and distresses." The saving acts of God are emphasized in the previous verse: "I brought up Israel out of Egypt, and I delivered you from the hand of the Egyptians and from the hand of all the kingdoms that were oppressing you." The אֱלֹהֵי of v 18 draws the attention to Yahweh, the God of Israel who has delivered them. The focus thus is on the subject of the action more than on the action itself. Chapter 11 then provides a model for how Yahweh delivers Israel. This message is made clear by v 13: "for today the Lord has wrought deliverance in Israel." And finally in 12:12 this is brought together once more. Israel asked for a king to save them from the Ammonites when Yahweh was king, i.e. Yahweh was the one they should have looked to to save them from this threat.

The whole account of the rise of kingship is thus permeated by the view that Israel's request for a king was a rejection of Yahweh in his role as Israel's defender. 1 Samuel 8-12 does not, however, reject kingship on this basis. Rather, 1 Samuel 8-12 affirms that kingship was instituted by Yahweh, and the first king was chosen by Yahweh. "Kingship is in no way 'fundamentally' rejected; it goes back to an explicit act (*Setzung*) of Yahweh, and from that it receives its religious dignity."[129] (Translation mine). In this way the Deuteronomist affirms kingship, but warns that kingship in Israel cannot be allowed to replace Yahweh in this crucial area. As we learned from our study of 2 Kings 18-20 and the account of King Hezekiah, the king's responsibility in this area was to trust Yahweh to deliver.

1 Samuel 8-12 Integrates Kingship with Israelite Theology. It has frequently been noted that for approximately two centuries a kind of Israel existed without kingship. Israel was very aware of the fact that it had not had kingship from the beginning, and that this was not the only possible form of government for her. This fact was especially important since the origin of Israelite law and most of her national institutions was traced back to this pre-kingship period. In other words, Israel's basic constitution did not assume the existence of kingship. Kingship was thus not seen as a necessary aspect of Israelite existence but a form of rule which Israel only adopted after some time without it. No doubt this change in structure was accompanied by considerable debate, conflict, and change. In light of this background, kingship could not simply be assumed, but had to be justified and supported. Kingship had to be adapted to Israel's self understanding before it could be accepted.

The fact that Israel's original request for kingship was interpreted as a rejection of Yahweh and so an act of rebellion also made it important that

---

[129]Boecker, *Die Beurteilung der Anfänge des Königtums, 35.*

kingship be consciously integrated into Israelite theology, and her understanding of her relationship with God. According to Israelite tradition
Yahweh had been Israel's king before the time of kingship, and this kingship of Yahweh was seen by at least some to exclude the possibility of
human kingship. The story of Gideon and his refusal of the offer of kingship makes it clear that kingship could not simply be adopted without
rethinking the theology, at least in the tradition. The rise of kingship,
grounded in Israel's sinful request but instituted by Yahweh, posed a
theological problem which required resolution. A very significant function
of 1 Samuel 8-12, especially of chapter 12, was to do this very thing.

Dennis J. McCarthy has made a literary analysis of 1 Samuel 8-12 in
which he proposes that the Deuteronomist has accomplished this through
the skillful combining of sources and his own writing.[130] 1 Samuel 8-12 is
not only about kingship, but about kingship as a problem. It is truly history
writing in that it attempts to give a new message and interpretation of
the evidence. McCarthy accepts the traditional division of 1 Samuel 8-12
into five literary units. He has noted that these five units alternate
between report and story. Throughout there is also an alternation between
passages which question the validity of the new institution, and passages
which affirm it. In this way the Deuteronomist has made his case for
kingship, and its incorporation into the thought and structure of Israel.
This now needs to be examined a little more closely.

The problem of kingship is first posed in 1 Samuel 8. This first scene
"focuses attention on the request for a king as an evil because it is a
rejection of the divinely ordained institution of the judgeship represented
by Samuel."[131] The practical burdens of kingship are emphasized in the
"ways of the king." The question or problem has now been raised, and
1 Samuel 9-12 then resolves it while continually reminding us of the problem. Weiser had earlier already argued that these four chapters show how
Samuel succeeded in starting a kingship which had its own unique Israelite
stamp.[132] The major difference between Weiser and McCarthy at this
point is that whereas Weiser sees this resolution as the historical contribution of Samuel, McCarthy sees this as the literary contribution of the
Deuteronomist.[133]

---

[130]McCarthy, "The Inauguration of the Monarchy."

[131]Ibid, p. 403.

[132]Weiser, *Samuel*, 44.

[133]Mayes, "The Rise of the Israelite Monarchy," essentially agrees with
McCarthy on this.
Volkmar Fritz ("I Sam 9-11,") sees 1 Samuel 9-11 as composed of three

The report of chapter 8 is followed by the well-told story of how Saul
went out to search for the lost asses and found a kingdom. In this story
Saul, the future king, is introduced to us in a manner which is bound to
make the readers like him. In this story Yahweh says that Saul "shall save
my people from the hand of the Philistines; for I have seen the affliction[134] of my people, because their cry has come to me." The similarity
between this verse and Exod 3:7 where Yahweh calls Moses to deliver his
people from Egypt cannot be missed. Yahweh's people are in need and
have cried to him for help. This verse raises hope that Yahweh will again
act on behalf of his people by choosing an agent to deliver them. An
attitude of openness and anticipation is aroused; what will God do now?
Clearly, a closed attitude toward the possibility of kingship is now not
possible. The story concludes with the account of Samuel anointing Saul to
be this special agent who will reign over the people of the Lord and save
them from the enemies round about.[135] As is proposed by a number of

---

accounts redacted together before the time of the Deuteronomist which
legitimize the kingship of Saul. Chapter 12 is then the Deuteronomist's
contribution. This is also fairly close to McCarthy, at least in terms of the
present role of 1 Samuel 9-12, even if not in terms of their literary
history.

[134]The Masoretic Text does not include the term "affliction" (עֳנִי). The
reading is based on the Septuagint, which is accepted by most commentators. Note Hans Joachim Stoebe, *Das erste Buch Samuelis*, KAT, Bd.8, T.1
(Gütersloh: Gütersloher Verlagshaus Gerd Mohn, 1973) 196—"Mit G
ταπεινωσιν (T?) wird allgemein und mit Recht עֳנִי ergänzt."

[135]A number of scholars have made much of the fact that this account
does not speak of Saul being anointed as king, but as "prince" (נָגִיד). It has
been suggested that נָגִיד is a term derived from pre-kingship days, and
originally meant commander of the militia of the tribal league. It is then
suggested that 9:1-10:16 do not really speak of Yahweh choosing Saul to
be king but that it can only be used in support of Saul as a tribal military
commander, or at least that the term sets a limitation on the kingship of
Saul. Note Cross, *Canaanite Myth and Hebrew Epic*, 220; W. F. Albright,
Samuel and the Beginnings of the Prophetic Movement, The Goldenson
Lecture for 1961 (Cincinnati: Hebrew Union College, 1961) 15-16; W.
Richter, "Die *nāgīd*-Formel," *BZ* 9 (1965); 71-84; and others.
It is questionable whether this emphasis can be accepted, however. A
number of scholars have recently argued that originally the term נָגִיד
probably meant "heir-apparent to the throne" or "crown prince." Originally the term thus probably had no religious connotations, and simply
applied to that person who would become king. 1 Kgs 1:35, rather than
being an exception to the rule, is probably the earliest example of the

scholars, an early tradition about Saul has been reworked on the basis of
the structure of the prophetic call narrative to affirm that through
Samuel Yahweh chose Saul to be his special agent.[136]

The tension is still not resolved, however, as becomes clear in the
report found in 10:17-27. In vv 17-19 the problems of kingship, and the
sinful nature of Israel's request are again emphasized. Yahweh has always
been Israel's deliverer in the past, and this Israel has failed to recognize.
Still, the narrative continues by describing how Saul is chosen by lot to be
king of Israel.[137] That the method used implies that it is Yahweh who
does the choosing is stated in v 24: "Do you see him whom the Lord has
chosen?" The "ways of the kingdom" in v 25 reminds us both "of the ways
of the king" in 8:11-17 with its negative connotations, and the institution
of a new order with the king having a specified place in it as is assumed
by chapter 12. The report then concludes with a question which again
raises the issue of what value the king can have for Israel—"How can this
man save us?" The question reminds us of Yahweh's statement in 9:16 and
points ahead to the story of chapter 11.

1 Samuel 11 then answers the question of 10:27. As McCarthy says:

> And then comes a story where Saul acts the inspired hero. In

---

term in the OT. Later, however, the term was theologized and came to
mean that person who had been chosen to be king by Yahweh. T. C. G.
Thornton, "Charismatic Kingship"; E. Lipinski, *"NAGID*, der Kronprinz,"
VT 24 (1974) 497-99; Mettinger, *King and Messiah*, 151-84.

[136]Birch, *The Rise of the Israelite Monarchy*, 29-42; Wolfgang Richter,
*Die sogenannten vorprophetischen Berufungsberichte. Eine literatur-
wissenschaftliche Studie zu I Sam 9,1-10,16, Ex 3f. und Ri 6,11b-17*,
FRLANT, Hft. 101 (Göttingen: Vandenhoeck & Ruprecht, 1970) 13-56;
Ludwig Schmidt, *Menschlicher Erfolg und Jahwes Initiative. Studien zu
Tradition, Interpretation und Historie in Überlieferungen von Gideon, Saul
und David*, WMANT, Bd 38 (Neukirchen: Neukirchener, 1970) 58-102;
Mettinger, *King and Messiah*, 64-79.

[137]It has been argued that 1 Sam 10:20-24 contains two traditions, one
about Saul being elected by lot, and the other about Saul being chosen
through an oracle which proclaimed him king who stood a head above all
the rest, or that the Deuteronomist has added the version of the lot to the
earlier tradition of the oracle. This may be correct literarily. In the
present text, however, the message is meant to focus on the lot and
Yahweh's choice of Saul by this method. Note Mettinger, *King and Messiah*, 179-84; and Boecker, *Die Beurteilung der Anfänge des Königtums*,
44-50 for a discussion of the issue.

chapter 8 kingship was condemned precisely because it went against the tradition of the judge-deliverer who represented Yahweh the savior. Now the chosen king is revealed as just such a deliverer. The use of the language of the judgeship to refer to the problem of the king is seen to have special significance. The Saul cycle had shown him as a hero-deliverer. Hence he could be presented as a king *not* like those of the nations (cf. 8:20). The condemnation of chapter 8 has been met on its own terms and reversed, and this has been done by retaining the favorable picture of Saul from the old cycle and giving it more force by the contrast with the negative chapters. The people can convene and confirm Saul's kingship with rejoicing.[138]

Saul can save when he allows the spirit of God to act through him (11:6). As 11:13 affirms, ultimately it is God who has wrought deliverance. Here the Deuteronomist's view comes out clearly even if most of chapter 11 was adopted from tradition and not composed by him. Kingship can be incorporated into Israel's structure and faith if it continues to allow Yahweh to be ultimately responsible for Israel's protection.

1 Samuel 12 then completes the Deuteronomistic account of the rise of kingship, and initiates the new era in Israel's history. This chapter needs to be treated as one of the key Deuteronomistic chapters in the whole history inserted at important turning points. It has already been shown that it is possible for the king to be Yahweh's agent of deliverance as Moses, Joshua and the judges had been. The matter of the people's faithless request still needs to be taken care of, however. 1 Sam 12:12 thus returns to the request of chapter 8. V 13 then emphasizes that Yahweh has taken over and acted. The king which the people had sinfully requested has now been set over Israel by Yahweh himself. Vv 14-15 now give the conditions of the new order. Both the king and the people need to fear Yahweh and serve him; they need to hearken to his voice and not rebel against his commandments.[139] It has been suggested that chapter 12 is meant to describe a covenant renewal ceremony which had been made necessary by Israel's sinful request, and which now initiates the new era of kingship.[140] This may very well be so. In any case, chapter 12 concludes

---

[138]McCarthy, "The Inauguration of the Monarchy," pp. 411-12.

[139]Note the discussion of Boecker, *Die Beurteilung der Anfänge des Königtums,* 77-82, on the translation of the difficult v 14.

[140]Dennis J. McCarthy, *Treaty and Covenant. A Study in Form in the Ancient Oriental Documents and in the Old Testament,* AnBib, no. 21A

with the problem of kingship resolved, at least theoretically. Kingship has been incorporated and integrated into Israel's relationship and covenant with Yahweh. After chapter 12 kingship itself is no longer a problem, but only whether the kings themselves will fulfill their expected role, both in terms of the law, and in terms of their responsibility to trust Yahweh for the defence of the nation.

> The fundamental thing threatened by Israel's action was the covenant relationship, and this is the formal restoration of that relationship with the king now explicitly included in it.
>
> . . . A crisis has been described and resolved in narrative terms and in theological, and a new era can begin.[141] Dennis J. McCarthy

> The demand for a king was fulfilled by Yahweh which made kinghip into a new historical act of Yahweh. In this way kingship is pulled into a sequence with the other great historical acts of Yahweh, the gift of the land, the election of Jerusalem.[142] (Translation mine). Hans Jochen Boecker.

The Rejection of Saul, 1 Samuel 13-15

The kingship which was established in 1 Samuel 8-12 very quickly comes under question. Saul is disobedient to Yahweh. Saul, who had so explicitly and repeatedly been shown to have been elected by Yahweh, is now rejected from his new position. Does this mean that kingship itself was a mistake and a step in the wrong direction? Can this failure and rejection of Saul be used to argue that the Deuteronomist was opposed to

---

(Rome: Biblical Institute, 1978) 206-242; Baltzer, *Covenant Formulary*, 66-68; James Muilenburg, "The Form and Structure of the Covenantal Formulations," *VT* 9 (1959) 347-65; Weiser, *Samuel*, 47-94; J. Robert Vannoy, *Covenant Renewal at Gilgal. A Study of I Samuel 11:14-12:25* (Cherry Hill, NJ: Mack, 1978).

Note also Vannoy's interesting proposal that the term "kingdom" in 1 Sam 11:14 does not refer to the kingdom of Saul as is usually assumed, but to the kingdom of Yahweh. The phrase is thus interpreted as not referring to the installation of Saul as king in 11:15, but to the covenant renewal ceremony described in 1 Samuel 12.

[141]McCarthy, "The Inauguration of the Monarchy," p. 412.

[142]Boecker, *Die Beurteilung der Anfänge des Königtums*, 77.

kingship? The Deuteronomist's account of these events needs to be examined more closely in order to determine this.

1 Samuel 13-14 needs to be treated as a separate unit apart from what precedes it and what follows it. 1 Samuel 8-12 records how kingship arose in Israel, and how Saul became the first king. The new era of kingship was formally begun by chapter 12. 1 Sam 13:1 is then the typical Deuteronomistic introduction to the reign of a king, and begins the description of the reign of Saul as king after the problem of kingship has been resolved. After chapter 15, Saul is not again the center of the story as our focus shifts to the battle for the throne between Saul and David. This creates the distinct unit of 1 Samuel 13-15.[143]

The role which these three chapters play in the History can be described as twofold. First of all, they play a narrative function. These chapters describe the rejection of Saul and his descendents from the throne of Israel thus preparing the way for the rise of David. The history of David's rise assumes that Saul has been rejected by Yahweh. Regardless of the nature or intention of the traditions used by the Deuteronomist in the production of these chapters, in the present form and location they explain why Saul, whom Yahweh had expressly chosen to be the first king, was rejected from this position. These chapters give the necessary background for the accounts following it. This is most clear in chapter 16 where vv 1-13 record how David was anointed to be king, and v 14 which states "Now the Spirit of the Lord departed from Saul." Both of these need chapters 13-15 as a background. The primary function of these chapters is thus the narrative one of leading the story from the account of the rise of kingship and the installation of Saul to the story of the anointing of David and the ensuing battle for the throne.

The above is in no way a sufficient explanation of these chapters, however. In them the Deuteronomist develops and emphasizes his understanding of the form which kingship should take in Israel. In this they continue some of the themes of 1 Samuel 8-12. Whereas in 1 Samuel 8-12 the Deuteronomist warned against some of the dangers of kingship through speech, here this warning is expressed in example. Saul was rejected from his position due to his disobedience of the commandment of

---

[143]Describing 1 Samuel 13-15 as a "unit" does not imply anything in terms of its literary history. It also does not speak to the question of whether 1 Samuel 13:7b-15a and 1 Samuel 15 originally were based on the same incident. For a discussion of these issues check the appropriate commentaries.

the Lord (13:13; 15:24). This was a vivid warning to future kings. Clearly a king, even though king, still had to obey Yahweh's commandments. This point had been made in the law of kingship, had been pointed at in the account of the rise of kingship, and now had been demonstrated in the life of the first king. On one level 1 Samuel 13-15 thus emphasizes that in Israel the king was to be under the covenant. Disobedience could lead to rejection.

But more can be ascertained from these chapters than the simple statement that in Israel the king was to be obedient to the covenant. An examination of the nature of Saul's disobedience, and Samuel's response to it can give us further information on the way the Deuteronomist looked at kingship. It has often been suggested that Saul's disobedience in chapter 13 was that he offered a sacrifice when he did not have the right to do this. His offence was taking a priestly role upon himself as a king did not have the right to offer sacrifice. This position cannot be accepted. The mere fact of a king offering a sacrifice would not have been a problem for the Deuteronomist, for whom the king was ultimately responsible for the cult,[144] nor for the people of the time of Saul when it would have been natural for the king as the leader of the people to offer sacrifice just as the patriarchal leaders had.[145] As Birch says, "It is not simply that Saul offered sacrifice, but that he proceeded with those sacral observances which precede the entry into battle without the presence of Samuel. We submit that these sacral acts are related to the holy war and the circles in which this tradition was preserved regarded the presence of the prophet as necessary."[146] The issue was then not simply a cultic one, but one related to the institution or ideology of holy war.

This ties the disobedience of chapter 13 to the incident in chapter 15 where the offence is more clearly the transgression of the holy war ritual of חֵרֶם, commanded by Samuel in 15:3.[147] Samuel had commanded Saul to

---

[144]As has been noticed by other scholars, the Deuteronomist has no problem with David and Solomon offering sacrifices, and Hezekiah and Josiah are clearly commended for interfering with the cult whereas other kings are condemned for not doing so.

A different problem for the Deuteronomist in these chapters would have been that the sacrifice was not offered in Jerusalem.

[145]Note Aelred Cody, *A History of Old Testament Priesthood*, AnBib, no. 35 (Rome: Pontifical Biblical Institute, 1969) 12, 98-107.

[146]Birch, *The Rise of the Israelite Monarchy*, 84.

[147]Birch, Ibid, pp. 74-108, argues that the punishment of chapter 13 is distinctly different from that of chapter 15. Whereas in chapter 13 Saul is

utterly destroy the Amalakites in keeping with the ritual of חֵרֶם. But Saul had failed to do this, and as a result Samuel was commanded by Yahweh to bring an announcement of judgment to Saul: Yahweh had rejected Saul from being king over Israel. In both chapters the central issue is then the king's obedience of Yahweh's word as communicated to him by the prophet Samuel. Saul had to learn through negative experience that although he had been appointed king, Yahweh was still responsible for the defence of the nation, and the king could not take affairs into his own hands. In Israel the king was expected to obey Yahweh in all areas, but this was especially important here since this was where the temptation was the greatest for the king to usurp Yahweh's position. In war and in defence of his people, Yahweh was king, and the human king was subservient to him.[148]

In defining the role of the king in this way these chapters also help to define the role of the prophet over against the king. To this extent it is possible to consider these chapters an apology for the prophet. In Israel the history of prophets largely coincides with the history of kingship. Historically it is probably correct to say that 1 Samuel 8-15 not only record the rise of kingship but also the rise of prophecy. In 1 Samuel 13-15 Samuel is very much portrayed as a typical prophet, at least as he appears in the Deuteronomistic History.[149] Right at the start of this history the role of the prophet over against the king is brought out. It is the prophet who communicates the word of Yahweh to the king. This would be valid in most areas, but is especially important in the field of holy war, and in the pronouncement of judgment. This is a role which the prophet fulfills throughout the rest of the history.

The account of Saul's disobedience and the resulting rejection in no way suggests that kingship itself needs to be rejected, or that the Deuterono-

---

simply told that he will not be allowed to establish a dynasty, in chapter 15 he is told that his kingship itself has been rejected. This may be so. For our purposes, however, this is not as important as the fact that in both cases Saul is condemned for not following Yahweh's command for holy war.

[148]Is this an example of the Deuteronomist using an incident to make his point by interpreting it in an especially harsh way since it is right at the beginning of the time of kingship? A parallel might be enforcing a new law especially strictly right at the beginning to make the point that it cannot be taken lightly.

[149]This is in contrast to 1 Samuel 8-12 where he appears to be seen primarily as the last judge, although prophetic characteristics already begin to show.

mist is opposed to the new institution. After all, the rejection of Saul does not lead to an Israel without a king but to an Israel with a king who fulfills his proper function. The narrative in 1 Samuel 13-15 thus performs the important function of being a bridge between 1 Samuel 8-12 and 1 Samuel 16ff, and also provides the Deuteronomist with the opportunity to emphasize some key elements of his understanding of the role of the king in this new era.

This emphasis is in keeping with the understanding of kingship reflected by 2 Kings 18-23. The king must obey the law. Both ideal kings, Hezekiah and Josiah are described as having done this. The king's responsibility in the area of defence is to trust Yahweh, and to follow his commands as communicated to him by the prophet. Hezekiah did this. Josiah also heeded the words of the prophet. This was how a king should act.

KING DAVID IN THE DEUTERONOMISTIC HISTORY

Preliminary Critical Concerns

When the Deuteronomistic History is examined from the perspective of proportion, it immediately becomes clear that a disproportionate amount of the history deals with David. A total of 40 chapters (1 Samuel 16 - 1 Kings 1) have David as the center of attention whereas the whole history from David to the end of the two kingdoms is dealt with in only 46 chapters. David receives more coverage than any other king, and almost as much as all other kings together. Literarily the David stories are right at the center of the history. It could be argued that this is also the case thematically. The history opens with the promise of the land, and this is only fulfilled completely during the reign of David. The remainder of the history then records the loss of the land. From this vantage point the history reaches its climax in David. This heavy emphasis on David in the history requires some examination and explanation.

The way David is treated in the history, and the amount of material on him can be explained in different ways. It is possible to say that this is due to the nature of the Deuteronomist's sources, and the prevailing thought within Judah. The Deuteronomist's sources on David were simply much more extensive than those on the other kings. Special note should be made of the survival of the two major documents on the time of David, the history of David's rise to the throne, and the succession narrative. In addition to these two major documents many other traditions about David had managed to survive till the time of the Deuteronomist. Thus on the one hand the Deuteronomist had the extensive sources on David. On the other hand, the esteem in which David was held in Judah made it virtually necessary that the Deuteronomist include this literature in the history. There is also truth in this. Historically David had been the king who had defeated the Philistines as well as other enemies of Israel, and made Israel a major kingdom. Further, David had clearly been a very charismatic figure about whom traditions naturally arose. He had also founded a dynasty which lasted about 400 years. David was thus the king par excellence. People awaited another king like David who would succeed in restoring the Davidic kingdom.[150] Exilic and later messianic thought built on the ideal picture of David which had developed within Judah. It is then possible that the extensive nature of the sources on David, and the image of David prevalent at the time of the Deuteronomist's writing gave the Deuteronomist little choice but to make David the center of his history.

If the above explanation were sufficient reason to explain the attention given David in the history, then it would be possible to say that the Deuteronomist might have had a somewhat different view of David than is expressed in the history, but that circumstances dictated the treatment of David in the history. This is the option that must be chosen by those who argue that the Deuteronomist himself was opposed to the institution of kingship. How else could one explain a history which was supposedly antikingship, but which focussed so extensively upon King David who had been anointed by Yahweh, who was used by Yahweh to fulfill his promise of the land, and who later became the model for hopes in Yahweh's future acts on behalf of Israel? The value of this explanation is that it does point to certain significant features of the David accounts—obviously the Deuteronomist's sources on David were extensive, and probably somewhat different in kind than his other sources, and clearly David had become a hero beyond history by the time of the Deuteronomist. But it is questionable whether this is a sufficient explanation.

A number of scholars have argued that not only do the David sources and traditions form a major part of the Deuteronomistic History, but that they are also at the heart of the Deuteronomist's thinking. According to von Rad the key force for the Deuteronomist was the word of the Lord. This word was expressed as law in the Mosaic covenant, and as promise in the Davidic covenant. "Thus the Deuteronomist sees the main problem of the history of Israel as lying in the question of the correct correlation of

---

[150]For a discussion of Biblical evidence for the hope of the restoration of the Davidic kingdom see J. Mauchline, "Implicit Signs of a Persistent Belief in the Davidic Empire," *VT* 20 (1970) 287-303.

Moses and David."[151] The destructive force of the law had been fulfilled in the punishment of 587 B.C., but the salvation promised in the Davidic covenant still lay ahead. Von Rad considered 2 Kgs 25:17ff as a sign that Yahweh could still resume his salvation history through the house of David. David, as the receiver of the Nathan oracle, is thus seen as standing at the center of the Deuteronomist's theology. Cross also sees the promise to David as one of the major two themes running through the history. He argues that the Deuteronomist has adopted the ideology of the Judaean royal cult, and that the fate of Judah was with the Davidic dynasty.[152] Perhaps even more significantly, McCarthy has argued that structurally the important 2 Samuel 7 with its record of the Nathan oracle is at the center and climax of the history.[153] If these scholars are correct, and we believe they are, then the David narratives need to be examined to see if they support our thesis so far, or if they conflict with it.

The Davidic Covenant[154]

   The Prophecy of Nathan, 2 Samuel 7. Just as the David stories are at the center of the whole Deuteronomistic History, so the account of Nathan's prophecy to David is at the center of the David stories, both literarily and thematically. The history of David's rise which precedes 2 Samuel 7 reaches its climax in this important chapter with David securely on the throne and in a state of rest from the enemies round about. The succession narrative which follows it then deals with the question of who will succeed David on the throne. This is clearly an important chapter within the David stories.

---

[151]Von Rad, *OTT,* I:339.

[152]Cross, *Canaanite Myth and Hebrew Epic,* 278-85.

[153]McCarthy, "II Samuel 7."

[154]The phrase "Davidic Covenant" is used in this dissertation because it seems to best describe that complex of ideas centered around the promise of II Samuel 7 even though it is not used within the Deuteronomistic History. In fact, the term "covenant" is really not used at all in the History of the Davidic promise. The two possible exceptions to this might be 1 Sam 23:5 and 1 Kgs 8:23. In 1 Sam 23:5 the term "covenant" is clearly meant to refer to the Davidic promise, but it is usually argued that 1 Samuel 21-24 are appendices to the History. 1 Kings 8:23 was part of the History, but it is questionable whether the term "covenant" here is meant to refer to the Davidic promise. More probably the reference here is to the Mosaic covenant, or perhaps to the patriarchal covenant.

The significance of 2 Samuel 7 and the prophecy of Nathan goes much beyond the David stories, however. Probably no chapter in the whole Deuteronomistic History has produced more debate and literature. It is not possible nor necessary to review all of this research within the confines of this present work.[155] Here we will simply point at some of the major issues under dispute.

Ever since Rost's work on the succession narrative with its analysis of 2 Samuel 7 a major concern of scholars has been to determine the different layers of composition in the chapter.[156] The majority of scholars have concluded that 2 Samuel 7 is not a literary unity, and so the task was to discover the different traditions in the chapter, where the remnants of the earliest tradition could be found, and what contributions the redactors had made. According to Rost vv 11b and 16 were the kernel of the original tradition of the promise to David. Discussion of the role of the Deuteronomist in the production of the final form has also been part of this. Some have argued against such analyses that the text was an original literary unity based on analogy with the Egyptian *Königsnovelle*.[157] Such literary questions have then been the object of one type of discussion.

A second issue arising from 2 Samuel 7 and related passages concerns the history of the promise related. Was the promise originally conditional or unconditional? Does the promise really go back to the time of David? What was the role of the Deuteronomist in formulating the promise as it is now found in Israel's literature? Were there originally two oracles, one focussing on the building of the temple, and the other on David's dynasty? These are some of the questions that are debated here, and so far there is little consensus on their answers.[158]

It is not our task to deal with the above questions. Rather, we will

---

[155]Note the reviews of research in the following works: Mettinger, *King and Messiah*, 48-50; Cross, *Canaanite Myth and Hebrew Epic*, 141-49; Veijola, *Die Ewige Dynastie*, 68-72; Manfred Görg, *Gott-König-Reden in Israel und Ägypten*, BWANT, Hft. 105 (Stuttgart: W. Kohlhammer, 1975) 178-82.

[156]Leonhard Rost, *Die Überlieferung von der Thronnachfolge Davids*, BWANT, Hft. 42 (Stuttgart: W. Kohlhammer, 1926) 47-74.

[157]Siegfried Herrmann, "Die Königsnovelle in Ägypten und in Israel," *Wissenschaftliche Zeitschrift der Karl Marx Universität* 3 (1953-54) 51-62. Cf. Görg, *Gott-König-Reden in Israel und Ägypten*.

[158]These issues are discussed very well by Cross (*Canaanite Myth and Hebrew Epic*, 229-65) and Mettinger (*King and Messiah*, 48-63, 275-93), although with conflicting conclusions.

examine the account of Nathan's prophecy as it is presently recorded, and disregard its past history. In this we are not implying any answers to the above issues, nor suggesting that they are not important. We are simply assuming that 2 Samuel 7 was part of the Deuteronomistic History, and that it made sense within the History.[159] Regardless of whether the Deuteronomist here inserted a tradition largely as he had received it, or whether he played a major role in producing the chapter, there is reason to believe that within the whole history it functioned as one of the key Deuteronomistic passages inserted in the history at important turning points.[160]

Now we must take a brief look at the content of 2 Samuel 7. A key verse in the thought of this passage is v 5: "Thus says the Lord: Would you build me a house to dwell in?" Various proposals have been made as to what this question really implied. Was the issue here who would build the temple? Or whether a temple should be built at all for Yahweh? Or was the issue here one of who was to take the initiative to build such a temple for Yahweh? Or was the question stating that Yahweh does not *dwell* in a temple? Cross is probably correct when he argues that originally this question, together with vv 6-7, permanently prohibited building a temple for Yahweh who moves about in a tent.[161] As Cross admits, however, the Deuteronomist did not interpret vv 5-7 as a permanent prohibition, but merely as a temporary one. This is confirmed by the later verses in the chapter, by verses such as 1 Kgs 5:3-5, as well as by the positive emphasis on the temple throughout the remainder of the history. Thus an earlier opposition to the building of the temple for Yahweh has been transformed into one which denies this for David.[162]

---

[159]Although there is considerable disagreement on an analysis of 2 Samuel 7, it has never been seriously questioned that it was part of the original Deuteronomistic History.

[160]Note: McCarthy, "II Samuel 7."

We thus agree with Noth on how the Deuteronomist operated, but disagree with him on his analysis of 2 Samuel 7. Noth argued that the Deuteronomist added vv 13a and 22-24 to 2 Samuel 7, but that otherwise the chapter was not that significant for the Deuteronomist since "weder die Ablehnung des Tempelbaus noch die starke Betonung der positiven Bedeutung der Institution des Königtums im Sinne von Dtr sind." (*ÜgS,* 64).

[161]Cross, *Canaanite Myth and Hebrew Epic,* 242-46. Cross also argues that different interpretations of v 5 are false attempts at harmonization.

[162]Note the work of Sigmund Mowinckel ("Natanforjettelsen 2 Sam. kap. 7," *Svensk Exegetsk Arsbok* 12 [1947] 220-29) who argued that the

In the present text the question in v 5 is answered in v 11 and 13. This is the case regardless of whether v 13a is a Deuteronomistic addition to the text, and v 5 was originally connected to v 11, or whether v 5 originally pointed ahead to v 13 and was later added to the tradition of the dynasty. The first answer to the question emphasizes that David need not build a house for Yahweh, but Yahweh will build a house for David. Much of the remainder of the passage focusses on this theme. Here is then perhaps the most significant formulation of the promise to David of a steadfast house, or of an everlasting dynasty.[163] Yahweh here promises that he will not remove his חֶסֶד from the house of David as he did from Saul. David, as a typical king of that time, had wanted to build a temple for his god. Yahweh's response had been that this should not be done, but that Yahweh would make his house and kingdom sure for ever—"your throne shall be established for ever."

The second answer to the question in v 5 is found in v 13. Here it is stated that not David shall build the house for Yahweh, but his offspring who shall come forth from his body—"He shall build a house for my name." Within the History this is an obvious reference to Solomon. This verse could be interpreted both as a justification for Solomon's building the temple, and as a sign legitimating his rise to the throne (the one who builds the temple is the God-chosen successor to David). The two major themes of the passage are bound together by the term "house." In terms of the History these are the two major passages of the prophecy.

Two further features of the passage require some attention at this point. V 14 is the only place within the Deuteronomistic History where the relationship between the king and Yahweh is spoken of in terms of sonship. Here Yahweh is quoted as saying "I will be his father, and he shall be my son." This is most probably language directly quoted from the official Judaean cult, and was perhaps used as part of the coronation ceremony of

---

original purpose of the text was to explain why David did not build the temple.

[163]The three major accounts of the Nathan prophecy are found in 2 Sam 7:1-17; 1 Chr 17:1-15; and Ps 89:19-37. One issue of debate has been the literary relationship of these three. The tendency has been to give preference to 2 Samuel 7, but note John L. McKenzie, "The Dynastic Oracle: 2 Samuel 7," *TS* 8 (1947) 187-218; and H. van den Busshe, "Le Texte de la Prophetie de Nathan sur Dynastie Davidique," *Ephemerides Theologicae Lovanienses* 24 (1948) 354-94.

Two other significant references to the promise are found in 2 Sam 23:1-7 and Ps 132:11-12.

a new king.[164] This line reflects the ancient Near Eastern background of the institution of kingship in Israel. Although such language had divine kingship implications in its original setting, it is usually recognized that it did not have this meaning within the Deuteronomistic History. Further, it is also probable that it did not have such connotations within the Israelite cult, at least during the time of the Deuteronomist. Either the language had been adapted to Israelite thought before it was adopted, or this process occurred within Israel's cult. This is indicated by the fact that the Deuteronomist apparently had no problems using the phrase in his history even though it clearly was not his favorite imagery for the king. This phrase thus points to the cultural background of Judah's royal cult, and it indicates the willingness of the Deuteronomist to use such official language even though it differed from his own.

The second interesting feature is found in vv 14b-15. These verses have usually been taken to emphasize the unconditional nature of the prophecy made to David by Nathan. Regardless of what David's descendents do, Yahweh will not remove his steadfast love from them. The promise is eternal and unconditional. Although they may point in that direction, it is striking that a passage so clearly grounded in the royal cults of that time would emphasize that Yahweh will punish the king for disobeying the law. This must be seen as at least qualifying the promise if not making it conditional. These verses point out that kings are not to use the Davidic promise as a justification for any style of behavior.

The Davidic Promise in the Remainder of the Deuteronomistic History. In order to describe how the Deuteronomist understood the promise to David we must examine how the promise enters the story at other points in the history. First we need to look at the narratives immediately surrounding the important 2 Samuel 7. Mettinger has argued that the majority of 2 Samuel 7 was composed by the author of the history of David's rise, and that it forms the conclusion and climax of this account.[165] Even

---

[164]For a discussion of this sonship language see the following: Mettinger, *King and Messiah,* 259-68; Gerald Cooke, "The Israelite King as Son of God," *ZAW* 73 (1961) 202-25.

[165]Mettinger, *King and Messiah,* 33-63.

The significant works on the history of David's rise include: Jakob H. Grønbaek, *Die Geschichte vom Aufstieg Davids* (1 Samuel 15-2 Samuel 5) *Tradition und Komposition,* Acta Theologica Danica, Vol. 10 (Copenhagen: Protestant Apud Munksgaard, 1971); J. Conrad, "Zum geschichtlichen Hintergrund der Darstellung von David's Aufstieg," *TLZ* 97 (1972) 321-32;

if one does not accept Mettinger's conclusion on the authorship of 2 Samuel 7, there is justification for speaking of the chapter as the climax of the account. Those passages in the history of David's rise which look forward to a lasting kingship for David probably anticipate the prophecy. One example of this occurs in the speech of Abigail to David where she says: "for the Lord will certainly make my lord a sure house." (2 Sam 25:8). Similarly the succession narrative builds on the prophecy. In fact, Rost and others have considered 2 Samuel 7 to be part of the beginning of the succession narrative.[166] The narratives about Solomon following the succession narrative continue in this vein, and in 1 Kings 8 the building of the temple is seen in direct fulfillment of the prophecy of Nathan. As McCarthy has said: "The promise, therefore, provides the literary framework for the account of the events which followed it. It is at once the climax of the narrative which precedes it and the program for what follows; in a word, it is central to its immediate context."[167] This shows that 2 Samuel 7 was not merely a tradition which the Deuteronomist included in his history, but it became an important structural block in the production of the history.

The importance of the promise to David for the Deuteronomist is confirmed by further references or hints to it later in the History, especially in passages where the Deuteronomist is considered to have had a more significant role in the composition. It is most helpful to divide these references into three categories. First, there are those passages which simply mention the fact that David had received this promise. An example of this is 1 Kgs 2:45 where Solomon says: "But King Solomon shall be blessed, and the throne of David shall be established for ever." Other passages mention the second theme in the prophecy which spoke to the issue of the building of the temple (e.g. 1 Kgs 5:5; 8:19). These references may not be that helpful in determining exactly how the Deuteronomist understood the promise, but they bring out that he was very conscious of

---

R. Rendtorff, "Beobachtungen zur altisraelitischen Geschichtsschreibung anhand der Geschichte vom Aufstieg Davids," in *Probleme biblischer Theologie* (München: Chr. Kaiser, 1971) 428-39; Artur Weiser, "Die Legitimation des Königs David. Zur Eigenart und Entstehung der sogen. Geschichte von Davids Aufstieg," *VT* 16 (1966) 325-354.

[166]Rost, *Die Überlieferung von der Thronnachfolge Davids.*

A good examination of past research on the succession narrative can be found in D. M. Gunn, *The Story of King David. Genre and Interpretation,* JSOTSup, no. 6 (Sheffield: The University of Sheffield, 1978) 19-33.

[167]McCarthy, "II Samuel 7," p. 134.

the contents of 2 Samuel 7 as he produced the remainder of the history.[168]

The second category of references to the Davidic promise is much more significant. A number of passages speak of Yahweh acting generously for the "sake of David my servant," or, so "that David my servant may always have a *nîr*[169] before me in Jerusalem." Such statements are found at four different points in history. First, this idea is found five times within 1 Kings 11 (vv 12, 13, 32, 34 and 36). Because of David, Solomon's punishment will be delayed till after his death, and because of David, not all of the kingdom will be lost to the Davidic dynasty. In 1 Kgs 15:4-5 it is stated that because of David the dynasty was allowed to remain on the throne despite the sins of Abijam. Then in 2 Kgs 8:19 this saving power of David has extended beyond his dynasty to the people of Judah.[170] It is stated that "for the sake of David" Yahweh did not destroy Judah. Finally, in the Hezekiah narratives it is twice stated that Yahweh will save Jerusalem for his own sake and for the sake of David his servant (2 Kgs 19:34; 20:6). Although these verses do not directly quote from the Davidic promise, they can only be explained within the History in light of the promise. According to the Deuteronomist this promise to David was an operative force within the history of Judah. This confirms the views of von Rad[171] and Cross[172] who emphasized the role of the Davidic promise for the Deuteronomist. The promise given to David in 2 Samuel 7 is effective for the Davidic dynasty, and for all of Judah despite the sins of individual kings.

The third category consists of those passages where references to the

---

[168]Other examples of this category would be: 1 Kgs 2:33; 8:15,24,26, (66?); 11:38; 2 Kgs 21:7.

[169]Three of these passages contain the Hebrew term נִיר. As a rule it has been translated "lamp" and taken as parallel to נֵר. Note, however, the interesting and rather convincing study by Paul Hanson ("The Song of Heshbon and David's NÎR," HTR 61 [1968] 297-320) in which he argues that it needs to be distinguished from נֵר, and be translated "dominion."

[170]Abijam and Jehoram were the first two kings of Judah who received totally negative evaluations from the Deuteronomist. In each case it is then stated that this did not cause the end because of David. The Deuteronomist's logic has thus been explained, and this reason no longer needs to be given at later negative evaluations.

Note also that here the significance of David and the king for the salvation of the people is considered to be important.

[171]von Rad, OTT, II:339-47.

[172]Cross, Canaanite Myth and Hebrew Epic, 281-85.

promise are associated with some statement about obedience to the law. In 1 Kgs 3:6 and 15:4-5 it is stated that Yahweh acted as he did toward David because David "did what was right in the eyes of the Lord, and did not turn aside from anything he commanded him." A similar idea is implied by 1 Kgs 11:38 where Jeroboam is told that if he hearkens to Yahweh's commands as David did, Yahweh will build him a sure house as he did for David. In other words, the Deuteronomist assumed that David had received the promise *because* of his faithfulness.

More important for the discussion, and more controversial, are those passages which make the promise itself contingent upon obedience to the law. An example of this is found in 1 Kgs 9:4-5.

> And as for you, if you will walk before me, as David your father walked, with integrity of heart and uprightness, doing according to all that I have commanded you, and keeping my statutes and my ordinances, then I will establish your royal throne over Israel for ever, as I promised David your father, saying, 'There shall never fail you a man upon the throne of Israel.'

Similar statements are made at 1 Kgs 2:3-4 and 8:25.[173] Ever since Rost the tendency within OT scholarship has been to say that in these passages the Deuteronomist conditionalized the unconditional promise which was part of the official Judaean ideology, and which is found in 2 Samuel 7.[174] Those passages outside of the Deuteronomistic History which speak of a conditional promise to David are then seen as having been influenced by the Deuteronomistic change.[175] In fact, some have considered this conversion of an unconditional promise to a conditional one to be one of his major theological points. Cross is one of the few who has argued against

---

[173] 1 Kgs 6:12 also speaks of the promise conditionally, but there the focus of attention appears to be on the building of the temple, the second theme of 2 Samuel 7.

[174] Rost, *Die Überlieferung von der Thronnachfolge Davids*, 89-90.

Some others who have held this position are: Martin Noth, *Könige I*, BKAT, Bd. 9, T.1 (Neukirchen-Vluyn: Neukirchener, 1968) 30; Wolff, "Kerygma"; Nicholson, *Deuteronomy and Tradition*, 109-112; Mettinger, *King and Messiah*, 275-83.

[175] The best example of this is Psalm 132. Mettinger, *King and Messiah*, thus dates this psalm post-Deuteronomistic since it reflects Deuteronomistic influence.

this position.[176] Cross argues that although the promise was originally seen as conditional, it became unconditional within the Judaean royal ideology, and the Deuteronomist accepted this official view without adapting it. This position is defended by stating that the Deuteronomist's view is found in 2 Samuel 7, and those passages which conditionalize this promise are the contribution of the later exilic redactor of the history. Unfortunately he gives no literary or other support for this contention. Thus he sees the conditionalization of the promise in 1 Kgs 2:3-4; 8:25; and 9:4-5 to be exilic, but the conditional form found in Psalm 132 to be early. More recently Nelson has made the interesting proposal that the so-called conditionalization passages cannot be connected with the promise in 2 Samuel 7 but refer to a different promise to David which applied only to Solomon and which was conditional.[177]

Cross's solution of eliminating these passages from the work of the Deuteronomist almost appears to be a case of eliminating those passages which do not agree with one's theory.[178] Since we are attempting to determine the Deuteronomist's view of the promise, we should begin by trying to incorporate them into a total view. To do this all references to the promise, as well as the History as a whole must be kept in view. The second category of references to the promise indicated that the Deuteronomist truly did consider the promise to be a saving force for the Davidic dynasty and for Judah. It is thus clearly not possible to say that the Deuteronomist conditionalized the promise if by this is meant that the Deuteronomist believed that disobedience eliminated the validity of the promise. On the other hand, it is questionable whether the Deuteronomist considered the promise to be eternally unconditional. The passages just referred to as well as the tenor of the whole History make such a position very unlikely. It appears to us that the opposition of conditional versus unconditional is not the most helpful way to understand the Davidic promise in the Deuteronomistic History.

The way to get at the Deuteronomist's understanding of the Davidic promise is to see it in light of his understanding of the Mosaic covenant. Within the Deuteronomistic History the Davidic promise does not replace the covenant between Yahweh and Israel.[179] "Rather, for the D writer,

---

[176]Cross, *Canaanite Myth and Hebrew Epic*, 229-87.

[177]Nelson, "Redactional Duality."

[178]Note also that Nelson (Ibid) argues that these passages were part of the original history.

[179]It is also probable that it did not replace the Mosaic covenant within the Judaean cult as much as is often suggested. The fact that the

the Davidic covenant continues and specifies the older one. David's covenant does not compete with the people's covenant as an independent, parallel means to Yahweh's grace; rather, through David the whole people receives the divine favor."[180] There is both an unconditional as well as conditional aspect in this earlier covenant. The history begins with an emphasis on the promise of the land. This promise is both unconditional in that Israel's sin in the wilderness does not cancel the promise, and conditional in that continued rebellion against Yahweh may result in the loss of the land. Logic would suggest that the Davidic promise, seen within the larger relationship between Yahweh and Israel, would need to share some of this paradoxical nature, and could not be totally without condition.[181]

This now needs to be summarized. For the Deuteronomist the prophecy of Nathan to David was an important operative force within the history of Judah, bringing salvation to the Davidic dynasty and to Judah where otherwise death and destruction might have been expected. This promise had this force even though it was not totally unconditional, and continued rebellion could result in punishment which might include the temporary loss of the throne. Just as the Mosaic covenant was permanent, however, the Davidic covenant was permanent.[182] The way in which the promise is described in 2 Samuel 7 and the way in which it is pictured in the remainder of the history are not contradictory but complementary.[183] Although the Deuteronomist probably did his work before 587 B.C., both the loss of the throne at that time, and the rise of later messianic expectations would have fit with his emphasis on the Davidic promise.

---

reading of Deuteronomy had the effect that it did during the time of Josiah suggests that some aspects of it must have remained present.

[180]McCarthy, "II Samuel 7," p. 136.

[181]As has been said, if kingship is an organ within Israel, and if Israel's continued existence is conditional, kingship cannot be unconditional.

[182]Tsevat has argued that an "everlasting" covenant need not necessarily be unconditional; Matitiahu Tsevat, "The Steadfast House: What was David Promised in II Sam. 7:11b-16?" *HUCA* 34 (1963) 71-82.

[183]We earlier already drew attention to the fact that 2 Sam 7:14b-15 to some extent qualify the promise of v 11. Notice also that Mettinger (*King and Messiah*, 284-86), points to a number of terms in 2 Samuel 7 which he associates with contractural covenants, which would also warn against a too unconditional reading of the chapter.

King David and the Deuteronomist's View of Kingship

Throughout the OT there are indications that David was a great king. Kingship had a rocky start in Israel with Saul, but it was firmly put on its feet by David. Much has been made of David's shrewdness in making neutral Jerusalem the political capital of all Israel, and then bringing the ark there thus combining the political center of power with the older religious traditions. David's significance for the cult is probably reflected by his image as the father of psalmody. Perhaps most important for the history of Israel, David was a great military leader who first defeated the Philistines thereby eliminating the major threat to Israel's existence, and then continued by building a large kingdom making Israel a major power of the time. His dynasty succeeded in reigning from the throne in Jerusalem for more than 400 years, a rather significant feat especially when compared with the tenure of dynasties in surrounding nations. It is not surprising that throughout its history Israel hoped for a return to the days of glory of the Davidic kingdom, and awaited the rise of a new David.

This great stature of David is accurately reflected in the Deuteronomistic History. The mass of material devoted to David in the History is one indication of the significance of David for the Deuteronomist. It is also noteworthy that in 2 Samuel 7 Yahweh addresses David as "my servant," a phrase which the Deuteronomist uses many more times when speaking of David. This title emphasizes the close relationship envisioned between David and Yahweh, and points to a comparison between David and Moses, the only other figure in the whole History who is spoken of in exactly this way. David, the founder of a new era in the history of Israel is thus compared favorably with Moses, the founder of Israel's faith. More evidence could be found but this is enough to indicate the high esteem in which the Deuteronomist held David.

When the way in which the Deuteronomist built up David is examined, however, some interesting features arise. As was stated above, historically David was the great military leader who made Israel a powerful nation of the time, and there is sufficient evidence in the OT that this image of David remained strong in Israel and was an important reason for the people's hopes that a new David would arise who could restore the glory of the past. Surprisingly, there is not much emphasis in the Deuteronomistic History on this contribution of David. Although David is mentioned quite frequently in the History after his death, his role as a military leader and builder of a large kingdom is ignored. When the narratives on David are examined, a similar down-playing of this aspect is discernible. This comes out especially clearly in those narratives right at the center of the David stories connected with the prophecy of Nathan.[184] The first task of David after becoming king of all Israel was to eliminate the Philistine threat. Before going into battle David inquires of the Lord whether he should go into the battle. Yahweh answers: "Go up; for I will certainly give the Philistines into your hand." (2 Sam 5:19). When the battle is about to begin Yahweh gives instructions as to exactly how David is to fight, and then concludes with "for then the Lord has gone out before you to smite the army of the Philistines." (2 Sam 5:24). The holy war language in the passage cannot be missed. The contrast between this passage and 1 Sam 8:20 is also striking. Israel had asked for a king who would "go out before us and fight our battles." But such a kingship would have been a rejection of Yahweh's role as defender of Israel. David is depicted as recognizing this and allowing Yahweh his proper role in battle, and so he is a model for later kings. The battle to free Israel from the Philistine threat is Yahweh's battle and not David's.

A similar picture is found in the important 2 Samuel 7. The chapter opens with the statement "and the Lord had given him rest from all his enemies found about." (cf. v 11). As has been noted by others, the term "rest" (הֵנִיחַ) is virtually a technical term in the Deuteronomistic History "for Yahweh's ultimate blessing on Israel: rest from enemies in the promised land."[185] Although David was the king of Israel when it is pictured as finally receiving this rest, David is not depicted as achieving this rest for Israel, but rather Yahweh gives it to David and to Israel.[186] Again we see this important Deuteronomistic emphasis—it is Yahweh who gives Israel the land, and it is Yahweh who protects Israel from her enemies while on the land, thus giving her her rest. Of course Yahweh uses human agents in granting this protection. But the king, as this agent of Yahweh, fulfills a function similar to that of earlier leaders of Israel such as Moses, Joshua and the judges. The emphasis is not on their own military success, but on how Yahweh delivers through them. Thus Yahweh could use David, not because he was a great military leader, but because he was faithful. In this way a good king can be an agent by which the people are blessed.

---

[184]Is this perhaps due to the fact that this is between the history of David's rise and the succession narrative, and the Deuteronomist was more involved in the writing of these chapters?

[185]McCarthy, "II Samuel 7," p. 132.

[186]It is also significant to note that Israel does not receive this rest until the rise of kingship and the reign of the first king who did what was right in the eyes of the Lord. For the Deuteronomist the time of the judges was not ideal time, but the time of kingship.

Notice the emphasis on the people of Israel in the midst of the Nathan prophecy (v 10).

If the Deuteronomist did not emphasize David's military contribution, how then did he view King David? The way in which David is mentioned and treated in the history of Israel after his death is a good indication. When those passages which simply mention David historically, or speak of the city of David, are eliminated, the remaining passages can be divided into three groups: 1) those passages which focus on David as the recipient of the divine promise, (including both those passages which simply mention this fact, and those which stress the later saving power of David for a later time); 2) those passages which use David as a model of someone who did what was right in the eyes of the Lord, and obeyed his commandments; 3) those passages which associate the promise of a dynasty with obedience to the law.

The first group was treated adequately earlier in the discussion of the Davidic promise. For the Deuteronomist David was the king who had received a promise which remained an effective force in Israel's history.

The second group of references to David has frequently been noted. Many of the Deuteronomist's evaluations of the kings include a comparison with David. For the Deuteronomist a king was expected to obey the law.

Although we have already examined those passages which connect the Davidic promise with obedience to the law in trying to determine if the promise was conditional, some of these third category passages require some further attention. As we noted above, according to the Deuteronomist David had received the promise of a dynasty *because* he had obeyed the law (1 Kgs 3:6; 11:38; 15:4-5). Given this fact, it is striking that there is no reference to this in 2 Samuel 7. This suggests that we need to look at the context of the prophecy more closely. In 2 Samuel 6 we have the account of David bringing the ark, the central religious symbol of Israel (at least within the present story), to Jerusalem, and establishing the ark at the political center of the land. 2 Samuel 7 begins with David requesting permission to build a home for the ark. In other words, in both chapter 6 and chapter 7 David is acting as the one responsible for the cult of Israel, and in both chapters the cult is symbolized by the ark. More specifically, in this role as protector of the cult he is depicted as active in moving the cult towards centralization in Jerusalem. Although David was not allowed to build the temple as he had hoped, it is important for the Deuteronomist that he had intended to build it. Since the centralization of the cult was so important for the Deuteronomist, these acts of David would have been significant for him. In fact, we would suggest that when the Deuteronomist states at other points that David received the promise because he had obeyed the law, he is considering the acts of David in 2 Samuel 6 and 7 a central part of that obedience. It is thus not coincidental that the important 2 Samuel 7 follows the account of David bringing the ark to Jerusalem. 2 Samuel 6 provides the basis for 2 Samuel 7. David had been faithful to the law as king by making centralization of the cult possible by bringing the ark to Jerusalem, and by intending to build a temple which would have furthered this direction even more. The emphasis on David in Solomon's speech at the dedication of the temple[187] shows that this was an important part of the Deuteronomist's picture of David. The Chronicler's view of David as the initiator of the cult is already foreshadowed in the Deuteronomistic History.

We can now conclude this unit on David within the Deuteronomistic History. For the Deuteronomist King David was clearly the greatest king in all Israel's history. David gave kingship a new start after the problematic beginning of Saul, and he became the example or norm for all future kings. The way in which David became this norm, however, was considerably affected if not determined by the Deuteronomist's view of the role of the king. David is thus highlighted as a model of a king obedient to the law, but the emphasis is not on personal obedience but on his acts as the one responsible for the law and cult. David's moves towards centralization were a central aspect of this obedience. Further, David is pictured as allowing Yahweh to remain Israel's defender. In this he has shown that it is possible to be a successful king without succumbing to the temptation of trying to replace Yahweh at this point. Because of his faithfulness David received the promise of an eternal dynasty. In David already the Mosaic law and the Davidic promise are combined. The Deuteronomist considers both to be effective within Israel; it is up to the king to follow and guarantee the Mosaic law, and, as the recipient of the Davidic promise, to be a sign and medium of God's grace.

I AND II KINGS

Much of the significant material in 1 and 2 Kings has already been dealt with in our examination of 2 Kings 18-23, and in the discussion of the Davidic covenant. In the following we want to look at a few further passages in 1 and 2 Kings which reflect the Deuteronomist's understanding of kingship.

---

[187]Note especially 1 Kgs 8:15-21.

The Deuteronomist and King Solomon

Although the history of David's rise had gone to great lengths to show that David's accession to the throne was a valid succession of Saul, the succession from David to Solomon was the first case of a "normal" succession within the kingship of Israel.[188] A change in kings is always a crisis, and this would have been the case even more so in Israel at this time when patterns of succession would still not have been developed. Very probably the Deuteronomist saw the method of determining a successor employed here (i.e. the reigning king appointing who among his sons was to succeed him upon his death) as the best one for ensuring the continued role of the king in the affairs of Israel.

Most interesting then is David's charge to Solomon just before his death.

> When David's time to die drew near, he charged Solomon his son, saying, "I am about to go the way of all the earth. Be strong, and show yourself a man, and keep the charge of the Lord your God, walking in his ways and keeping his statutes, his commandments, his ordinances, and his testimonies, as it is written in the law of Moses, that you may prosper in all that you do and wherever you turn; that the Lord may establish his word which he spoke concerning me, saying, 'If your sons take heed to their way, to walk before me in faithfulness with all their heart and with all their soul, there shall not fail you a man on the throne of Israel. (1 Kgs 2:1-4)

Noth and many others have emphasized the Deuteronomistic nature of the charge found in this passage.[189] The exhortation given here was thus no doubt meant to apply to all kings as they came to the throne, and not only to Solomon. Porter has argued that the charge given here is not a free composition, but came from actual existing practice. He has noted that somewhat similar installation formulae were used at the formal induction into various offices in Israel, but only in the case of a royal installation

---

[188]David succeeding Saul was clearly not a typical change of kings. Ishbosheth succeeding Saul was possibly a typical dynastic succession, but it does not really become part of the Deuteronomistic History.

[189]Noth, *Könige I*, 30; cf. Würthwein, *Das Erste Buch der Könige, 1-16*, 20.

was there the emphasis on keeping the law of Moses.[190] The charge itself reminds us of Deut 17:14-20 and Josh 1:7-9. The law of kingship commands the king to write for himself a copy of the law, to read it, and then to keep it. Joshua is given a similar charge at his installation as leader of Israel.[191] Like Solomon, Joshua is given a word of encouragement, and is then exhorted to keep the law in order that he may be prosperous and successful as leader. The necessity for Israel's leader to follow the law is thus emphasized in the law of kingship, as well as in the charge to Joshua and to Solomon. This emphasis naturally will have included the idea that it is important for the king (or leader) as an Israelite to be faithful to the law, but it is questionable whether this is a sufficient explanation for the emphasis. The fact that this stress on the law was apparently present only in the installation of the king, or the leader of Israel, suggests that there is a more formal connection between the law and the position itself. Thus Joshua is described as leading Israel in a ceremony of commitment to the covenant (Josh 8:30-35), and is shown active in calling on the people to follow the covenant (Joshua 23). Similar expectations are now placed on Solomon, since the law of kingship and the model of Joshua must be remembered when the charge to Solomon is read. The king has important public responsibilities to fulfill, and a king is judged on whether or not he fulfills them. It is up to the king to ensure justice and righteousness in the land, and in so doing bring blessing to the nation. Thus the queen of Sheba says to Solomon: "Blessed be the Lord your God, who has delighted in you and set you on the throne of Israel! Because the Lord loved Israel for ever, he has made you king, that you may execute justice and righteousness." (1 Kgs 10:9). Yahweh's love for Israel has been expressed in that he made Solomon king. If Solomon now follows the law as king, and fulfills his royal responsibilities with regard to the law, then "there shall never fail you a man on the throne of Israel," for only then will there continue to be an Israel on the promised land.

Understanding the charge to Solomon in 1 Kgs 2:1-4 as calling on Solomon to fulfill his leadership responsibility with law also helps to understand a different strange feature of the Deuteronomist's account of Solomon. There is fairly extensive agreement among scholars on the kind of kingship Solomon exercised.[192] It was Solomon who was king when

---

[190]Porter, "The Succession of Joshua," 110-118.

[191]This reflects the fact that Joshua was seen as a type for kingship within the Deuteronomistic History.

[192]J. Alberto Soggin, "Der offiziel geförderte Synkretismus;" Soggin,

Israel's kingship most closely resembled that of the surrounding nations. During his time the cult became quite syncretistic as more and more foreign elements were adopted. Solomon developed harsh policies which forced the people to provide for his extensive court, as well as his major building projects. It is usually agreed that it was Solomon's internal policies which were largely responsible for the division of the kingdom which occurred after his death. Thus it has even been suggested that the "ways of the king" of 1 Sam 8:11-17 was originally an example of anti-Solomonic polemic. Although most of these conclusions are based on the Deuteronomist's account of the reign of Solomon, they do not agree with the Deuteronomist's view of him.

For the Deuteronomist Solomon was a very significant king, if not one of the greatest. This view comes through at various points. The account of Solomon's birth had earlier already indicated that Yahweh loved Solomon (2 Sam 12:24). The narrative of Solomon's vision and request for wisdom is certainly meant to reflect positively on him. Solomon's wise decision in the case of the two harlots makes him a model as a judge. Sheba's statement quoted above basically agrees with the Deuteronomist's evaluation. Thus it is said in 1 Kgs 3:3—"Solomon loved the Lord, walking in the statutes of David his father."

When the reason for the Deuteronomist's positive picture of Solomon is sought, it is not too hard to find. When Solomon came to the throne, Israel still offered sacrifice wherever it chose. After affirming that Solomon loved Yahweh, and did what was right, the Deuteronomist continues with "only, he sacrificed and burned incense at the high places." Solomon's important contribution was that he built the temple, allowing for the centralization of worship which according to the Deuteronomist was so important in following the covenant. At the center of the account of Solomon is the detailed account of this building project, climaxing with Solomon's lengthy speech and prayer given at the dedication of the temple. Despite the fact that David had not been allowed to build the temple, he is commended for having had the idea in his heart (1 Kgs 8:18). Solomon had built the temple fulfilling the prophecy of 2 Sam 7:13.[193] For the Deuteronomist the temple was of central importance. Jerusalem was the city which Yahweh had chosen, and the temple was the place

---

Das Königtum in Israel, 77-89; Cross, *Canaanite Myth and Hebrew Epic,* 237-41; Crüsemann, *Der Widerstand gegen das Königtum.*

[193]Note that 1 Kgs 8:20 specifically mentions the fulfillment of the two major themes of 2 Samuel 7.

Yahweh would put his name. By building the temple Solomon had made possible obedience to the law of Deuteronomy 12. In this Solomon had made a very significant contribution toward covenant obedience in Israel, and had thus acted as a king should act, in keeping with the charge given him at his installation. In building the temple Solomon is depicted as faithfully fulfilling his responsibility as protector of the cult, and continuing in the model provided by David.

The Deuteronomist's picture of Solomon changes quite strikingly in 1 Kings 11, however. Here the Deuteronomist expresses a strong indictment of Solomon. Solomon has married foreign women who have succeeded in turning his heart after other gods. It is even stated that Solomon built high places for these rival deities. Solomon had clearly violated the Deuteronomic command for exclusive worship of Yahweh. Such an act would have been wrong for any Israelite, but it had more serious implications when a king became involved in this, since in doing this Solomon was not only disobeying the law himself, but also leading Israel in such rebellion. 1 Kings 11 thus records how Solomon failed as leader of Israel, as the one who was responsible for ensuring obedience to the law, and by virtue of this protector of the cult.

Both the high and the low in the Deuteronomist's description of the reign of Solomon are explainable within the Deuteronomist's view of kingship. The charge to the king to obey the law implied that the king was to lead Israel in such obedience. In building the temple Solomon fulfilled this responsibility, and furthered covenant faithfulness in Israel. But in turning to other gods, Solomon failed to lead as a king should, and is appropriately indicted by the Deuteronomist.

The Sin of Jeroboam, and the End of the North

As is well known, the kings of the North are consistently given negative evaluations in the Deuteronomistic History.[194] The typical evaluation had the following structure: 1) X did what was evil in the eyes of the Lord, 2) he continued in the sin of Jeroboam, 3) which he made Israel to sin, 4) he did not depart from it.[195] The validity of the Deuteronomist's

---

[194]The one king who receives a somewhat conditional negative evaluation is the last king of the North, King Hoshea, 2 Kings 17:2.

[195]Jörg DeBus, *Die Sünde Jeroboams. Studien zur Darstellung Jeroboams und der Geschichte des Nordreichs in der deuteronomistischen Geschichtsschreibung,* FRLANT, Hft. 93 (Göttingen: Vandenhoeck & Ruprecht, 1967) 93.

evaluations has often been questioned. It has been suggested that his evaluations of the kings of the North were based totally on religious considerations, and ignored political or economic considerations, or it has been argued that they were simply very biased.[196] A modern historian would probably agree with these criticisms of the Deuteronomist. After all, how could Omri be dismissed with just a few verses? Such accusations are somewhat simplistic, however. The Deuteronomist's evaluations of the kings of the North, as well as his analysis of why the North succumbed to Assyria make sense given his understanding of the relationship between Yahweh and Israel, and the role of kings within this relationship.

In 2 Kgs 17:7-23 the Deuteronomist gives his explanation for why the North had to go into exile.[197] "And this was so, because the people of Israel had sinned against the Lord their God, who had brought them up out of the land of Egypt . . ." (v 7). Yahweh had warned them to turn from their disobedience, but they "despised his statutes, and his covenant that he had made with their fathers." (v 15). Yahweh punished the North and sent her into exile because the people of the North had not obeyed Yahweh's covenant law. The specific accusations within the passage reflect the Deuteronomist's emphasis on cultic purity, and total loyalty to Yahweh requiring cultic centralization. The North had not obeyed this Deuteronomic law. Since Israel's remaining on the land was dependent upon her obedience to the covenant law as expressed in Deuteronomy, this continued disobedience resulted in the loss of the land.

In vv 21-23 the Deuteronomist summarizes his analysis. Here, however, the emphasis is on Jeroboam the king who is mentioned three times. It has been suggested that these verses reflect a different understanding of the end of the North, and came from a different redactor.[198] This is not a necessary conclusion. V 22 still states: "The people of Israel walked in all the sins which Jeroboam did; they did not depart from them." The reason

---

[196] An example of this is found in the article: C. F. Whitley, "The Deuteronomic Presentation of the House of Omri," *VT* 2 (1952) 137-52.

[197] Many different literary analyses of these verses have been proposed. See the appropriate commentaries. Noth, (*ÜgS*, 6) considers 2 Kgs 17:7ff. to be one of the key Deuteronomistic passages. With Cross (*Canaanite Myth and Hebrew Epic*), however, we would consider only v 19 as secondary, or coming from the later Deuteronomistic redactor.

[198] The following consider vv 21-23 to come from a different editor than vv 7-18: J. Robinson, *Second Kings,* 157; Montgomery, *Kings,* 470. Montgomery mentions Stade, Benzinger, Sanda, Eissfeldt and Burney as others who hold this position.

given for the loss of the land is still that the people did not obey the Deuteronomic law of centralization, and worshipped at the cultic centers established by Jeroboam. The difference is that here the role of the king in this is pointed at. It was Jeroboam the king who "drove Israel from following the Lord and made them commit great sin." (v 21). For the Deuteronomist the king was responsible for guaranteeing covenant law with its emphasis on the centralization and purity of the cult. This Jeroboam had failed to do. In fact, he had caused Israel to sin by establishing the cultic centers at Bethel and Dan. The extremely significant role which the Deuteronomist attributed to the king is reflected here. As king, as the leader of Yahweh's people, and thus successor to Moses and Joshua, he was to lead the people in covenant obedience so that the people would be allowed to remain on the promised land. Jeroboam and all his successors had failed in this, and were thus ultimately responsible for the sin of the North, and then its demise.[199]

Once this is realized, then it becomes clear that the narratives about Jeroboam, and the evaluations of the kings of the North all fit into this pattern. In the Deuteronomistic History the division of Israel is considered to be punishment of the house of David for the sin of Solomon. Jeroboam is then chosen by Yahweh to be king of the ten northern tribes. No criticism of Jeroboam enters the narrative until it is recorded that he built the worship centers at Bethel and Dan, and made houses on the high places. Although Jeroboam had been chosen for his position by Yahweh, he had rejected the Deuteronomic law.[200] The emphasis on total obedience

---

[199]The so-called myth and ritual school has emphasized the importance of the king for the well being of the community. According to Hooke, "The ritual pattern represents the things which were done to and by the king in order to secure prosperity of the community in every sense for the coming year." (S. H. Hooke, "The Myth and Ritual Pattern," p. 8). It would be our contention that for the Deuteronomist the king was extremely important for the well being of the community, but not in the way Hooke proposed. The king did not guarantee the security of Israel through participation in the cult, but through fulfilling his role as the one responsible for covenant law, and thus the cult.

[200]DeBus (*Die Sünde Jerobeams*) has argued that the portrayal of Jeroboam in the Deuteronomistic History as the one ultimately responsible for the end of the North by his setting up of the sanctuaries at Bethel and Dan is a product of the Deuteronomist. This was his way of accounting for the destruction of that kingdom. If he is correct, our analysis would only be strengthened.

Note also: Ina Plein, "Erwägungen zur Überlieferung von I Reg 11, 26-14,20," *ZAW* 78 (1966) 8-24.

to the word of the Lord in 1 Kings 13, and the consequences of disobedience, suggest the final fate of Jeroboam.[201] This is then specified in
1 Kgs 14:16—"And he will give Israel up because of the sins of Jeroboam,
which he sinned and which he made Israel to sin." The fate of Jeroboam's
house, as well as that of the whole North, is already sealed. Each of the
judgments on the Northern kings then continues in this vein. Regardless of
what else they did in their reign, they failed to correct the sin of Jeroboam by eliminating the cultic centers at Bethel and Dan. By not doing
this they made the people sin. It is not that their personal sin was so
significant because they were king, but that their sin was a neglect of
their responsibility to oversee the covenant, and this naturally then had
consequences for the whole nation. The kings had failed to do what was
necessary to insure the North's continued existence on the land.

Given the Deuteronomist's understanding of the history of the North it
is simply not valid to say that he focussed on only the religious elements
in the king's reign. According to the Deuteronomist the king's religious
policies (failure to lead the North in adherence of the covenant law) were
the direct cause of the loss of the land. What could be more political than
the end of a nation's existence? The military battles the kings may have
won, or the economic contributions they may have made were in the final
analysis failures. In fact, the defence of the nation against the surrounding enemies was Yahweh's duty, and so the king would never be credited
very highly for this within the Deuteronomistic History. But the king
could be judged on the basis of his central responsibility, and in this all of
the Northern kings failed the test.

Prophets, Kings, and the Battles of Israel

When Jerusalem was threatened by the Assyrians, King Hezekiah asked
Isaiah to call upon Yahweh to help. Yahweh then announced through Isaiah

---

There has also been considerable discussion on the historical details of
Jeroboam's rise to power, and the nature of his cultic centers. This does
not need to be discussed here.

[201] Werner E. Lemke, "The Way of Obedience: I Kings 13 and the
Structure of the Deuteronomistic History," in *Magnalia Dei,* Essays on the
Bible and Archaeology in memory of G. Ernest Wright, ed. F. M. Cross, W.
E. Lemke, and Patrick D. Miller (Garden City: Doubleday, 1976) 301-326.

Note also: Uriel Simon, "I Kings 13: A Prophetic Sign—Denial and
Persistence," *HUCA* 47 (1976) 81-117.

that he would deliver the city and its inhabitants. Samuel as prophet announced to Saul that Yahweh would use Saul to deliver Israel from its enemies. Later Samuel confronted Saul with the accusation that he had not followed the commands of Yahweh in waging war. In the Deuteronomistic History it is Yahweh who fights Israel's battles, and it is the prophets who deliver his word and commands to Israel's leaders, the kings. There are a few further passages in the books of Kings which reflect this view.

When Syria threatens Israel, a prophet comes to Ahab the king of Israel and announces that Yahweh will give Israel the victory over the enemy—"Behold, I will give it into your hand this day; and you shall know that I am the Lord." (1 Kgs 20:13). It is then recorded how the Syrians were defeated. But in the following spring the Syrians threaten again, this time determining to fight the battle in the plains since Yahweh, the god of Israel must be a god of the hills. Yahweh again speaks to Ahab through his prophet—"therefore I will give all this great multitude into your hand, and you shall know that I am the Lord." (1 Kgs 20:28). Again Syria is defeated. By defeating the Syrians and defending Israel Yahweh has shown the people who he is.

Jehoshaphat is one of the kings of Judah who receives a positive, although qualified, evaluation from the Deuteronomist. It is then perhaps also significant that twice he is recorded to have sought out prophets to inquire of the Lord as to the outcome of battles. In 1 Kings 22 Jehoshaphat suggests this procedure, and is not satisfied with the positive word from the 400 prophets, and pushes Ahab to call up Micaiah ben Imlah. In 2 Kings 3 Jehoshaphat calls upon Elisha to deliver the word of the Lord to him. Elisha responds by announcing that Yahweh will give the Moabites into his hand. In both of these incidents the prophets react negatively toward the king of the North, but appear to respect Jehoshaphat. Although it is true that in each of these accounts the prophet acts more as a fortune teller than as an initiator of the action, it is significant that the accounts of these battles point out Yahweh's role in them, and the prophet communicates this to the king. In the first account Yahweh is depicted as causing Ahab's defeat, and in the second account Yahweh gives the victory. The fact that in each case Jehoshaphat is the one who initiates the inquiry suggests that he understands the role of Yahweh, and the role of a king, in such military conflicts.

The account of Elisha and the Syrian forces in 2 Kings 6 is clearly meant to communicate the true state of affairs in Israel's battles. When Syria sends out a force to take Elisha so that he will not be able to help the king of Israel, Elisha's servant exclaims "Alas, my master! What shall

we do?" (v 15). Elisha responds with "Fear not, for those who are with us
are more than those who are with them." (v 16). He then prays to Yahweh
to reveal the truth of this statement to the servant. The servant's eyes
are opened and he sees the mountains full of horses and chariots of fire.
Yahweh is there to protect them. The passage then continues to tell of
Yahweh blinding the Syrians allowing them to be led into the city of
Samaria. The fact that the horses and chariots of fire are not involved in
the larger account has been taken to imply that vv 14-17 were a later
addition to the story to emphasize its message.[202] This may very well be
so, but even the original story focusses more on the message of Yahweh's
protection, than on a battle between Israel and Syria. This is supported by
the conclusion of the story—the Syrians are not killed in Samaria but are
given a feast and sent home. No one could miss the point of this "object
lesson." Yahweh's forces were in control of the battle. Despite the forces
of the enemy, Israel was not to fear. Their task was to trust Yahweh to
deliver, and to await his word from the prophets. The king, although
Israel's leader, had to obey the prophet's message.

The Coronation of Joash, 2 Kings 11

2 Kings 11 records how Athaliah, the usurper to the Davidic throne, is
overthrown by a coalition of the priests and the people of the land.[203]
Joash, the son of Ahaziah and so a descendent of David is then made king.
This is one of only two accounts of a royal coronation in the OT. This
chapter may thus reveal some features of the normal ceremonies at such
an occasion. Since both the coronation of Solomon and this one were under
somewhat unusual circumstances, however, one must be careful not to
draw too firm conclusions from such an account.

There are two verses in this chapter which have attracted considerable
attention among scholars, and which could both have some bearing on the
thesis of this dissertation. The RSV translation of v 12 is typical of most

---

[202]Fricke, *Das zweite Buch von den Königen,* 82-84.

[203]Here we are not arguing for the historical accuracy of the account,
but simply affirming that in the present account the overthrow of
Athaliah is seen as caused by such a coalition. It has been argued that
historically the change was more possibly caused by a palace *coup de tat,*
and that the inclusion of the people of the land was a later addition. Such
an analysis could be strengthened by the fact that the people of the land
are largely emphasized in vv 13-18, verses which may have been a later
addition to the original.

translations: "Then he brought out the king's son, and put the crown upon him, and gave him the testimony; and they proclaimed him king, and anointed him; and they clapped their hands, and said, 'Long live the king!'" This verse appears to describe the central acts of the coronation ceremony. The Hebrew term עֵדוּת has caused considerable discussion. In the past the tendency was to emend it to הַצְּעָדוֹת on the basis of 2 Sam 1:10 producing a reading of "and put the crown and armlets upon him."[204] Von Rad has argued that such an emendation is not necessary, and he has been followed by most scholars on this.[205] No agreement has arisen among these scholars, however, as to what עֵדוּת implies in this particular context.[206] Von Rad interpreted the term as referring to a kind of Israelite parallel to the Egyptian royal protocol. Only in Israel the focus has shifted from the notion of the divine sonship of the king to an emphasis on the promise of the Davidic covenant.[207] Some scholars have accepted von Rad's conclusion that עֵדוּת points to the Davidic covenant, but instead of emphasizing the promise aspect of it, they argue that it signified the king's obligation within the Davidic covenant.[208] Others have emphasized the covenant or law connotations of the term without connecting it to the Davidic covenant. Widengren considers it to refer to the two tables of the

---

[204]An example of this is: Wellhausen, *Composition des Hexateuchs*, 292. For further examples of this see Aubrey Johnson, *Sacral Kingship in Ancient Israel* (Cardiff: University of Wales, 1955) 21.

[205]Gerhard von Rad, "The Royal Ritual in Judah," originally written in 1947, now in *The Problem of the Hexateuch and Other Essays* (Edinburgh: Oliver & Boyd, 1966) 222-31.

[206]For a summary of different conclusions see Mettinger, *King and Messiah*, 286-88.

[207]Von Rad, "The Royal Ritual in Judah," p. 228.
Some scholars who have followed von Rad in his conclusions are: Sigmund Mowinckel, *The Psalms in Israel's Worship*, 2 vols. (Oxford: Basil Blackwell, 1962), 1:62; Hans Joachim Kraus, *Psalmen*, 2 vols., BKAT, Bd. 15 (Neukirchen Kreis Moers: Neukirchener 1960) 2:886; Fricke, *Das zweite Buch von den Königen*, 150.

[208]Johnson, *Sacral Kingship in Ancient Israel*, 20-21.
He is followed in this by Gray, *I & II Kings*, 518. As Gray says: "The covenant , as we learn from the *locus classicus*, the oracle of Nathan (2 Sam 7.12-16), contained both promise of divine grace and obligations upon the king, and from Ps 132.12 (*ʿēdōt zūᵃlamᵉdēm*) it seems obvious that *ʿēdūt* or *ʿēdōt* signified specifically the king's obligations in the covenant."

law,[209] and Cross simply translates it "covenant stipulations."[210] This is sufficient to indicate the diversity of opinion on the subject.

We suspect that von Rad is probably correct in seeing the term as originally referring to some royal object, probably a written document, which was given or placed upon the king at his coronation. It was an Israelite adaptation of the Egyptian practice of presenting the king with the royal protocol at the coronation. In light of the significance of the Davidic covenant in the Judaean royal ritual, and in light of the context in which the term is used in Psalm 132, it is likely that the עֵדוּת symbolized or confirmed the Davidic covenant.[211] It is questionable, however, whether one needs to choose between the promise element of the covenant, or the obligation element. It is difficult to comprehend a Judaean royal ritual focussing on the Davidic covenant which did not emphasize the fact that Yahweh had chosen the Davidic dynasty and promised it an everlasting throne. On the other hand, all OT references to the Davidic covenant or promise include some reference to the king's obligation to obey the law.[212] This suggests that this was also the case in the royal עֵדוּת. It thus seems likely that historically at the coronation of a king the king received a "testimony" which confirmed Yahweh's choice of the Davidic dynasty, and pointed out the obligations of the king.

Given what we have seen thus far about the Deuteronomist's view of kingship, we would now suggest the Deuteronomist interpreted the "testimony" of 2 Kgs 11:12 as confirming the Davidic covenant, and the king's responsibility to ensure the Mosaic covenant. This interpretation is supported by the fact that, as Mettinger has pointed out, Jewish mediaeval exegesis "connected 2 R 11,12 with the injunction in Dt 17,18-19 that the king should have a copy of the Law," and then understood עֵדוּת to refer to that copy of the law.[213] One can obviously not put too much emphasis on

---

[209]Widengren, "King and Covenant," p. 6. Cf. Widengren, *Sakrales Königtum im Alten Testament und im Judentum,* Franz Delitsch-Vorlesungen, 1952 (Stuttgart: W. Kohlhammer, 1955) 28ff.

[210]Cross, *Canaanite Myth and Hebrew Epic,* 260.

[211]Widengren may be right in emphasizing the law aspect of עֵדוּת but not in separating it from the Davidic covenant.

[212]In the debate over whether the Davidic covenant was conditional or unconditional not enough emphasis has been placed on the fact that even in those passages which have been considered to speak of the Davidic covenant as unconditional (especially 2 Samuel 7 and Psalm 89), it is explicitly stated that the king is obligated to obey the law.

[213]Mettinger, *King and Messiah,* 287.

such a late interpretation, but it does fit with our understanding of the
Deuteronomist, and there are hints of such an assumption on the relationship between the king and the law throughout the history. Thus in Deut
17:14-20 the king is commanded to write out a copy of the law for himself. In Josh 1:8 Joshua is commanded to meditate on the law day and
night.[214] In 1 Sam 10:25 Samuel tells the people the rights and duties of
kingship, and writes them in a book. The verse just studied, and the
account of Josiah and the lawbook all fit into this pattern as well. At a
king's coronation he was formally granted a document which both confirmed that Yahweh had chosen him to continue the Davidic dynasty, and
confirmed his responsibility to obey the law, and as the leader of Israel, to
lead the people in obedience.

The second striking verse in the chapter is v 17—"And Jehoida made a
covenant between the Lord and the king and the people, that they should
be the Lord's people; and also between the king and the people." Despite
proposals to the contrary,[215] the last part of the verse needs to be
retained. The question then is how many, and which covenants are
referred to in this verse. The last part of the verse seems to be a clear
reference to a covenant between the king and the people. There is sufficient evidence in the OT that in Israel the king had a covenantal or con-
tractual relationship with the people. David made a covenant with Israel
at Hebron (2 Sam 5:3), and Rehoboam negotiated with the North for such
an agreement.[216] V 17b thus refers to the confirmation of such a covenant between Joash, the new king, and the people of Judah.

The first part of the verse has resulted in considerably more disagree-

---

[214]This proposal is similar to the one made by Porter, "The Succession
of Joshua," pp. 111-13.

[215]Von Rad, *Studies in Deuteronomy*, 64, has argued that v 17b needs
to be considered dittography, and thus not original.

It is true that the present verse is an awkward construction, but von
Rad's proposal is not satisfactory. Mettinger has made a more helpful
suggestion. He argues that v 17b was part of the original account of the
coronation of Joash. The Deuteronomist composed vv 13-18 of this
account, and in v 17 included the original reference to the covenant
between the king and the people. V 17a would then have been the Deuteronomist's contribution. The LXX, seeing the repetition, then omitted
v 17b (*King and Messiah*, 143).

[216]For a discussion of the covenant between the king and the people
see: Georg Fohrer, "Der Vertrag zwischen König und Volk in Israel," *ZAW*
71 (1959) 1-22.

Cf. Mettinger, *King and Messiah*, 137-50.

ment. Gray, for example, speaks of a threefold covenant in v 17, the third
phase consisting of the covenant between the king and the people, and the
first two phases, presumably described in v 17a, consisting of a renewal of
the Davidic covenant, and a renewal of the Sinaitic covenant.[217] It is
questionable whether v 17a contains any reference to the Davidic covenant. This covenant would, after all, have already been confirmed by the
handing over of the "testimony" in v 12. Rather, the focus of v 17a is a
renewal of the Mosaic covenant between Yahweh and the people. This is
confirmed by the purpose given for this covenant—"that they should be
the Lord's people." As is indicated in Deut 27:9, through the renewal or
confirmation of the Mosaic covenant Israel becomes the people of Yahweh.[218] The first formal act of the new administration is then to lead the
people in a renewal of the Mosaic covenant. In this passage Jehoida must
be seen as the surrogate for the minor King Joash.[219] The passage itself
does not give any indication as to why such a ceremony was held at this
point, and one must be circumspect about concluding too much from this
passage. Was the covenant renewal deemed necessary because of the
lawlessness of the reign of the non-Davidic Athaliah? Or was this a regular feature of all coronation ceremonies, times at which leadership
changed thus requiring a reaffirmation of the covenant? Or was this even
an annual event?[220] Such questions cannot be answered without caution

---

[217]Gray, *I & II Kings*, 523-24. Fricke, *Das zweite buch von den
Königen*, 152, holds a similar view.

[218]For a discussion of the significance of the phrase "people of
Yahweh" see: Norbert Lohfink, "Beobachtungen zur Geschichte des Aus-
drucks יהוה עַם," in *Probleme biblischer Theologie*, Fs Gerhard von Rad
(München: Chr. Kaiser, 1971) 275-305; A. R. Hulst, "גּוֹי/עַם," in *Theolo-
gisches Handwörterbuch zum Alten Testament*, ed. Ernst Jenni & Claus
Westermann (München: Chr. Kaiser, 1976), 2:290-326.

[219]McCarthy, *Treaty and Covenant*, 261; Geo Widengren, "King and
Covenant," p. 7.

[220]Baltzer, *Covenant Formulary*, is probably correct when he argues
that a covenant renewal was necessary at a change in leadership. This fits
both with the Biblical evidence (note the emphasis on covenant at the
change of leadership from Moses to Joshua, at the end of Joshua's life, at
the beginning of kingship, at the succession of Solomon, and now at the
coronation of Joash) as well as non-Biblical evidence (pp. 81-83 of
Covenant Formulary). Perhaps the reason why the covenant renewal of
Joash is described is that it had been made necessary both by the fact
that a new leader was coming to the throne, and the fact that this had
been a time of crisis. None of this gives any support, however, to the
proposal of an annual covenant renewal ceremony.

on the basis of this passage. It is noteworthy, however, that the new king, represented by the priest Jehoida, acts as the mediator in the renewal of the covenant.[221]

The similarity between 2 Kgs 11:17 and the covenant renewal led by Josiah has been noted by many. In both cases the leader of Judah leads the people in a covenant renewal ceremony. But further parallels can be found. Immediately after the covenant renewal it is stated: "Then all the people of the land went to the house of Baal, and tore it down; his altars and his images they broke in pieces, and they slew Mattan the priest of Baal before the altars." The Mosaic covenant, as expressed in Deuteronomy, required total loyalty to Yahweh. In both 2 Kings 11 and 23 covenant renewal immediately leads to reform of the cult. There is a necessary and natural connection between the two. It is also interesting that Joash is depicted as repairing the temple. It is clear that the Deuteronomist considered Joash's kind of leadership to be proper, and in keeping with his responsibilities. When Joash is evaluated, it is stated that "he did what was right in the eyes of the Lord because Jehoida instructed him." (2 Kgs 12:2).

---

[221]McCarthy, *Treaty and Covenant*, 260-61, confirms this direction when he states: "Moreover, there are some indications of a special position of Israel's chiefs in regard to the covenant with Yahweh. At least the kings of Judah seem to have had such a position from texts like 2 Kings 11,17 and 23,3 where the king is named separately from the people when the covenant is renewed. The king himself or the high-priest as surrogate for a minor made a covenant with God for the people. Even though much is different in Ex 34, for example, Yahweh and not the mediator makes the covenant, the fact of the mediator is there . . . This merely emphasizes what is already clear, the importance of the mediator role in Israelite religious covenant." During the time of kingship, the king was expected to play this mediator role with regard to the covenant. In fact, it has been suggested that Moses' mediator role at Mount Sinai has been modelled on the royal role in covenant making. See: Porter, *Moses and Monarchy*; Barnabas Lindars, "Torah in Deuteronomy," in *Words and Meanings*, Essays Presented to David Winston Thomas, (Cambridge: At the University, 1968) 117-36.

4

Summary and Conclusion

When Martin Noth proposed that Deuteronomy to Kings had been produced by a systematic Deuteronomistic Historian, he also argued that this historian was fundamentally opposed to the institution of kingship. This quickly became the standard position, and is still a common view. This is true even though a number of articles and books have been published more recently which have shown that at the very least it is inadequate to say that the Deuteronomistic Historian was opposed to kingship, and more probably, that it is wrong. The major weaknesses of these recent critiques of the traditional position were however, that they did not propose a comprehensive alternative to the traditional view, and that they continued to focus primarily upon the narratives on the rise of kingship in Israel in 1 Samuel 8-12. Our purpose was thus to describe the Deuteronomist's view of kingship as reflected by the whole Deuteronomistic History. Such a task could only be accomplished if the proper question were asked, and to merely ask whether the Deuteronomist was anti-kingship or pro-kingship is inadequate and unproductive. Rather, we needed to ask what kind of kingship the Deuteronomist saw as ideal for Israel, or what role he expected the king to fulfill within Israel.

The Deuteronomist's description of the reigns of Josiah and Hezekiah was chosen as the starting point of this study. In this we followed Veijola's suggestion of not starting with 1 Samuel 8-12, a passage which is weighted down with so many hypotheses, but searched for some other passages which also reflected the Deuteronomist's view.[1] 2 Kings 18-20 and 22-23 were admirably suited for this. First, Josiah and Hezekiah were kings of the relatively recent past for the Deuteronomist, and it is probable that their way of fulfilling the position might have influenced him, either

---

[1]Veijola, *Das Königtum*, 13.

positively or negatively. Second, these two kings received the highest
praise in the whole history of Israel. This suggests that the way in which
these two kings fulfilled their responsibilities came fairly close to the
Deuteronomist's ideal. We thus began with these two sets of narratives.

The analysis of 2 Kings 18-20 and 22-23 revealed that the Deuteronomist attributed a very significant role to the kings within the structures
of Israel. This role had two sides to it. On the one hand, the Deuteronomist considered the king to be the official within Israel who was responsible for insuring adherence to the covenant within Israel. Practically he
became the covenant administrator. Since Israel's existence as a nation on
the land was dependent upon her obeying the covenant, the king did not
have direct responsiblity for the defence of the nation. This was then the
other side of his role. In time of military crisis his responsibility was to
trust Yahweh; Yahweh was the one who had created Israel, and who would
protect her from her enemies. The Deuteronomist's view on the role of
the king thus ultimately coincided with the ancient Near Eastern pattern,
but it was expressed in the light of his historical view of Israel. An Israelite king insured the well-being of his people through fulfilling his responsibility as covenant administrator, and then trusting Yahweh to protect
and bless them.

The examination of the remainder of the Deuteronomistic History
confirmed the proposal based on 2 Kings 18-20 and 22-23. The law of
kingship is not opposed to kingship even while it does place some
restraints upon the king. Key to this is the assumption that the king is a
brother and so also under the covenant. This had not been emphasized
within 2 Kings 18-20 and 22-23 but it had certainly been assumed there as
well. The Deuteronomistic addition to the law of kingship emphasizes the
king's relationship to the law, and gives the groundwork for his role as
administrator of that law. The command to the king to write for himself a
copy of the law, and to read it all the days of his life may possibly come
from the formal liturgy of the installation of a new king.

In the Deuteronomistic History Joshua foreshadows the rise of kingship.
He is also commanded to follow the law of Moses, and to meditate on it
day and night. Later he is depicted as leading Israel in covenant renewal.
Although he is the military commander of Israel during the time of the
conquest, the emphasis on the holy war pattern makes it clear that
Yahweh is the true deliverer. A king was expected to lead Israel as Joshua
had.

The book of Judges then describes a period of sin and rebellion. Sin led
to oppression by an enemy. But Yahweh always heard the cries of his
people and sent "judges" whom he used to deliver his people. The story of

Gideon clearly warns Israel of the danger of assuming she can deliver herself. Gideon rejects an offer of kingship which did not recognize Yahweh's role in this domain. The Abimelech incident is used to show the consequences of a kingship based on force and violence. Judges 17-21 show that a different kind of kingship is needed within Israel. Already it is indicated that the king's responsibility would include administering the law thus not allowing every man to do what was right in his own eyes. Gideon's rejection of the offered kingship, and the obvious repudiation of Abimelech's kingship do not indicate a fundamental rejection of kingship as such, but are used by the Deuteronomist to warn against possible abuses of kingship. The book ends, however, with the clear message that kingship is needed in order that justice can be administered.

The narratives on the rise of kingship in Israel are also used in order to warn Israel of the dangers of the new institution. The request for kingship itself is rejected because the request has assumed that the king would replace Yahweh as Israel's protector. The narratives emphasize that Yahweh has delivered Israel in the past, and can continue to do so. These chapters also warn kings against abusing their power and oppressing the people. The king is expected to treat fellow Israelites as brothers under the covenant. Despite the warnings, however, the narratives bring out over and over that Yahweh has instituted kingship, and that he has chosen Saul to be the first king. The very significant 1 Samuel 12 then inaugurates this new era and incorporates the new institution into Israel's constitution. Samuel, the last judge of the previous era, leads Israel in a covenant renewal. From now on this will be the responsibility of the new leaders of Israel, the kings.

The David narratives also support the Deuteronomist's picture. David was obviously seen as the greatest king of Israel's history, and the Deuteronomist accepted this and built upon it. Despite David's very important contribution to the establishment of Israel as a power of that time, David is depicted as receiving the promise of an eternal dynasty because he had fulfilled his responsibility as the one responsible for covenant law, including its emphasis on cultic centralization. This Davidic promise then remained an effective force within the history of Israel. The Davidic kings were expected to follow and guarantee the Mosaic law, and, as the recipients of the Davidic promise, to be a sign and medium of God's grace.

King Solomon's major contribution according to the Deuteronomist was building the temple in Jerusalem. The Deuteronomic law required the cult to be centralized and so this was an important act on his part as covenant administrator. He was thus considered very highly by the Deuteronomist. The Deuteronomist's description of him is not totally positive, however, and he receives a very negative evaluation when he fails to fulfill his official responsibilities and allows foreign pagan influences to enter the cult of Israel. Jeroboam and his successors in the North of course also failed in their responsibilities since they did not unify and centralize the cult. The Deuteronomistic accounts of the battles of Israel continually emphasize that Yahweh is totally in command. At various points the prophets bring Yahweh's decisions and commands to the kings. Finally, Joash, acting through his substitute, the priest, leads Israel in a renewal of the covenant. The "testimony" which Joash received at his coronation probably symbolized his responsibility for the law in Israel.

We would thus argue that the whole Deuteronomistic History reflects a unified concept of kingship. His view of kingship was probably one which arose out of the context of his time, be it in the last years of the Southern Kingdom, or early in the exile. In light of this it would be helpful to briefly place his view into the larger historical context. It is usually agreed that historically speaking the institution of kingship was adopted by Israel in response to the Philistine threat. A more centralized form of government was required to lead the defence of the tribes at that time. It is probable that in light of the obvious danger a majority of the people favored the new institution, but it is improbable that approval of even a limited form of kingship was unanimous. The fact that these tribes had lived on the land for approximately two centuries before such an innovation was accomplished suggests that there were factors which worked against the rise of such a centralized institution. These factors will have been both social and religious. Centralized kingship would have been seen as a threat to local autonomy and freedom, and as in conflict with Yahweh's kingship. The threat of the Philistines, however, was sufficiently great and real to overcome these contrary influences.

The kingship which arose in Israel began in a rather limited form with the first king Saul, but in a very short time it changed dramatically. As soon as the Philistines had been defeated it became possible to devote fuller attention to establishing a powerful centralized kingship. David established Jerusalem as the capital of both political and religious life. A significant court was established and a major temple built. Soon the kingship in Israel became typical of kingship of that time. Such rapid growth in state officialdom, in bureaucracy, and in building naturally put severe pressure on the people. Taxation and forced labor became the necessary means to maintain this kingship in its adopted style. The opposition to kingship which had been overcome in light of the Philistine threat now reasserted itself. It is very possible that the rebellions of Absalon and Sheba were at least influenced by such opposition. Some of the writings of this time, although supportive of kingship, may also have been affected by these criticisms and may have worked for a more limited kind of kingship.

With the division of the kingdom after the death of Solomon kingship in Israel entered a new era. In the South a stable kingship of the Davidic House was established. For various reasons the North never succeeded in establishing such a state dynasty, but kingship is clearly the accepted form of government. It is likely that in neither kingdom did the kings ever again have the total power which David and Solomon had had. It is also likely that kingship became somewhat less oppressive for the people. It is significant that the prophets, in all their criticism of the oppression of the poor, never emphasize the role of the kings in this. The role of the people of the land in the South also suggests that kingship was less than totally autocratic or self-sufficient. Kingship had become the natural form of government for both the North and the South. There is no evidence that any segment of society in the North or the South rejected this form of government for either religious, social or political reasons.[2]

Josiah then became king of Judah during the 7th century B.C. During his reign he led the South in significant reform. Various factors contributed to the reform. The decline in Assyria made the assertion of independence attractive, and allowed for the hope of a re-establishment of a unified Davidic kingdom to rise. But even more significant, however, was the discovery of a lawbook in the temple. Although the Davidic covenant or promise had become prominent in the South, the Mosaic covenant had not been totally forgotten and was still formally affirmed. The discovered lawbook received at least some immediate authority from this formal affirmation. Josiah's reform received new inspiration from this discovery. A covenant renewal ceremony was held, a centralized passover was instigated, and attempts were made to purify and centralize the cult. Josiah led in a reform which aimed at making the requirements of the law, especially with regard to total loyalty of Yahweh as expressed in a pure centralized cult, normative for all Israel. The negative example of the North will have spurred this on in the hope that its fate could be avoided.

The Deuteronomistic History was then produced under the influence of Josiah's reform, and the lawbook which he discovered.[3] Josiah's reform affected the understanding of the lawbook, and Josiah himself became the model for kingship. The various sources available to the Deuteronomist

---

[2]This description is adapted from Crüsemann, *Der Widerstand gegen das Königtum.*

[3]This would be true whether the Deuteronomist wrote immediately after the reform during the reign of Josiah, or during the exile.

were adopted, adapted or rejected to produce a history which reflected the Deuteronomist's view of history arising out of this time. Israel had received the promised land as a gift of grace in fulfillment of the promise to the patriarchs. But in order to remain on the land Israel was expected to follow the law and remain totally loyal to Yahweh. Much of the history was a record of Israel's disregard of this condition, and in the North it had led to exile and loss of land. Obedience, however, would lead to Yahweh's blessing and protection from enemies.

Although the history was about Israel as a people, Israel's leaders dominate the history throughout. First there was Moses, then Joshua, then the judges, then Samuel, and finally the kings. At each point in the history the fate of the people was largely tied up with that of the leader. This was not because of some magical understanding of the leader, but because Israel's leaders set the direction for the people. Moses and Joshua had led the people in covenant obedience and the people were led out of Egypt into the promised land. The judges were used by Yahweh to defeat certain enemies but they were not successful in leading Israel in the covenant. With the rise of kingship this responsibility of the leader shifted to the kings. David and Solomon are depicted as leading the people in covenant loyalty, and at each point it is stated that Yahweh gave the people rest from their enemies. Throughout the rest of the History each king is judged by whether or not he fulfilled this central responsibility. Since political existence on the land was dependent upon covenant obedience, it is totally false to say that the Deuteronomist judged the kings by religious criteria only, and not political. Rather, according to the Deuteronomist the political success or failure of a king was entirely dependent upon the degree to which Israel obeyed the covenant. Political success could thus only be achieved by a king through fulfilling his responsibility as covenant administrator. Given this view, it is also clear that military success was not a major accomplishment of a king, but the act of Yahweh in his role as protector of the people. The king's role in this was to trust Yahweh to deliver, and then to be obedient to his word.

The king thus had an extremely important role within the structure of Israel for the Deuteronomist. Ultimately this role of the king was really quite similar to that assumed by all nations of that time. But the way in which the Israelite king was expected to insure this well-being was dependent upon Israel's unique covenant relationship with Yahweh. In Israel the king was expected to lead the people in covenant obedience and loyalty to Yahweh. Then the king and the people could trust Yahweh and rely upon him to bless them and deliver them from their enemies as they lived in the land of milk and honey.

Appendix:
A Review of Research on
2 Kings 22-23

In 1805 de Wette argued for a thesis which had already been suggested by early church fathers but which had never been examined critically.[1] According to de Wette the lawbook found in the temple during the time of Josiah was the book which later entered the canon as Deuteronomy. Graf and Wellhausen then used this correspondence as the basis of their reconstruction of the history of OT literature. As Wellhausen stated, "About the origin of Deuteronomy there is still less dispute; in all circles where appreciation of scientific results can be looked for at all, it is recognized that it was composed in the same age as that in which it was discovered, and that it was made the rule of Josiah's reformation, which took place about a generation before the destruction of Jerusalem by the Chaldeans."[2] Once the date of Deuteronomy was assured, the dates of much OT literature could be determined by their relationship to Deuteronomy.

The centrality of 2 Kings 22-23 for this thesis and structure naturally gave these two chapters an extremely important place in OT studies. In 1910 F. Puukko could write that these two chapters belong "zu den wichtigsten Resten der altisraelitische Literatur" since they are the "Ausgangspunkt für die neuere Pentateuchforschung" and so are a "Voraussetzung des moderne Verständnisses vom Alten Testament."[3] A whole understanding of the OT had been built upon de Wette's thesis based on a

---

[1] W. M. L. de Wette, *Dissertatio critica exegetica qua Deuteronomium a prioribus Pentateuchi libris diversum, alius cuiusdam recentioris auctoris opus esse monstratur* (Halle: np, 1805).

[2] Wellhausen, *Prolegomena*, 9.

[3] A. F. Puukko, *Das Deuteronomium. Eine Literarkritische Untersuchung*, BWAT, Nr. 5 (Leipzig: J. C. Hinrichs, 1910). This is quoted in Dietrich, "Josia und das Gesetzbuch," p. 13.

particular interpretation of 2 Kings 22-23. A significant role for these chapters within OT studies had been assured.

This whole structure underwent considerable attack during the 1920's when quite a number of scholars questioned the accuracy of de Wette's thesis. On the one hand, scholars like Kegel, Löhr, Oestreicher, Staerk, Welch and Wiener argued that Deuteronomy was much older than the 7th century B.C. and so in all probability was not the lawbook found by Josiah. On the other hand, scholars like Berry, Hölscher, Horst and Kennet stated that Deuteronomy had only been written after Josiah's reform and so could not have been the lawbook found in the temple. Still others defended the traditional view. The intensity of this "Kampf um das Deuteronomium"[4] is reflected by the number of articles and books published on this topic during this period.[5] Despite the battle, when calm returned consensus was not that different from before. The opponents of de Wette's thesis had attracted attention to some of its weaknesses but they had not managed to replace it as the most commonly accepted position. Thus most authors who have written during the past twenty years on the subject still assume that Deuteronomy was the lawbook of Josiah,[6] and focus on related issues such as the origin of Deuteronomy,[7] or the historical reconstruction of the events of Josiah's reign and reform.[8]

Probably the single most significant work published during this "Kampf um das Deuteronomium" was Th. Oestreicher's *Das Deuteronomische*

---

[4]This is the title of an article which Walter Baumgartner published in 1929 in which he described the debate. Walter Baumgartner, "Der Kampf um das Deuteronomium," *TRu* 1 (1929) 7-25.

[5]In his article of 1929 Baumgartner gives a good description of the debate of that decade. He begins by listing 32 articles and books on the topic, all of which had been published between 1919 and 1929. Ibid, pp. 1-2.

[6]The following is a representative sample of authors who accept this: Ronald Clements, *God's Chosen People. A Theological Interpretation of the Book of Deuteronomy* (Valley Forge: Judson, 1968) 18; Nicholson, *Deuteronomy and Tradition*, 1-18; Lohfink, "Die Bundesurkunde des Königs Josias"; Anderson, *Understanding*, 309; Jepsen, "Die Reform des Josia," 97-108.

[7]Note especially Johannes Lindblom, *Erwägungen zur Herkunft der Josianischen Tempelurkunde* (Lund: CWK Gleerup, 1971).

[8]A few examples of this would be: Jepsen "Die Reform des Josia;" Donald W. B. Robinson, *Josiah's Reform and the Book of the Law* (London: Tyndale, 1951); F. M. Cross & David Noel Freedman, "Josiah's Revolt Against Assyria," *JNES* 12 (1953) 56-58.

Grundgesetz of 1923. Although his view that Deuteronomy had been written long before the 7th century B.C., very possibly by Moses himself, convinced very few, two other emphases of Oestreicher's had a far reaching effect. First of all, Oestreicher presented a new and convincing literary analysis of 2 Kings 22-23. Oestreicher argued, largely on the basis of stylistic differences, that a distinction needed to be made between the narrative of the discovery of the lawbook, 2 Kgs 22:3-23:3, 16-18, 20-24, and the report of the reform, 2 Kgs 23:4-14, 15, 19. Oestreicher noted that the narrative of the lawbook had an expansive style in which numerous details of the events described were recorded. In contrast to this, the report of the reform was "knapp und gedrängt" without any extra details or description. As Oestreicher concluded, "Wir haben hier offenbar einen aus ganz anderer Feder geflossene Bericht über die Reinigung des Gottesdienstes in Juda vor uns, der mit dem völlig andersartigen Stück über die Gesetzesauffindung vom Verfasser der Königsbücher nachträglich zusammengestellt wurde."[9] This conclusion of Oestreicher's has been accepted by most scholars since then.[10] There are some disagreements among scholars over the extent of these two accounts, and also over the question of whether the Deuteronomist himself wrote the narrative of the lawbook discovery, or whether he used a source at this point. Despite these differences, Oestreicher's work has had tremendous influence at this point, and Albrecht Alt considered this conclusion of Oestreicher's to be the "fruchtbarste Ergebnis von Oestreichers Untersuchungen."[11]

A second aspect of Oestreicher's work which has had considerable influence was his picture of Josiah's reform. Oestreicher used both the parallel account in Chronicles, and the history of the ancient Near East of this period to help him reconstruct the events of 2 Kings 22-23. He argued that Josiah's reform was primarily motivated by the struggle for freedom from Assyrian overlordship. By eliminating the Assyrian cult symbols in Judah, and especially in the temple, Josiah was expressing his independence from Assyria and actually rebelling against it. He also noted that Chronicles spoke of the reform as taking place in stages, and that even in

---

[9]Theodor Oestreicher, *Das Deuteronomische Grundgesetz.*

[10]The following commentaries and articles accept this division: Gray, *Kings;* Fricke, *Das zweite Buch von den Königen;* Jepsen, "Die Reform des Josia"; Dietrich, "Josia und das Gesetzbuch"; Hollenstein, "2 Kön. XXIII 4ff"; Würthwein, "Die Josianische Reform."

[11]Albrecht Alt, "Die Heimat des Deuteronomiums," in *Kleine Schriften zur Geschichte des Volkes Israel,* II, by Albrecht Alt (München: C. H. Beck'sche, 1953) 253.

Kings it is stated that temple repairs were taking place before the lawbook was found. This emphasis of Oestreicher's has also had many followers, both in its use of Chronicles as an important source for the reconstruction of the historical details of Josiah's reform, and in its pointing to the connections between Josiah's religious reform and his movement towards political independence from Assyria.[12] It should be noted, however, that the works of John McKay and Morton Cogan have seriously questioned the validity of seeing Josiah's reform as primarily a product of nationalism and anti-Assyrian actions. They have once again suggested that religious motivation may have been the major reason for the actions of Josiah.[13]

It would probably be correct to describe the present state of affairs as one in which most scholars still accept de Wette's thesis of equating the lawbook of Josiah with Deuteronomy, or at least its core,[14] but they will tend to analyze 2 Kings 22-23 making use of Oestreicher's observations.[15] 2 Kings 22-23 thus still plays a very important role in OT studies because of its value in reconstructing the history of OT literature.

---

[12]Cross & Freedman, "Josiah's Revolt Against Assyria"; Nicholson, *Deuteronomy and Tradition*; Jepsen, "Die Reform des Josia"; Robinson, *Josiah's Reform*; Bright, *History*.

[13]McKay, *Religion in Judah under the Assyrians*; Cogan, *Imperialism and Religion*.

Both McKay and Cogan argue that it is dangerous to connect Josiah's reform as described in 2 Kings 22-23 too closely with a struggle for independence from Assyria. McKay begins by looking at the Kings passage, and argues that all of the cultic house cleaning done by Josiah is better explained as acts against Canaanite cultic practices rather than against official Assyrian symbols. He then concludes with an examination of Assyrian practices and discovers nothing which would indicate that Assyria required its vassals to formally worship Assyrian gods. Cogan begins with an examination of Assyrian practices, and then proceeds to the Biblical text, and arrives at conclusions similar to those of McKay. Although Assyrian religion will no doubt have entered Israel and Judah during its time of control, this will have been due to local influence. The cleansing of the Jahwistic religion by Josiah (as well as by Hezekiah) can thus not be explained largely from a political perspective.

[14]See footnote 6, p. 196. One exception to this would be Lundbom, "The Lawbook of the Josianic Reform." Lundbom argues that the lawbook found in the temple by Josiah was the Song of Moses found in Deuteronomy 32.

[15]Not all commentaries or articles emphasize this division, but none systematically argue against it.

A new direction in the study of 2 Kings 22-23 has been suggested, however, by the very recent articles of Walter Dietrich,[16] Ernst Würthwein[17] and Helmut Hollenstein.[18] All three have observed that the starting point for both sides of the debate during the 1920's was the assumption that 2 Kings 22-23 were historically trustworthy, and thus a valid source for reconstructing the events of Josiah's time. This assumption was made by both those who argued against de Wette's thesis (including both those who thought Deuteronomy was much earlier, and those who thought it was later) and those who defended it. Hölscher expressed the sentiment of both sides on this issue.

> Zuerst ist festzustellen, dass dieser Bericht in seinem wesentlichen Bestande von vorzüglichem geschichtlichem Wert ist. Das zeigen die unerfindlichen Einzelheiten, die genaue Datierung des Ereignisses, all die genauen Namen der königlichen Beamten, der Propheten und ihre Ehemannes, des Stadhauptmanns und des Eunuchen, und alle die merkwürdigen Kulteinrichtunge, die Josia beseitigt, wie die Bockgeisterhöhe, die Sonnenrosse und der Sonnenwage. Wenn hier nicht eine geradezu authentische Geschichtsüberlieferung vorliegt, so gäbe es überhaupt keine.[19]

It is this assumption which has now been challenged. After examining these two chapters Würthwein concluded that "2 Kön 22f können keinen Anspruch auf geschichtliche Glaubwürdigkeit erheben (abgesehen von der vordeuteronomistischen Schicht des Reformberichts, der auf die Auseinandersetzung Josias mit Assur zu beziehen ist)," and that thus they cannot be used for the dating of Deuteronomy.[20] Rather, Würthwein saw these two chapters as largely produced by the Deuteronomistic community in their battle to instill the cultic requirements of Deuteronomy upon the Jewish people of their time. In other words, Würthwein did not question that these two chapters meant to point to the book of Deuteronomy, but he considered this to be a fiction and thus not helpful for any dating of Deuteronomy. Dietrich also found only a very brief source behind the narrative, and saw most of these two chapters as having been written by

---

[16]Dietrich, "Josia und das Gesetzbuch."
[17]Würthwein, "Die Josianische Reform."
[18]Hollenstein, "2 Kön. XXIII 4ff."
[19]Hölscher, "Das Buch der Könige," p. 208.
[20]Würthwein, "Die Josianische Reform."

the Deuteronomistic community (he divided this into DtrG, DtrP and DtrN) in order to communicate their particular theology. For all three of these scholars these chapters are much more valuable for discerning the theology of the different Deuteronomistic authors than for getting at the details of Josiah's reform, if indeed, there was such a reform. If these scholars' conclusions find a following, it is very possible that a new "battle over Deuteronomy" will result.

Bibliography

Ackroyd, Peter R. *The First Book of Samuel.* The Cambridge Bible Commentary. Cambridge: Cambridge University Press, 1971. 237 pp.

_____ "An Interpretation of the Babylonian Exile: A Study of 1 Kings 20, Isaiah 38-39." *Scottish Journal of Theology* 27 (1974) 329-52.

_____ *The Second Book of Samuel.* The Cambridge Bible Commentary. Cambridge: Cambridge University Press, 1977. 247 pp.

Ahlström, G. W. "Die Königsideologie in Israel. Ein Diskussionsbeitrag." *Theologische Zeitschrift* 18 (1962) 205-10.

_____ "Der Prophet Nathan und der Tempelbau." *Vetus Testamentum* 11 (1961) 113-27.

Albright, William Foxwell. *The Biblical Period from Abraham to Ezra.* Harper Torchbooks. New York: Harper, 1963. 120 pp.

_____ *Samuel and the Beginnings of the Prophetic Movement.* The Goldenson Lecture for 1961. Cincinnati: Hebrew Union College Press, 1961. 28 pp.

Alt, Albrecht, "Der Anteil des Königtums an der sozialen Entwicklung in den Reichen Israel und Juda." In *Kleine Schriften zur Geschichte des Volkes Israel, III* by Albrecht Alt, pp. 348-72. München: C. H. Beck'sche Verlagsbuchhandlung, 1959.

_____ "The Formation of the Israelite State in Palestine," first published in 1930. In *Essays on Old Testament History and Religion,* pp. 171-237. Translated by R. A. Wilson. Oxford: Basil Blackwell, 1966.

_____ "Die Heimat des Deuteronomiums." In *Kleine Schriften zur Geschichte des Volkes Israel, II,* by Albrecht Alt, pp. 250-75. München: C. H. Beck'sche Verlagsbuchhandlung, 1953.

Anderson, Bernhard W. *Understanding the Old Testament.* 2nd edition, 1st published in 1957. Englewood Cliffs: Prentice-Hall, Inc., 1966. 586 pp.

Bächli, Otto. *Israel und die Volker. Eine Studie zum Deuteronomium.* Abhandlungen zur Theologie des Alten und Neuen Testaments, Nr. 41. Zürich: Zwingli Verlag, 1962. 235 pp.

Baltzer, Klaus. *The Covenant Formulary in Old Testament, Jewish and Early Christian Writings.* Translated by David Green from *Das Bundes Formular,* 1964. Philadelphia: Fortress Press, 1971. 221 pp.

Bardtke, H. "Samuel and Saul. Gedanken zur Entstehung des Königtums in Israel." *Biblical et orientalia* 25 (1968) 289-302.

Baumgartner, Walter. "Der Kampf um das Deuteronomium," *Theologische Rundschau* 1 (1929) 7-25.

Begrich, J. *Die Chronologie der Könige von Israel und Juda und die Quellen des Rahmens der Königsbucher.* Beiträge zur historischen Theologie, Nr. 3. Tübingen: J. C. B. Mohr (Paul Siebeck), 1929. 214 pp.

Bentzen, A. "The Cultic Use of the Story of the Ark in Samuel." *Journal of Biblical Literature* 67 (1958) 37-53.

Benzinger, I. *Die Bücher der Könige.* Kurzer Hand-Commentar zum Alten Testament, Abteilung 9. Freiburg: J. C. B. Mohr (Paul Siebeck), 1899. 216 pp.

Bernhardt, Karl-Heinz. *Das Problem der altorientalischen Königsideologie im Alten Testament unter besonderer Berücksichtung der Geschichte der Psalmenexegese dargestellt und kritisch gewürdigt.* Vetus Testamentum, Supplement, Vol. 8, Leiden: E. J. Brill, 1961. 351 pp.

Beyerlin, Walter. "Gattung und Herkunft des Rahmens im Richterbuch." In *Tradition und Situation. Studien zur alttestamentlichen Prophetie,* pp. 1-29. Festschrift für Artur Weiser. Edited by Ernst Würthwein & Otto Kaiser. Göttingen: Vandenhoeck & Ruprecht, 1963.

_____ "Geschichte und Heilsgeschichtliche Traditionsbildung im Alten Testament. Ein Beitrag zur Traditionsgeschichte von Richter VI-VIII." *Vetus Testamentum* 13 (1963) 1-25.

_____ "Das Königscharisma bei Saul." *Zeitschrift für die alttestamentliche Wissenschaft* 73 (1961) 186-201.

Bič, Miloš. "Saul sucht die Eselinnen (I Sam. IX)." *Vetus Testamentum* 7 (1957) 92-97.

Bin-Nun, Shoshana R. "Formulas from the Royal Records of Israel and of Judah." *Vetus Testamentum* 18 (1968) 414-32.

Birch, Bruce C. "The Choosing of Saul at Mizpah." *Catholic Biblical Quarterly* 37 (1975) 447-57.

_____ "Development of the Tradition on the Anointing of Saul in I Sam. 9:1-10:16." *Journal of Biblical Literature* 90 (1971) 55-68.

_____ *The Rise of the Israelite Monarchy: The Growth and Development of I Samuel 7-15.* SBL Dissertation Series, no. 27. Missoula: Scholars Press, 1976. 170 pp.

Blenkinsopp, Joseph. "The Quest of the Historical Saul." In *No Famine in the Land,* pp. 75-99. Studies in honor of John L. McKenzie. Edited by James Flanagan & Anita Weisbrod Robinson. Missoula: Scholars Press, 1975.

Boecker, Hans Jochen. *Die Beurteilung der Anfänge des Königtums in den deuteronomistischen Abschnitten. Ein Beitrag zum Problem des "deuteronomistischen Geschichtswerks."* Wissenschaftliche Monographien zum Alten und Neuen Testament, Bd. 31. Neukirchen: Neukirchener Verlag, 1969. 99 pp.

Boling, Robert G. "'In Those Days There Was No King In Israel.'" In *A Light Unto My Path,* pp. 33-48. In honor of Jacob Meyers. Edited by Howard N. Bream, Ralph D. Heim, and Carey A. Moore. Philadelphia: Temple University Press, 1974.

_____ *Judges.* The Anchor Bible. Garden City: Doubleday & Company, Inc., 1975. 338 pp.

Braulik, G. "Spuren einer Neuarbeitung des deuteronomistischen Geschichtswerk in I K 8:52-53, 59-60." *Biblica* 52 (1971) 20-33.

Bright, John. *A History of Israel.* 2nd edition. 1st published in 1959. Philadelphia: The Westminster Press, 1972. 519 pp.

_____ "Introduction to and Exegesis of the Book of Joshua." In *Interpreter's Bible,* 2:541-673. Edited by George Buttrick. New York: Abingdon Press, 1955.

Brueggemann, Walter. "The Kerygma of the Deuteronomistic Historian." *Interpretation* 22 (1968) 387-402.

_____ *The Land.* Overtures to Biblical Theology. Philadelphia: Fortress Press, 1977. 203 pp.

_____ "Wolff's Kerygmatic Methodology." In *The Vitality of Old Testament Traditions,* pp. 29-40. By Walter Brueggemann and Hans Walter Wolff. Atlanta: John Knox Press, 1975.

Buber, Martin. "Der Gesalbte." Originally written in 1939, and earlier published as three articles: "Das Volksbegehren," "Die Erzählung von Sauls Königswahl," and "Samuel und die Abfolge der Gewahlten." In *Martin Buber Werke*, Zweiter Band, Schriften zur Bibel, pp. 725-846. München: Kösel-Verlag, 1964.

_____ *Kingship of God.* Translated by Richard Scheimann from the 3rd edition of *Königtum Gottes,* 1st published in 1932. New York: Harper & Row, Publishers, 1967. 228 pp.

Buccellati, Giorgio. *Cities and Nations in Ancient Syria.* Studi Semitica, Nr. 26. Rome: Universita di Roma, 1967. 264 pp.

Budde, Karl. *Das Buch der Richter.* Kurzer Hand-Commentar zum Alten Testament, Abt. 7. Freiburg: Verlag von J. C. B. Mohr (Paul Siebeck), 1897. 147 pp.

_____ *Die Bücher Richter und Samuel. Ihre Quellen und ihr Aufbau.* Giessen: J. Ricker, 1890. 276 pp.

_____ *Die Bücher Samuel.* Kurzer Hand-Commentar zum Alten Testament, Abt. 18. Tübingen: Verlag von J. C. B. Mohr (Paul Siebeck), 1902. 343 pp.

Burney, C. F. *The Book of Judges.* London: Rivingtons, 1918. 528 pp.

_____ *Notes on the Hebrew Text of the Books of Kings.* Oxford: At the Clarendon Press, 1903. 384 pp.

Busshe, H. van den. "Le Texte de la Prophetie de Nathan sur Dynastie Davidique." *Ephemerides Theologicae Lovanienses* 24 (1948) 354-94.

Caird, G. B. "Introduction to and Exegesis of the First and Second Books of Samuel." *Interpreter's Bible,* 2:855-1176. Edited by George Buttrick. New York: Abingdon Press, 1955.

Calderone, Philip J. *Dynastic Oracle and Suzerainty Treaty* Logos, no. 1. Manila: Ateno de Manila University, 1966. 80 pp.

Caquot, A. "Remarques sur la 'loi royale' du Deutéronome (17:14-20)." *Semitica* 9 (1959) 21-33.

Carlson, R. A. *David, the Chosen King. A Traditio-Historical Approach to the Second Book of Samuel.* Translated by Eric J. Sharpe and Stanley Rudman. Stockholm: Almqvist & Wiksell, 1964. 304 pp.

Carmichael, Calum M. *The Laws of Deuteronomy.* Ithaca: Cornell University Press, 1974. 277 pp.

Childs, Brevard S. *Isaiah and the Assyrian Crisis.* Studies in Biblical Theology, Ser. 2, no. 3. Naperville: Alec R. Allenson, Inc., 1967. 144 pp.

Claburn, W. Eugene. "The Fiscal Basis of Josiah's Reforms." *Journal of Biblical Literature* 92 (1973) 11-22.

Clements, R. E., "The Deuteronomistic Interpretation of the Founding of the Monarchy in I Sam. 8." *Vetus Testamentum* 24 (1974) 398-410.

_____ "Deuteronomy and the Jerusalem Cult Tradition." *Vetus Testamentum* 15 (1965) 300-312.

_____ *God's Chosen People. A Theological Interpretation of the Book of Deuteronomy.* Valley Forge: The Judson Press, 1968. 126 pp.

_____ *One Hundred Years of Old Testament Interpretation.* Philadelphia: The Westminster Press, 1976. 152 pp.

Cody, Aelred. *A History of Old Testament Priesthood.* Analecta Biblica, no. 35. Rome: Pontifical Biblical Institute, 1969. 216 pp.

Cogan, Morton. *Imperialism and Religion. Assyria, Judah and Israel in the Eighth and Seventh Centuries B. C. E.* SBL Monograph Series, no. 19. Missoula: Scholars Press, 1974. 136 pp.

Conrad, J. "Zum geschichtlichen Hintergrund der Darstellung von David's Aufstieg." *Theologische Literaturzeitung* 97 (1972) 321-32.

Cooke, Gerald. "The Israelite King as Son of God." *Zeitschrift für die alttestamentliche Wissenschaft* 73 (1961) 202-225.

Cornill, Carl. *Introduction to the Canonical Books of the Old Testament.* Translated by G. H. Box from the 5th revised edition of *Einleitung in das Alte Testament,* 1st published in 1891. New York: G. P. Putnam's Sons, 1907. 556 pp.

Craigie, Peter C. *The Book of Deuteronomy.* The New International Commentary on the Old Testament. Grand Rapids: William B. Eerdmans Publishing Company, 1976. 424 pp.

Cross, Frank M. *Canaanite Myth and Hebrew Epic.* Cambridge: Harvard University Press, 1973. 376 pp.

_____ "The Structure of the Deuteronomic History." *Perspectives in Jewish Learning.* Vol. 3. Chicago: Spertus College of Judaica Press, 1967. pp. 9-24.

_____ and Freedman, David Noel. "Josiah's Revolt Against Assyria." *Journal of Near Eastern Studies* 12 (1953) 56-58.

Crüsemann, Frank. *Der Widerstand gegen das Königtum. Die antiköniglichen Texte des Alten Testaments und der Kampf um den frühen israelitischen Staat.* Wissenschaftliche Monographien zum Alten und

Neuen Testament, Bd. 49. Neukirchen: Neukirchener Verlag, 1978. 257 pp.

Cundall, Arthur E. "Antecedents of the Monarchy in Ancient Israel." In *Vox Evangelica III*, pp. 178-181. Edited by Ralph P. Martin. London: The Epworth Press, 1964.

_____ "Judges—An Apology for the Monarchy?" *Expository Times* 81 (1969/70) 178-81.

Daube, David. "'One from among your brethren shall you set king over you.'" *Journal of Biblical Literature* 90 (1971) 480-81.

_____ *Studies in Biblical Law.* Cambridge: University Press, 1947. 328 pp.

Davies, G. Henton. "Judges VIII 22-23." *Vetus Testamentum* 13 (1963) 151-57.

DeBus, Jörg. *Die Sünde Jerobeams. Studien zur Darstellung Jerobeams und der Geschichte des Nordreichs in der deuteronomistischen Geschichtsschreibung.* Forschungen zur Religion und Literatur des Alten und Neuen Testaments, Hft. 93. Göttingen: Vandenhoeck & Ruprecht, 1967. 122 pp.

Dietrich, Walter, "Josia und das Gesetzbuch (2 Reg. XXII)." *Vetus Testamentum* 27 (1977) 13-35.

_____ *Prophetie und Geschichte. Eine redaktionsgeschichtliche Untersuchung zum deuteronomistischen Geschichtswerk.* Forschungen zur Religion und Literatur des Alten Testaments, Nr. 108. Göttingen: Vandenhoeck & Ruprecht, 1972. 158 pp.

Driver, S. R. *Deuteronomy.* The International Critical Commentary. New York: Charles Scribner's Sons, 1895. 434 pp.

Eichrodt, Walther. *Der Herr der Geschichte. Jesaja 13-23 und 28-39.* Die Botschaft des Altes Testaments, Bd. 17, T. 2. Stuttgart: Calwer Verlag, 1967. 282 pp.

Eissfeldt, Otto. *Einleitung in das Alte Testament.* Neue theologische Grundrisse. Tübingen: Verlag von J. C. B. Mohr (Paul Siebeck), 1934. 752 pp.

_____ "Die Geschichtswerke im Alten Testament." *Theologische Literaturzeitung* 72 (1947) 71-76.

_____ *The Old Testament. An Introduction.* Translated by Peter R. Ackroyd from the 3rd edition (1964) of *Einleitung in das Alte Testament,* 1st published in 1934. New York: Harper & Row, Publishers, 1965. 861 pp.

Engnell, Ivan. *Gamla Testamentet. En Traditionshistorisk Inledning.* Stockholm: Svensk Kyrkans Diakonistyrelses Bokföflag, 1945. 289 pp.

_____ *A Rigid Scrutiny: Critical Essays on the Old Testament.* Translated and edited by John T. Willis. Nashville: Vanderbilt University Press, 1969. 303 pp.

_____ *Studies in Divine Kingship in the Ancient Near East.* 2nd edition, 1st published in 1943. Oxford: Basil Blackwell, 1967. 261 pp.

Eppstein, V. "Was Saul also among the Prophets?" *Zeitschrift für die alttestamentliche Wissenschaft* 81 (1969) 287-304.

Fichtner, Johannes. *Das erste Buch von den Königen.* Die Botschaft des Alten Testaments, Bd. 12, T. 1. Stuttgart: Calwer Verlag, 1964. 547 pp.

Flanders, Henry Jackson, Jr.; Crapps, Robert Wilson; and Smith, David Anthony. *People of the Covenant. An Introduction to the Old Testament.* New York: The Ronald Press Company, 1963. 479 pp.

Fohrer, Georg. *History of Israelite Religion.* Translated by David E. Green from *Geschichte der Israelitischen Religion,* 1968. Nashville: Abingdon Press, 1972. 416 pp.

_____ *Introduction to the Old Testament.* Translated by David E. Green from the 10th edition (1965) of *Einleitung in das Alte Testament,* originally written by Ernst Sellin in 1910, then revised by Leonhard Rost, and then revised and rewritten by Georg Fohrer. Nashville: Abingdon Press, 1968. 540 pp.

_____ "Der Vertrag zwischen König und Volk in Israel." *Zeitschrift für die alttestamentliche Wissenschaft* 71 (1959) 1-22.

Frankfort, Henri. *Kingship and the Gods. A Study of Ancient Near Eastern Religion as the Integration of Society and Nature.* Chicago: The University of Chicago Press, 1948. 444 pp.

Fricke, Klaus Dietrich. *Das zweite Buch von den Königen.* Die Botschaft des Alten Testaments, Bd. 12, T. 2. Stuttgart: Calwer Verlag, 1972. 381 pp.

Fritz, Volkmar. "Die Deutungen des Königtums Sauls in den Überlieferungen von seiner Entstehung I Sam 9-11." *Zeitschrift für die alttestamentliche Wissenschaft* 88 (1976) 346-62.

Frost, S. B. "The Death of Josiah: A Conspiracy of Silence." *Journal of Biblical Literature* 87 (1968) 369-382.

Gadd, C. J. *Ideas of Divine Rule in the Ancient East.* The Schweich Lectures of the British Academy, 1945. London: Oxford University Press, 1948. 101 pp.

Galling, Kurt. "Das Königsgesetz im Deuteronomium." *Theologische Literaturzeitung* 76 (1951) 133-38.

Gaster, T. H. "Divine Kingship in the Ancient Near East." *Review of Religion* 9 (1944-45) 267-81.

Geisler, Norman L. *A Popular Survey of the Old Testament*. Grand Rapids: Baker Book House, 1977. 299 pp.

Gese, Hartmut. "Der Davidsbund und die Zionserwählung." *Zeitschrift für Theologie und Kirche* 62 (1964) 10-26.

Geus, C. H. J. de. *The Tribes of Israel. An Investigation into some of the Presuppositions of Martin Noth's Amphictyony Hypothesis*. Studia Semitica Neerlandia, nr. 18. Amsterdam: Van Gorcum, 1976. 258 pp.

Geyer, J. B. "2 Kings 18:14-16 and the Annals of Sennacherib." *Vetus Testamentum* 21 (1971) 604-6.

Görg, Manfred. *Gott-König-Reden in Israel und Ägypten*. Beiträge zur Wissenschaft vom Alten und Neuen Testament, Hft. 105. Stuttgart: Verlag W. Kohlhammer, 1975. 295 pp.

Good, E. M. "Joshua Son of Nun." *Interpreter's Dictionary of the Bible*. 2:995-96.

Gottwald, Norman K. *A Light to the Nations. An Introduction to the Old Testament*. New York: Harper & Brothers, Publishers, 1959. 615 pp.

Gray, John. "The Hebrew Conception of the Kingship of God." *Vetus Testamentum* 6 (1956) 168-87.

_____ *Joshua, Judges and Ruth*. The Century Bible. London: Thomas Nelson and Sons, 1967. 424 pp.

_____ *I & II Kings*. Old Testament Library. Philadelphia: The Westminster Press, 1964. 744 pp.

Greenwood, David C. "On the Jewish Hope for a Restored Northern Kingdom." *Zeitschrift für die alttestamentliche Wissenschaft* 88 (1976) 376-85.

Grønbaek, Jakob H. *Die Geschichte vom Aufstieg Davids (1. Sam. 15-2. Sam. 5). Tradition und Komposition*. Acta Theologica Danica, Vol. 10. Copenhagen: Protestant Apud Munksgaard, 1971. 302 pp.

Gunn, D. M. *The Story of King David. Genre and Interpretation*. Journal for the Study of Old Testament, Supplements, no. 6. Sheffield: The University of Sheffield, 1978. 164 pp.

Gunneweg, A. H. J. "Sinaibund und Davidsbund." *Vetus Testamentum* 10 (1960) 335-41.

Haag, H. "Gideon—Jerubbaal—Abimelek." *Zeitschrift für die alttestamentliche Wissenschaft* 79 (1967) 305-314.

Hanson, Paul. "The Song of Heshbon and David's NÎR." *Harvard Theological Review* 61 (1968) 297-320.

Hermann, Siegfried. "Die Königsnovelle in Ägypten und in Israel." *Wissenschaftliche Zeitschrift der Karl Marx Universität* 3 (1953-54) 51-62.

Hertzberg, Hans Wilhelm. *Die Bücher Josua, Richter, Ruth.* Das Alte Testament Deutsch, Teilband 9. Göttingen: Vandenhoeck & Ruprecht, 1959.

_____ *I & II Samuel.* Old Testament Library. Translated by J. S. bowden from the 2nd edition (1960) of *Die Samuelbücher,* 1st published in 1956. Philadelphia: The Westminster Press, 1964. 416 pp.

Hölscher, Gustav. *Die Anfänge der hebräischen Geschichtsschreibung.* Sitzungsberichte der Heidelberger Akademie der Wissenschaften, Philosophisch-historische Klasse, Jahrgang 1941/42, 3 Abh. Heidelberg: Carl Winter's Universitätsbuchhandlung, 1942. 115 pp.

_____ "Das Buch der Könige, seine Quellen und seine Redaktion." In *Eucharistērion,* pp. 158-213. Festschrift für Hermann Gunkel. Forschungen zur Religion und Literatur des Alten und Neuen Testaments, hft. 36, T. 1. Edited by Hans Schmidt. Göttingen: Vandenhoeck & Ruprecht, 1923.

_____ *Geschichtsschreibung in Israel. Untersuchungen zum Jahwisten und Elohisten.* Skrifter Utgivna av Kungl. Humanistiska Vetenskapssamfundet I Lund, Nr. 50. Lund: C. W. K. Gleerup, 1952. 411 pp.

Hollenstein, Helmut. "Literarkritische Ersägungen zum Bericht über die Reformamassnahmen Josias, 2 Kön. XXIII 4ff." *Vetus Testamentum* 27 (1977) 321-36.

Honor, L. L. *Sennacherib's Invasion of Palestine.* New York: Columbia University Press, 1926. 122 pp.

Hooke, S. H., ed. *The Labyrinth. Further Studies in the Relation between Myth and Ritual in the Ancient World.* London: Society for Promoting Christian Knowledge, 1935. 288 pp.

_____ *Myth, Ritual, and Kingship. Essays on the Theory and Practice of Kingship in the Ancient Near East and in Israel.* Oxford: At the Clarendon Press, 1958. 308 pp.

_____. *Myth and Ritual. Essays on the Myth and Ritual of the Hebrews in relation to the Culture Pattern of the Ancient East*. London: Oxford University Press, 1933. 204 pp.

Horn, S. H., "Did Sennacherib Campaign Once or Twice Against Hezekiah?" *Andrews University Seminary Studies* 4 (1966) 1-28.

Hulst, A. R. "עַם גּוֹי." In *Theologisches Handwörterbuch zum Alten Testament*, 2:290-326. Edited by Ernst Jenni and Claus Westermann. München: Chr. Kaiser Verlag, 1976.

Irvin, W. A. "Samuel and the Rise of the Monarchy." *American Journal of Semitic Languages and Literature* 58 (1941) 113-34.

Ishida, Tomoo. "נגיד: A Term for the Legitimation of the Kingship." *Annual of the Japanese Biblical Institue* 3 (1977) 35-51.

_____. *The Royal Dynasties in Ancient Israel. A Study on the Formation and Development of Royal-Dynastic Ideology*. Beiheft zur Zeitschrift für die alttestamentliche Wissenschaft, Nr. 142. Berlin: Walter de Gruyter, 1977. 211 pp.

Jenni, Ernst. "Zwei Jahrzehnte Forschung an den Büchern Josua bis Könige." *Theologische Rundschau* 27 (1961) 1-32, 97-146.

Jenkins, A. K. "Hezekiah's Fourteenth Year. A New Interpretation of 2 Kings xviii 13-xix 37." *Vetus Testamentum* 26 (1976) 284-98.

Jepsen, Alfred. "בטח, batach." In *Theological Dictionary of the Old Testament*, 2:88-94. Edited by G. Johannes Botterweck and Helmer Ringgren. Translated by John T. Willis. Grand Rapids: William B. Eerdmans Publishing Company, 1975.

_____. *Die Quellen des Königsbuches*. Halle: VEB Max Niemeyer Verlag, 1953. 114 pp.

_____. "Die Reform des Josia." In *Festschrift für Friedrich Baumgärtel*, pp. 97-108. Edited by Johannes Herrmann & Leonhard Rost. Erlangen Forschungen, Reihe A, Bd. 10. Erlangen: Universitätsbund, 1959.

_____. "Zur Chronologie der Könige von Israel und Judah." In *Untersuchungen zur Israelitisch-Jüdischen Chronologie*, pp. 4-47. Beiheft zur Zeitschrift für die alttestamentliche Wissenschaft, Nr. 88. Berlin: verlag Alfred Töpelmann, 1964.

Jobling, David. "Saul's Fall and Jonathan's Rise: Tradition and Redaction in I Sam 14:1-46." *Journal of Biblical Literature* 95 (1976) 367-76.

Johnson, Aubrey R. "Hebrew Conceptions of Kingship." In *Myth, Ritual and Kingship. Essays on the Theory and Practice of Kingship in the*

Ancient Near East and in Israel, pp. 204-235. Edited by S. H. Hooke. Oxford: At the Clarendon Press, 1958.

_____ "The Role of the King in the Jerusalem Cultus." In *The Labyrinth. Further Studies in the Relation Between Myth and Ritual in the Ancient World,* pp. 71-112. Edited by S. H. Hooke. London: Society for Promoting Christian Knowledge, 1935.

_____ *Sacral Kinship in Ancient Israel.* Cardiff: University of Wales Press, 1955. 154 pp.

_____ Summary of Karl-Heinz Bernhardt, *Das Problem der altorientalischen Königsideologie im Alten Testament unter Berücksichtigung der Geschichte der Psalmenexegese dargestellt und kritisch gewürdigt.* In *A Decade of Bible Bibliography. The Book Lists of the Society for Old Testament Study, 1957-1966,* p. 352. Edited by G. W. Anderson. Oxford: Basil Blackwell, 1967.

Kaiser, Otto. *Introduction to the Old Testament.* Translated by John Sturdy from a revised form of the 2nd edition (1970) of *Einleitung in das Alte Testament,* 1st published in 1969. Minneapolis: Augsburg Publishing House, 1975. 420 pp.

_____ *Isaiah 13-39.* Old Testament Library. Translated by R. A. Wilson from *Der Prophet Jesaja. Kap. 13-39,* 1973. Philadelphia: The Westminster Press, 1974. 412 pp.

_____ "Die Verkündigung des Prophet jesaja im Jahre 701. Von der Menschen Vertrauen und Gottes Hilfe. Eine Studie über II Reg 18 17 ff, par Jes 36 1ff." *Zeitschrift für die alttestamentliche Wissenschaft* 81 (1969) 304-315.

Kapelrud, A. S. "Temple Building, A Task for Gods and Kings." *Orientalia* 32 (1963) 56-62.

Kaufmann, Y. *The Book of Judges* (Hebrew). Jerusalem: Kiryat Sepher Ltd., 1962. 315 pp.

Keil, C. F. *The Books of the Kings.* 2nd ed. Translated by James Martin. Clark's Foreign Theological Library, Ser. 4, Vol. 33. Edinburgh: T. & T. Clark, 1877. 523 pp.

Kittel, Rudolf, ed. *Biblia Hebraica.* Masoretic text edited by Paul Kahle, 7th edition, with additions and corrections by Albrecht Alt and Otto Eissfeldt. Stuttgart: Württembergische Bibelanstalt, 1951. 1434 pp.

_____ *Die Bücher der Könige.* Handkommentar zum Alten Testament, Abt. 1, Bd. 5. Göttingen: Vandenhoeck & Ruprecht, 1900. 312 pp.

Kraus, Hans-Joachim. *Geschichte der historisch-kritischen Erforschung des Alten Testaments von der Reformation bis zur Gegenwart.* Neukirchen Kries Moers: Verlag der Buchhandlung des Erziehungsvereins, 1956. 478 pp.

_____ *Psalmen.* 2 vols. Biblischer Kommentar: Altes Testament, Bd. 15. Neukirchen Kreis Moers: Neukirchener Verlag der Buchhandlung der Erziehungsvereins, 1960. 994 pp.

_____ *Worship in Israel. A Cultic History of the Old Testament.* Translated by Geoffrey Buswell from the 1962 publication. Oxford: Basil Blackwell, 1966. 246 pp.

_____ *Die Königsherrschaft Gottes im Alten Testament. Untersuchungen zu den Liedern von Jahwes Thronbesteigung.* Beiträge zur historischen Theologie, Nr. 13. Tübingen: Verlag J. C. B. Mohr (Paul Siebeck), 1951. 155 pp.

Kuenen, Abraham. Historisch kritisch Einleitung in die Bücher des Alten Testaments. Translated by Th. Weber from the 2nd edition (1865) of *Historisch-kritischen Onderzoek naar hat antstaan en de verzameling van de Boeken des Ouden Verbonds.* Leipzig: Verlag von Otto Schulze, 1887-92.

Kutsch, Ernst. "Die Dynastie von Gottes Gnaden. Probleme der Nathanweissagung in 2 Sam 7." *Zeitschrift für Theologie und Kirche* 58 (1961) 137-53.

_____ *Salbung als Rechtsact im Alten Testament und im Alten Orient.* Beiheft zur Zeitschrift für die alttestamentliche Wissenschaft, Nr. 87. Berlin: Verlag Alfred Töpelmann, 1963. 78 pp.

Labuschagne, C. J. "Some Remarks on the Prayer of David in II Sam 7." In *Studies on the Books of Samuel,* pp. 28-35. Papers Read at 3rd Meeting Held at Stellenbosch, 26-28 January, 1960. Pretoria: Die Ou Testamentiese Werkgemeenskap in Suid-Africa, 1960.

Lamparter, Helmut. *Der Aufruf zum Gehorsam. Das fünfte Buch Mose.* Die Botschaft des Alten Testaments, Bd. 9. Stuttgart Calwer Verlag, 1977. 178 pp.

Lance, H. D. "The Royal Stamps and the Kingdom of Josiah." *Harvard Theological Review* 64 (1971) 315-32.

Landersdorfer, Simon. *Die Bücher der Könige.* Die Heilige Schrift des Alten Testaments, 3 Bd. 2 Abt. Bonn: Peter Hanstein, 1927. 251 pp.

Langlamet, F. "Les recits de l'institution de la royaute (I Sam. 7-12)." *Revue biblique* 77 (1970) 161-200.

Lemke, Werner E. "The Way of Obedience: I Kings 13 and the Structure of the Deuteronomistic History." In *Magnalia Dei*, pp. 301-326. Essays on the Bible and Archaeology in memory of G. Ernest Wright. Edited by F. M. Cross, W. E. Lemke, and Patrick D. Miller. Garden City: Doubleday, 1976.

Levenson, Jon D. "Who Inserted the Book of the Torah?" *Harvard Theological Review* 68 (1975) 203-233.

Lindars, Barnabas, "Gideon and Kingship." *Journal of Theological Studies* 16 (1965) 315-26.

_____ "Jotham's Fable—A New Form-Critical Analysis." *Journal of Theological Studies* 24 (1973) 355-66.

_____ "Torah in Deuteronomy." In *Words and Meanings*, pp. 117-36. Essays Presented to David Winson Thomas. Edited by Peter Ackroyd and Barnabas Lindars. Cambridge: At the University Press, 1968.

Lindblom, Johannes. *Erwägungen zur Herkunft der Josianischen Tempelurkunde*. Lund: CWK Gleerup, 1971. 82 pp.

Lipinski, E. "*NĀGÎD*, der Kronprinz." *Vetus Testamentum* 24 (1974) 497-99.

Lohfink, Norbert. "Beobactungen zur Geschichte des Ausdrucks In *Probleme biblischer Theologie*, pp. 275-305. Festschrift für Gerhard von Rad. Edited by Hans W. Wolff. München: Chr. Kaiser Verlag, 1971.

_____ "Bilanz nach der Katastrophe. Das deuteronomistische Geschichtswerk." In *Wort und Botschaft*, pp. 196-208. Edited by J. Schreiner. Würzburg: Echter-Verlag, 1967.

_____ "Die Bundesurkunde des Königs Josias. Eine Frage an die Deuteronomiumsforschung." *Biblica* 44 (1963) 261-88, 461-98.

_____ "Die deuteronomistische Darstellung des Übergangs der Führung Israels von Moses auf Josue." *Scholastik* 37 (1962) 32-44.

_____ *Das Hauptgebot. Eine Untersuchung literarischer Einleitungsfragen zu Dtn 5-11*. Analecta Biblica, Nr. 20. Romae: E Pontificio Instituto Biblico, 1963. 317 pp.

Long, Burke O. review of *Das Königtum in der Beurteilung der deuteronomistischen Historiographie. Eine redaktionsgeschichtliche Untersuchung*, by Timo Veijola, 1977. *Journal of Biblical Literature* 98 (1979) 119-120.

Lundbom, Jack R. "The Lawbook of the Josianic Reform." *Catholic Biblical Quarterly* 38 (1976) 293-302.

McCarthy, Dennis J. "The Inauguration of the Monarchy in Israel." *Interpretation* 27 (1973) 401-412.

_____ "II Samuel 7 and the Structure of the Deuteronomic History." *Journal of Biblical Literature* 84 (1965) 131-38.

_____ "The Theology of Leadership in Joshua 1-9." *Biblica* 52 (1971) 165-75.

_____ *Treaty and Covenant. A Study in Form in the Ancient Oriental Documents and in the Old Testament.* 2nd edition, 1st published in 1963. Analecta Biblica, no. 21A. Rome: Biblical Institute Press, 1978. 368 pp.

_____ "The Wrath of Yahweh and the Structural Unity of the Deuteronomistic History." In *Essays in Old Testament Ethics,* pp. 99-110. In memory of J. Philip Hyatt. Edited by James L. Crenshaw and John T. Wallis. New York: KTAV Publishing House, Inc., 1974.

Macholz, G. Ch. "Die Stellung des Königs in der israelitischen Gerichtsverfassung." *Zeitschrift für die alttestamentliche Wissenschaft* 84 (1972) 157-82.

McHugh, John, "The Date of Hezekiah's Birth." *Vetus Testamentum* 14 (1964) 446-53.

McKay, John W. "Further Light on the Horses and Chariot of the Sun in the Jerusalem Temple." *Palestine Exploration Quarterly* 105 (1973) 167-69.

_____ *Religion in Judah under the Assyrians.* Studies in Biblical Theology, Ser. 2, No. 26. Naperville: Alec R. Allenson, Inc., 1973. 142 pp.

McKenzie, John L. "The Dynastic Oracle: II Samuel 7." *Theological Studies* 8 (1947) 187-218.

Maly, Eugene. "The Jothan Fable—Anti-monarchical?" *Catholic Biblical Quarterly* 22 (1960) 299-305.

Mann, Thomas W. *Divine Presence and Guidance in Israelite Traditions: The Typology of Exaltation.* The Johns Hopkins Near Eastern Studies. Baltimore: The Johns Hopkins Press, 1977. 310 pp.

Martin, James D. *The Book of Judges.* The Cambridge Bible Commentary. Cambridge: Cambridge University Press, 1975. 234 pp.

Mauchline, J. "Implicit Signs of a Persistent Belief in the Davidic Empire." *Vetus Testamentum* 20 (1970) 287-303.

Mayes, A. D. H. "The Rise of the Israelite Monarchy." *Zeitschrift für die alttestamentliche Wissenschaft* 90 (1978) 1-19.

Mendelsohn, Isaac. "Samuel's Denunciation of Kingship in the Light of Akkadian Documents from Ugarit." *Bulletin of the American Schools of Oriental Research* 143 (1956) 17-22.

Mendenhall, George E. "The Monarchy." *Interpretation* 29 (1975) 155-70.

_____ *The Tenth Generation. The Origins of the Biblical Tradition.* Baltimore: The Johns Hopkins Press, 1973. 248 pp.

Mettinger, Tryggve N. D. *King and Messiah. The Civil and Sacral Legitimation of the Israelite Kings.* Coniectanea Biblica, Old Testament Ser. 8. Lund: C. W. K. Gleerup, 1976. 342 pp.

Meyer, Rudolf. "Stilistische Bemerkungsn zu einem angeblichen Auszug aus der 'Geschichte der Könige von Juda'." In *Festschrift für Friedrich Baumgärtel*, pp. 114-123. Edited by Johannes Herrmann & Leonhard Rost. Erlangen Forschungen, Reihe A, Bd. 10. Erlangen: Universitätsbund, 1959.

Meyers, Jacob M. "Introduction to and Exegesis of the Book of Judges." In *Interpreter's Bible*, 2:677-826. Edited by George Buttrick. New York: Abingdon Press, 1955.

Miller, J. M. "Saul's Rise to Power: Some Observations concerning I Sam 9:1-10:16; 10:26-11:15 and 13:2-14:46." *Catholic Biblical Quarterly* 36 (1974) 157-74.

Miller, Larry. "An Exegetical Study of Deuteronomy 17:14-20." Elkhart, 1974 (mimeographed), 40 pp.

Miller, Patrick D., Jr. "The Gift of God. The Deuteronomic Theology of the Land." *Interpretation* 23 (1969) 451-65.

Montgomery, James A. and Gehman, Henry Snyder. *A Critical and Exegetical Commentary on the Books of Kings.* The International Critical Commentary. Edinburgh: T. & T. Clark, 1951. 575 pp.

Moore, George Foot. *Judges.* The International Critical Commentary. New York: Charles Scribner's Sons, 1903. 476 pp.

Moran, W. L. review of *Israel und die Völker*, Otto Bächli, 1962. *Biblica* 44 (1963) 375-377.

_____ "A Study of the Deuteronomic History." *Biblica* 46 (1965) 223-228.

Mowinckel, Sigmund. "Natanforjettelsen 2 Sem. kap. 7." *Svensk Exegetisk Arsbok* 12 (1947) 220-29.

_____ *The Psalms in Israel's Worship.* 2 vols. Translated by D. R. Ap-Thomas from a revised edition of *Offersang og Sangoffer*, 1951. Oxford: Basil Blackwell, 1962. Vol. I—246 pp., Vol. II—303 pp.

Muilenburg, James. "The Form and Stucture of the Covenantal Formulations." *Vetus Testamentum* 9 (1959) 347-65.

Mulder, E. S. "The Prophecy of Nathan in 2 Sam. 7." In *Studies on the Books of Samuel*, pp. 36-42, Papers Read at 3rd Meeting Held at Stellenbosch 26-28 January, 1960. Pretoria: Die Ou Testamentiese Werkgemeenskap in Suid-Africa, 1960.

Nelson, Richard Donald. "The Redactional Duality of the Deuteronomistic History." Th.D. dissertation, Union Theological Seminary of Virginia, 1973. 302 pp.

Nicholson, Ernst. "The Centralization of the Cult in Deuteronomy." *Vetus Testamentum* 13 (1963) 380-89.

_____ *Deuteronomy and Tradition. Literary and Historical Problems in the Book of Deuteronomy.* Philadelphia: Fortress Press, 1967. 145 pp.

Nielsen, Eduard. *Shechem. A Tradition-Historical Investigation.* Copenhagen: G. E. C. Gad, 1955. 384 pp.

North, C. R. "The Old Testament Estimate of the Monarchy." *American Journal of Semitic Languages and Literature* 48 (1931/32) 1-19.

Noth, Martin. "The Background of Judges 17-18." In *Israel's Prophetic Heritage*, pp. 68-85. Edited by Bernhard W. Anderson and Walter Harrelson. New York: Harper & Brothers, Publishers, 1962.

_____ "David and Israel in II Samuel 7." First published in 1957. In *The Laws of the Pentateuch and Other Studies*, by Martin Noth, pp. 250-59. Translated by D. R. Ap-Thomas. London: Oliver & Boyd, 1966.

_____ "God, King and Nation in the Old Testament." First published in 1950. In *The Laws of the Pentateuch and Other Essays*, by Martin Noth, pp. 145-78. Translated by D. R. Ap-Thomas. Edinburgh: Oliver & Boyd, 1966.

_____ *The History of Israel.* Translated by P. R. Ackroyd from the 2nd edition of *Geschichte Israels.* New York: Harper & Row, Publishers, 1960. 487 pp.

_____ *Könige I*, Biblischer Kommentar: Bd. 9, T. 1. Altes Testament. Neukirchen-Vluyn: Neukirchener Verlag, 1968. 366 pp.

_____ "The Laws in the Pentateuch: Their Assumption and Meaning." Written in 1940 as "Die Gesetze im Pentateuch (Ihre Voraussetzungen und ihr Sinn)." In *The Laws of the Pentateuch and Other Studies* by Martin Noth, pp. 1-107. Translated by D. R. Ap-Thomas. Edinburgh: Oliver & Boyd, 1966.

_____ *Überlieferungsgeschichtliche Studien I. Die sammelnden und bearbeitenden Geschichtswerke im Alten Testament.* Halle: Max Niemeyer Verlag, 1943. 266 pp.

Östborn, Gunnar. *tōrā in the Old Testament.* Lund: Häken Ohlssons Boktryckeri, 1945. 212 pp.

Oerstreicher, Theodor. *Das Deuteronomische Grundgesetz.* Beiträge zur Förderung christlicher Theologie, Bd. 27, hft. 4. Gütersloh: C. Bertelsmann, 1923. 120 pp.

Perlitt, Lothar. *Bundestheologie im Alten Testament.* Wissenschaftliche Monographien zum Alten und Neuen Testament, Bd. 36. Neukirchen-Vluyn: Neukirchener Verlag, 1969. 300 pp.

Pfeiffer, Robert. *Introduction to the Old Testament.* 2nd edition; 1st published in 1941. London: Adam and Charles Black, 1948. 909 pp.

Plein, Ina. "Erwägungen zur Überlieferung von I Reg 11,26-14,20." *Zeitschrift für die alttestamentliche Wissenschaft* 78 (1966) 8-24.

Plöger, Otto. *Die Prophetengeschichten der Samuel- und Königsbücher.* Greifswald: J. Adler, 1937. 67 pp.

_____ "Reden und Gebete im deuteronomistischen und chronistischen Geschichtswerk." In *Festschrift für Günther Dehn,* pp. 35-49. Edited by Wilhelm Schneemelcher. Neukirchen Kreis Moers: Verlag der Buchhandlung der Erziehungsvereins, 1957.

Porten, B. "The Structure and Theme of the Solomon Narrative." *Hebrew Union College Annual* 38 (1967) 93-128.

Porter, J. R. "The Interpretation of 2 Samuel 6 and Psalm 132." *Journal of Theological Studies* 5 (1954) 161-73.

_____ *Moses and Monarchy. A Study in the Biblical Tradition of Moses.* Oxford: Basil Blackwell, 1963. 28 pp.

_____ "The Succession of Joshua." In *Proclamation and Presence,* pp. 102-132. Essays in Honor of G. Henton Davies. Edited by J. I. Durham and J. R. Porter. London: SCM Press, 1970.

Pritchard, James B., ed. *Ancient Near Eastern Texts Relating to the Old Testament.* 3rd edition with supplement, 1st published in 1955. Princeton: Princeton University Press, 1969. 710 pp.

Prussner, Frederick C. "The Covenant of David and the Problem of Unity in Old Testament Theology." In *Transitions in Biblical Scholarship*, pp. 17-41. Essays in Divinity, no. 6. Edited by J. G. Rylaarsdam. Chicago: University of Chicago Press, 1968.

Puukko, A. F. *Das Deuteronomium. Eine literarkritische Untersuchung.* Beiträge zur Wissenschaft vom Alten Testament, Nr. 5. Leipzig: J. C. Hinrichs, 1910. 302 pp.

Rad, Gerhard von. *Deuteronomy.* Old Testament Library. Translated by Dorothea Barton from *Das fünfte Buch Mose: Deuteronomium*, 1964. Philadelphia: The Westminster Press, 1966. 211 pp.

_____ "The Form-critical Problem of the Hexateuch." First published as "Das Formgeschichtliche Problem des Hexateuch" in 1938. In *The Problem of the Hexateuch and Other Essays*, by Gernard von Rad, pp. 1-78. Translated by E. W. Trueman Dicken. Edinburgh: Oliver & Boyd, 1966.

_____ *Der Heilege Krieg im alten Israel,* 3 Aufl. Göttingen: Vandenhoeck & Ruprecht, 1958. 84 pp.

_____ "Hexateuch oder Pentateuch." *Verkündigung und Forschung* (1949/50), pp. 52-56.

_____ *Old Testament Theology.* 2 vols. Translated by D. M. G. Stalker from *Theologie des Alten Testaments,* 1957. New York: Harper & Row, Publishers, 1962. Vol. I—483 pp., Vol. II—470 pp.

_____ "The Promised Land and Yahweh's Land in the Hexateuch." First published in 1943. In by Gerhard von Rad, pp. 79-93. Translated by E. W. Trueman Dicken. Edinburgh: Oliver & Boyd, 1966.

_____ "The Royal Ritual in Judah." Originally written in 1947. In *The Problem of the Hexateuch and Other Essays,* by Gerhard von Rad, pp. 94-102. Translated by E. W. Trueman Dicken. Edinburgh: Oliver & Boyd, 1966.

_____ "There Remains Still a Rest for the People of God: An Investigation of a Biblical Conception." First published in 1933. In *The Problem of the Hexateuch and Other Essays,* by Gerhard von Rad, pp. 94-102. Translated by E. W. Trueman Dicken. Edinburgh: Oliver & Boyd, 1966.

_____ *Studies in Deuteronomy.* Studies in Biblical Theology, no. 9. Translated by David Stalker from *Deuteronomium Studien,* 1948. London: SCM Press, 1953. 91 pp.

_____ "Theologische Geschichtsschreibung im Alten Testament." *Theologische Zeitschrift* 4 (1948) 161-74.

Radjawane, Arnold Nicolaas. "Das deuteronomistische Geschichtswerk: Ein Forschungsbericht." *Theologische Rundschau* 38 (1974) 177-216.

Rendtorff, R. "Beobachtungen zur altisraelitischen Geschichtsschreibung anhand der Geschichte vom Aufstieg Davids." In *Probleme biblischer Theologie,* pp. 428-39. Festschrift für Gerhard von Rad. Edited by H. W. Wolff. München: Chr. Kaiser Verlag, 1971.

Richter, Wolfgang. *Die Bearbeitung des "Retterbuches" in der deuteronomistischen Epoche.* Bonner Biblische Beiträge, Nr. 21. Bonn: Peter Hanstein Verlag G.M.B.H., 1964. 148 pp.

_____ "Die nagid-Formel." *Biblische Zeitschrift* 9 (1965) 71-84.

_____ *Die sogenannten vorprophetischen Berufungsberichte. Eine literaturwissenschaftliche Studie zu I Sam 9,1-10,16. Ex 3f, und Ri 6,11b-17.* Forschungen zur Religion und Literatur des Alten und Neuen Testaments, Hft. 101. Göttingen: Vandenhoeck & Ruprecht, 1970. 203 pp.

_____ *Traditionsgeschichtliche Untersuchungen zum Richterbuch.* Bonner Biblische Beiträge, Nr. 18. Bonn: Peter Hanstein Verlag, GMBH, 1963. 411 pp.

Roberts, J. M. "The Davidic Origin of the Zion Tradition." *Journal of Biblical Literature* 92 (1973) 329-44.

Robinson, Donald W. B. *Josiah's Reform and the Book of the Law.* London: The Tyndale Press, 1951. 40 pp.

Robinson, J. *The First Book of Kings.* The Cambridge Bible Commentary. Cambridge: Cambridge University Press, 1976. 256 pp.

_____ *The Second Book of Kings.* The Cambridge Bible Commentary. Cambridge: Cambridge University Press, 1976. 256 pp.

Rose, Martin, "Bemerkungen zum historischen Fundament des Josia-Bildes in II Reg 22f." *Zeitschrift für die alttestamentliche Wissenschaft* 89 (1977) 50-63.

Rosenthal, E. I. J. "Some Aspects of the Hebrew Monarchy." *Journal of Jewish Studies* 9 (1958) 1-18.

Rost, Leonhard. "Josias Passa." Originally published in 1968. In *Studien zum Alten Testament,* pp. 87-93. Beiträge zur Wissenschaft vom Alten und Neuen Testament, Hft. 101. Stuttgart: Verlag W. Kohlhammer, 1974.

_____ "Sinaibund und Davidsbund." *Theologische Literaturzeitung* 72 (1947) 129-34.

_____ Die Überlieferung von der Thronnachfolge Davids. Beiträge zur Wissenschaft vom Alten und Neuen Testament, Hft. 42. Stuttgart: Verlag W. Kohlhammer, 1926. 142 pp.

_____ "Zur Vorgeschichte des Kultusreform des Josia." Vetus Testamentum 19 (1969) 113-20.

Roth, Wolfgang. "The Deuteronomic Rest Theology: A Redaction-Critical Study." Biblical Research 21 (1976) 5-14.

Rowley, H. H. The Growth of the Old Testament. London: Hutchinson's University Library, 1950. 192 pp.

_____ "Hezekiah's Reform and Rebellion." Bulletin of the John Rylands University Library of Manchester 44 (1961/62) 395-431.

_____ "Zadok and Nehushtan." Journal of Biblical Literature 58 (1939) 113-41.

Schmidt, Ludwig. Menschlicher Erfolg und Jahwes Initiative. Studien zu Tradition. Interpretation und Historie in Überlieferungen von Gideon, Saul und David. Wissenschaftliche Monographien zum Alten und Neuen Testament, Bd. 38. Neukirchen: Neukirchener Verlag, 1970. 246 pp.

Schmidt, W. H. "Kritik am Königtum." In Probleme biblischer Theologie, pp. 440-61. Festschrift für Gerhard von Rad. Edited by Hans W. Wolff. München: Chr. Kaiser Verlag. 1971.

Schulte, Hannelis. Die Entstehung der Geschichtsschreibung im alten Israel. Beiheft zur Zeitschrift für die alttestamentliche Wissenschaft, Nr. 128. Berlin: Walter de Gruyter, 1972. 109 pp.

Seebass, H. "I Sam. 15 als Schlüssel für das Verständnis der sogenannten königsfreundlichen Reihe I Sam. 9:1-10:16; 11:1-15; und 13:2-14:52." Zeitschrift für die alttestamentliche Wissenschaft 78 (1966) 149-79.

_____ "Traditionsgeschichte von I Sam. 8, 10:17ff., und 12." Zeitschrift für die alttestamentliche Wissenschaft 77 (1965) 286-96.

_____ "Die Vorgeschichte der Königserhebung Sauls." Zeitschrift für die alttestamentliche Wissenschaft 79 (1967) 155-71.

Seitz, Gottfried. Redaktionsgeschichtliche Studien zum Deuteronomium. Beiträge zur Wissenschaft vom Alten und Neuen Testament, hft. 93. Stuttgart: Verlag W. Kohlhammer, 1971. 338 pp.

Sekine, M. "Beobachtungen zu der josianischen Reform." Vetus Testamentum 22 (1972) 361-68.

Shafer, Byron E. "The root *bḥr* and Pre-Exilic Concepts of Chosenness in the Hebrew Bible." *Zeitschrift für die alttestamentliche Wissenschaft* 87 (1977) 20-42.

Sigrist, Christian. *Regulierte Anarchie. Untersuchungen zum Fehlen und zur Entstehung politischer Herrschaft in segmentären Gesellschaften Afrikas.* Freiburg: Walter-verlag, 1967. 275 pp.

Simon, Uriel. "I Kings 13: A Prophetic Sign—Denial and Persistence." *Hebrew Union College Annual* 47 (1976) 81-117.

Simpson, Cuthbert. *Composition of the Book of Judges.* Oxford: Basil Blackwell, 1957. 197 pp.

_____ *The Early Traditions of Israel. A Critical Analysis of the Pre-deuteronomic Narrative of the Hexateuch.* Oxford: Basil Blackwell, 1948. 675 pp.

Smend, Rudolf. "Das Gesetz und die Völker." In *Probleme biblischer Theologie,* pp. 494-509. Festschrift für Gerhard von Rad. Edited by Hans Walter Wolff. München: Chr. Kaiser Verlag, 1971.

Smith, Henry Preserved. *I & II Samuel.* International Critical Commentary. New York: Charles Scribner's Sons, 1899, 421 pp.

Snaith, Norman H. "The Historical Books." In *The Old Testament and Modern Study,* pp. 84-114. Edited by H. H. Rowley. London: Oxford University Press, 1961.

_____ "Introduction to and Exegesis of the First and Second Books of Kings." In *Interpreter's Bible,* 3:3-338. Edited by George A. Buttrick. New York: Abingdon Press, 1954.

Soggin, J. Alberto. "Der Beitrag des Königtums zur altisraelitischen Religion." In *Studies in the Religion of Ancient Israel,* pp. 9-26. Vetus Testamentum, Supplement, Vol. 23. Leiden: E. J. Brill, 1972.

_____ "Charisma und Institution im Königtum Sauls." *Zeitschrift für die alttestamentliche Wissenschaft* 75 (1963) 54-65.

_____ "Gilgal, Passah und Landnahme. Eine neue Untersuchung des kultischen Zusammenhangs der Kap. iii-vi des Josuabuches." In *Volume du Congrès. Genève, 1965,* pp. 263-77. Vetus Testamentum, Supplements, no. 15. Leiden: E. J. Brill, 1966.

_____ *Introduction to the Old Testament.* The Old Testament Library. Trandlated by John Bowden from the 2nd edition (1974) of *Introduzione all'Antico Testamento,* published in 1957. Philadelphia: The Westminster Press, 1976. 510 pp.

_____ . *Joshua*. Old Testament Library. Translated by R. A. Wilson from *Le Livre de Josue,* 1970. Philadelphia: The Westminster Press, 1972. 245 pp.

_____ . *Das Königtum in Israel. Ursprünge, Spannungen, Entwicklung.* Beiheft zur Zeitschrift für die alttestamentliche Wissenschaft, Nr. 104. Berlin: Verlag Alfred Töpelmann, 1967. 103 pp.

_____ . "Der judäische ʿ*ām hāʾāreṣ* und das Königtum in Juda." *Vetus Testamentum* 13 (1963) 187-95.

_____ . "Der offiziel geförderte Synkretismus in Israel während des 10 Jahrhunderts." *Zeitschrift für die alttestamentliche Wissenschaft* 78 (1966) 179-203.

_____ . "Zur Entstehung des alttestamentlichen Königtum." *Theologische Zeitschrift* 15 (1959) 401-418.

Stade, Bernhard. *Ausgewählte akademische Reden und Abhandlungen.* Giessen: np, 1899. 296 pp.

_____ . *Geschichte des Volkes Israel.* Allgemeine Geschichte in Einzeldarstellungen, 1 Hptabt., 6 T. Berlin: G. Grote'sche Verlagsbuchhandlung Separat-Tonto, 1886. 710 pp.

Stähli, H.-P. "ירא *jrʾ* fürchten." In *Theologisches Handwörterbuch zum Alten Testament,* 2:766-778. Edited by Ernst Jenni and Claus Westermann. München: Chr. Kaiser Verlag, 1971.

Steck, O. H. *Israel und das gewaltsame Geschick der Propheten: Zur Überlieferung des deuteronomistischen Geschichtsbildes im Alten Testament, Judentum und Urchristentum.* Wissenschaftliche Monographien zum Alten und Neuen Testament, Bd. 23. Neukirchen-Vluyn: Neukirchener Verlag, 1967. 380 pp.

Stoebe, Hans Joachim. *Das erste Buch Samuelis.* Kommentar zum Alten Testament, Bd. 8, T. 1. Gütersloh: Gütersloher Verlagshaus Gerd Mohn, 1973. 544 pp.

_____ . "Noch einmal die Eselinnen des Kis." *Vetus Testamentum* 7 (1957) 362-70.

Sturdy, J. "The Original Meaning of 'Is Saul also Among the Prophets?' (I Sam. 10:11,12; 19:24)." *Vetus Testamentum* 20 (1970) 206-213.

Tadmore, Hayim. "'The People' and the Kingship in Ancient Israel: The Role of Political Institutions in the Biblical Period." *Journal of World History* 11 (1968) 3-23.

Talmon, Shemaryahu. "Case of Faculty Harmonization (Is 37:18, II Kings 19:37)." *Vetus Testamentum* 5 (1955) 206-18.

_____ "In Those Days There Was No King in Israel." In *Proceedings of the 5th World Congress of Jewish Studies, August, 1959,* Hebrew: 1:135-44, English abstract: 1:242-43. Jerusalem: World Union of Jewish Studies, 1969.

Thornton, T. C. G. "Charismatic Kingship in Israel and Judah." *Journal of Theological Studies* 14 (1963) 1-11.   ·

Tillesse, G. Minette de. "Sections 'tu' et sections 'vous' dans le Deutéronome." *Vetus Testamentum* 12 (1962) 29-87.

Todd, E. W. "The Reforms of Hezekiah and Josiah." *Scottish Journal of Theology* 9 (1956) 288-93.

Tsevat, Matitiahu. "The House of David in Nathan's Prophecy." *Biblica* 46 (1965) 353-56.

_____ "The Steadfast House: What Was David Promised in II Samuel 7:11b-16?" *Hebrew Union College Annual* 34 (1963) 71-82.

Vannoy, J. Robert. *Covenant Renewal at Gilgal. A Study of I Samuel 11:14-12:25.* Cherry Hill, NJ: Mack Publishing Company, 1978. 277 pp.

Vaux, Roland de. *Les Livres des Rois.* Vol. 2, Fasc. 5 of *La Sainte Bible.* Sours le direction de l'Ecole Biblique de Jérusalem. Paris: Les Editions du Cerf, 1949. 234 pp.

Veijola, Timo. *Das Königtum in der Beurteilung der deuteronomistischen Historiographie. Eine redaktionsgeschichtlicht Untersuchung.* Suomalaisen Tiedeakatemian Toimituksia Annales Academiae Scietiarum Fennicae, Ser. B, Tom. 198. Helsinki: Suomalainen Tiedeakatemia, 1977. 147 pp.

_____ *Die Ewige Dynastie. David und die Entstehung seiner Dynastie nach der deuteronomistischen Historiographie.* Suomalaisen Tideakatemian Toimituksia Annales Academiae Scietiarum Fennicae, Ser. B., Tom. 192. Helsinki: Suomalainen Tiedeakatemia, 1975. 164 pp.

Wallis, Gerhard. *Geschichte und Überlieferung. Gedanken über alttestamentliche Darstellung der Frühgeschichte Israels und der Anfänge seines Königtums.* Arbeiten zur Theologie, Reihe 2, Bd. 13. Stuttgart: Calwer Verlag, 1968. 108.

Warner, Sean M. "The Period of the Judges within the Structure of Early Israel." *Hebrew Union College Annual* 47 (1976) 57-79.

Weinfeld, Moshe. "Cult Centralization in Israel in the Light of a Neo-Babylonian Analogy." *Journal of Near Eastern Studies* 23 (1964) 202-212.

_____ *Deuteronomy and the Deuteronomic School.* Oxford: At the Clarendon Press, 1972. 467 pp.

_____ "Deuteronomy—The Present State of Inquiry." *Journal of Biblical Literature* 86 (1967) 249-62.

_____ "The Period of the Conquest and of the Judges as seen by the Earlier and the Later Sources." *Vetus Testamentum* 17 (1967) 93-113.

Weippert, Helga. "Die 'deuteronomistischen' Beurteilungen der Könige von Israel und Juda und das Problem der Redaktion der Königsbücher." *Biblica* 53 (1972) 301-339.

Weiser, Artur. *Introduction to the Old Testament.* Translated by Dorothea Barton from the 4th edition (1957) of *Einleitung in das Alte Testament,* 1st published in 1948. New York: Association Press, 1961. 492 pp.

_____ "Die Legitimation des Königs David Zur Eigenart und Entstehung. der sogen. Geschichte von Davids Aufstieg." *Vetus Testamentum* 16 (1966) 325-54.

_____ *The Psalms.* Old Testament Library. Translated by Herbert Hartwell from the 5th revised edition of *Die Psalmen,* 1959. Philadelphia: The Westminster Press, 1962. 841 pp.

_____ "Samuel und die Vorgeschichte des israelitischen Königtums." *Zeitschrift für Theologie und Kirche* 57 (1960) 141-61.

_____ *Samuel: Seine geschichtliche Aufgabe und religiöse Bedeutung. Traditionsgeschichtliche Untersuchungen zu I Samuel 7-12.* Forschungen zur Religion und Literatur des Alten und Neuen Testamentes, hft. 81. Göttingen: Vandenhoeck & Ruprecht, 1962. 94 pp.

_____ "Die Tempelbaukrise unter David." *Zeitschrift für die alttestamentliche Wissenschaft* 77 (1965) 153-68.

Wellhausen, Julius. *Die Composition des Hexateuchs und der historischen Bücher des Alten Testaments.* 4 unveränderte Auflage, erste in 1894. Berlin: Walter de Gruyter & Co., 1963. 373 pp.

_____ *Prolegomena to the History of Ancient Israel.* Translated by Black & Menzies from a revised edition of *Geschichte Israels, I,* 1st published in 1878. Cleveland: Meridian Books, 1957. 552 pp.

Wenham, G. J. "Deuteronomic Theology of the Book of Joshua." *Journal of Biblical Literature* 90 (1971) 140-48.

Wette, W. M. L. de. *Dissertatio critica exegetica qua Deuteronomium a prioribus Pentateuchi libris diversum, alius cuiusdam recentioris auctoris opus esse monstratur.* Halle: np, 1805.

Whitley, C. F. "The Deuteronomic Presentation of the House of Omir." *Vetus Testamentum* 2 (1952) 137-52.

Widengren, Geo. "King and Covenant." *Journal of Semitic Studies* 2 (1957) 1-32.

_____ *Sakrales Königtum im Alten Testament und im Judentum.* Franz Delitsch-Vorlesungen, 1952. Stuttgart: Verlag W. Kohlhammer GMBH, 1955. 69 pp.

Wildberger, H. "Samuel und die Entstehung des israelitischen Königtums." *Theologische Zeitschrift* 13 (1957) 443-69.

Whybray, R. N. *The Succession Narrative.* Studies in Biblical Theology, Ser. 2, no. 9. London: SCM Press, 1969. 118 pp.

Wolff, Hans Walter. "The Kerygma of the Deuteronomic Historical Work." Translated by Frederick C. Prussner from an article of 1961. In *The Vitality of Old Testament Traditions*, pp. 83-100. By Walter Brueggemann & Hans Walter Wolff. Atlanta: John Knox Press, 1975.

Wright, George Ernest. "Introduction and Exegesis of the Book of Deuteronomy." In *Interpreter's Bible*, 2:311-537. Edited by George A. Buttrick. New York: Abingdon Press, 1954.

Würthwein, Ernst. *Das Erste Buch der Könige. Kapitel 1-16.* Das Alte Testament Deutsch, Teilband 11, 1 Göttingen: Vandenhoeck & Ruprecht, 1977. 204 pp.

_____ "Die Josianische Reform und das Deuteronomium." *Zeitschfift für Theologie und Kirche* 73 (2976) 395-423.

Yonick, Stephen S. "The Rejection of Saul: A Study of Sources." *Australian Journal of Biblical Archaeology* I (1968) 29-50.

Young, Edward J. *An Introduction to the Old Testament.* 2nd edition; 1st published in 1949. Grand Rapids: Wm. B. Eerdmans Publishing Co., 1970. 432 pp.

Zimmerli, W. "Jesaja und Hiskia." In *Wort und Geschichte*, pp. 199-208. Festschrift für Karl Elliger. Edited by Hartmut Gese und Hans Peter Rüger. Alter Orient und altes Testament. Neukirchen-Vluyn: Neukirchener Verlag, 1973.

Index

Ackroyd, P. R., 18, 87
Albright, W. F., 10, 151
Alt, A., 107, 197
Anderson, B. W., 7, 75

Bächli, O., 109, 113-4, 116
Baltzer, K., 62, 154
Barrick, W. B., 50
Baudissin, 20
Baumgartner, W., 196
Begrich, J., 46
Bentzen, A., 136
Benzinger, I., 178
Bernhardt, K. H., 15, 25-6, 34,
    37, 141
Berry, 196
Beyerlin, W., 13, 141, 151, 156
Bin-Nun, S. R., 16, 47
Birch, B., 31, 37-8
Blenkinsopp, J., 23
Boecker, H. J., 13, 27-8, 34, 37,
    126-8, 140-1, 146-54
Boling, R., 124
Bright, J., 10, 69, 124-5, 198
Brueggemann, W., 90-2, 98, 119
Buber, M., 124-6, 129, 135, 144
Buccellati, G., 107
Budde, K., 2, 3, 21, 135-6
Burney, C. F., 9, 47, 51-2, 125,
    178
Busshe, H. van den, 163

Caquot, A., 114
Carlson, R. A., 9
Carmichael, C., 106
Childs, B., 69-70, 74, 76, 80-84

Claburn, W. E., 65
Clements, R. E., 1, 30, 37-8, 196
Cody, A., 156
Cogan, M., 65, 82, 198
Conrad, J., 164
Cooke, G., 164
Cornill, C., 2-3
Craigie, P. C., 113
Crapps, R. W., 7, 22
Cross, F. M., 10, 16-8, 51, 60,
    90-2, 103, 108, 144, 151, 160-
    2, 166-8, 176, 178, 184, 196,
    198
Crüsemann, F., 15, 19, 34, 37,
    40, 125-35, 143-4, 147, 176,
    193
Cundall, A. E., 124, 126, 145

Daube, D., 111, 119
Davies, G. H., 124-6
Debus, J., 177, 179
Dietrich, W., 11, 14-5, 32, 45-6,
    57, 59-60, 70, 195, 197, 199
Driver, S. R., 108

Eichrodt, W., 86-7
Eissfeld, O., 3-4, 13, 21, 27, 136,
    142, 178
Engnell, I., 5-6

Flanders, H. J., 7, 22
Fohrer, G., 5, 47, 144, 185
Frankfort, H., 96-8
Freedman, D. N., 196, 198
Fricke, K., 53, 58, 70, 80-87,
    182-3, 186, 197

Fritz, V., 33-4, 37, 141, 150

Galling, K., 105-7
Gehman, H. S., 51
Geisler, N. L., 7
Geyer, J. B., 69
Good, E. M., 117-8
Görg, M., 161
Gottwald, N. K., 22
Gray, J., 10, 52, 58, 60, 65-6, 69, 71-2, 87, 123, 125, 131, 183, 186
Greenwood, D. C., 16
Gressmann, H., 125
Grønbaek, J. H., 164
Gunn, D. M., 165

Hanson, P., 166
Herrmann, S., 161
Hertzberg, H. W., 22-3, 25, 123, 136, 141
Hollenstein, H., 12, 45-6, 58, 65, 197, 199
Holscher, G., 3, 4, 13, 21, 52
Honor, L., 70
Hooke, S. H., 97-8, 179
Horst, 196
Hulst, A. R., 186

Ishida, T., 31-2, 34, 37, 40, 106

Jenkins, A. K., 70, 80-1
Jenni, E., 1
Jepsen, A., 5-6, 46-7, 58, 60, 65, 101, 196, 198
Johnson, A., 23, 26, 97-8, 183

Kaiser, O., 7, 12, 72
Kaufmann, Y., 29
Kegel, 196
Keil, C. F., 53
Kennet, 196
Kittel, R., 9, 52
Kraus, H. J., 1, 62, 66, 183
Kuenen, A., 9, 16, 20

Lamparter, H., 113
Landersdorfer, S., 53
Lemke, W. E., 180
Levenson, J. D., 11, 103
Lindars, B., 125, 129-31, 187

Lindblom, J., 196
Lipinski, E., 152
Lohfink, N., 54, 61, 118, 186, 196
Löhr, 196
Long, B., 14
Lundbom, J. R., 46, 198

Maly, E., 129-31
Mann, T. W., 117, 119-20
Martin, J. D., 123
Mauchline, J., 159
Mayes, A. D. H., 34, 43, 142, 146, 150
Mays, J. L., 96
McCarthy, D. J., 29-30, 34, 43, 117, 122, 142, 145, 150-54, 160, 162, 165, 168, 171, 187
McHugh, J., 69
McKay, J., 65, 198
McKenzie, J. L., 163
Mendelsohn, I., 24, 144, 147
Mendenhall, G., 134
Mettinger, T., 12, 30-1, 36-8, 152, 161, 164, 167, 169, 183-5
Meyer, R., 65
Miller, L., 113-4
Miller, P. D., 93-4, 96
Montgomery, J. A., 51-2, 59-62, 66, 68-70, 178
Moore, G. F., 125, 131
Moran, W. D., 114
Mowinckel, S., 162, 183
Muilenburg, J., 154

Nelson, R. D., 8-9, 16-7, 47-8, 168
Nicholson, E., 65, 105, 108, 113-4, 167, 196
Nielsen, E., 124
Noth, M., 1-18, 21, 24-8, 31, 34-43, 47, 55, 58, 63, 67-8, 90-4, 103-4, 121, 125, 135, 136, 140-2, 146, 162, 167, 174, 178, 189

Oestreicher, T., 57, 196-8
Östborn, G., 117

Perlitt, L., 94
Pfeiffer, R., 10
Plein, I., 179

Plöger, O., 20, 90
Porter, J. R., 116, 119-21, 174-5,
    185, 187
Pritchard, J. B., 69
Puukko, A. F., 195

von Rad, G., 7-8, 11, 84, 90-3,
    105, 107-9, 113, 159-60, 166,
    183, 185
Radjawane A. N., 1, 8
Rendtorff, R., 165
Richter, W., 13, 126, 151-2
Robinson, J., 52, 80, 178
Robinson, D. W. B., 196
Rost, L., 161, 165, 167
Roth, W., 12
Rowley, H. H., 10, 69-71

Sanda, 178
Schmidt, L., 152
Schulte, H., 4, 137
Schunck, 136
Seitz, G., 105, 137
Shafer, B. E., 107, 110
Sigrist, C., 35
Simon, U., 180
Simpson, C., 3-4
Smend, R., 11, 115, 137
Smith, D. A., 7, 22
Snaith, N., 1, 10, 51-2
Soggin, J. A., 7, 26-7, 34, 37-8,
    117, 120, 125-6, 136, 138, 175
Stade, B., 20, 59, 124
Staerk, 196
Stahli, H.-P., 84
Steuernagel, C., 20
Stöbe, H. J., 151

Talmon, S., 134-5
Täubler, 136
Thornton, T. C. G., 107, 152
de Tillese, M., 104-6, 137
Towner, S., 96
Tsevat, M., 169

Vannoy, J. R., 154
de Vaux, R., 10
Veijola, T., 12, 14, 15, 32-3, 37,
    41-2, 102, 136-9, 143-4, 161,
    189

Weinfeld, M., 28-9, 37, 65, 135-
    6, 139
Weippert, H., 16, 47
Weiser, A., 18, 23-9, 34, 36, 62,
    141, 147, 150, 154, 165
Welch, 196
Wellhausen, J., 2-3, 9, 18-28, 33-
    4, 36-7, 40-1, 47, 124-5, 140,
    142, 183, 195
de Wette, W. M. L., 195-9
Whitley, C. F., 178
Widengren, G., 61, 64, 114, 116-
    7, 183-4
Wiener, 196
Wildberger H., 110
Wolff, H. W., 10, 54, 59, 90-2,
    167
Wright, G. E., 54, 105
Wurthwein, E., 12, 45-6, 57-60,
    65-6, 70, 174, 197, 199

Young, E. J., 7

Zimmerli, W., 76